CITY IMAGES

J3

Cover photo: Giraudon/Art Resource, LA 160116. Marnille, Rue Bernard
de Palifoy.

CITY IMAGES
Perspectives from Literature, Philosophy, and Film

Edited by

MARY ANN CAWS

Graduate School
City University of New York

GORDON AND BREACH
USA Switzerland Australia Belgium France
Germany Great Britain India Japan Malaysia
Netherlands Russia Singapore

First published 1991
Second printing 1993

Gordon and Breach Science Publishers

Y-Parc
Chemin de la Sallaz
1400 Yverdon, Switzerland

Post Office Box 90
Reading, Berkshire RG1 8JL
Great Britain

Private Bag 8
Camberwell, Victoria 3124
Australia

3-14-9, Okubo
Shinjuku-ku, Tokyo 169
Japan

58, rue Lhomond
75005 Paris
France

Emmaplein 5
1075 AW Amsterdam
Netherlands

Glinkastrasse 13-15
O-1086 Berlin
Germany

820 Town Center Drive
Langhorne, Pennsylvania 19047
United States of America

Library of Congress Cataloging-in-Publication Data

City images: perspectives from literature, philosophy, and film /
    edited by Mary Ann Caws.
        p.   cm.
      ISBN 2-88124-426-2—ISBN 2-88124-464-5 (pbk.)
      1. Cities and towns in literature.   2. Literature—History and
criticism.   3. Geographical perception.   I. Caws, Mary Ann.
    PN56.C55C5   1991
    809'.93321732—dc20   90-30611
                                                                      CIP

CONTENTS

INTRODUCTION

THE CITY ON OUR MIND

.. the emergence of a structure of feeling . . .
Raymond Williams,
Writing in Society (1)

City-knowing

Knowing any real city, and still more so, knowing what it *is* to know a city, may be as much about passive as about active experience. What we read in the field—that field of the city in all its bizarre mixture of culture and nature—is bound to determine, to some non-fictional extent, what we know of it, what we imagine it could be, what we fear it may be, or become. For the actuality of the *place*—its ways and walks—is only partly the issue; of no less concern is the imagination of that city-ness in the sense that Raymond Williams uses the term in his "Tenses of Imagination." (2) It is "something fully knowable but not yet known." Now of course, for Williams, this future knowability is related to his political project, a socialism that could be, but is not yet. Whether or not we endorse his project, share or not his particular consciousness, it has to be taken into account in viewing his city views, and those about the knowledge connected with his imaginative hopes.

The sort of knowing that is textual enters often, also into the space of the present essays as an extension of the city's real space in its workings-out along the length and width of the mind. Williams' *The Country and the City* (3) takes Dickens' novels as paradigmatically important for exposing the double condition of a city: "the random and the systematic, the visible and the obscured, which is the true significance of the city . . . as a dominant social form." His experiments in fiction are slanted towards an explicit program of what Williams aptly calls the *creation of a consciousness*, communal in its essence, and to which writers of the city frequently allude. Intimately linked, in this consciousness, story and culture reinforce each other, so that, in some deep sense, "the fictional method is the experience of a city." (155)

These essays are meant to be, albeit in their critical mode, the recountings of knowing something through something else: they

1

are the projected imagination, through reading, of the reading by the self and/or others (a wide range of each) of a city, or cities as such, of what city-knowing or city-thinking is. The city as stage, market, and labyrinth, variously trafficked and aestheticized, dreamt and politicized, as passionately written by authors from Cicero to Kazin, from Wordsworth, Dickens, Whitman, and Woolf, to Williams, Ashbery, and Bonnefoy, is the place the essays play themselves out, through architecture and metaphor. The recurrence, almost obsessive, of some few great figures is at once to be expected and to be reflected on—as if the very notion of city were to call up recent phantoms in all of us. To this obsession, this preface will return, having wanted to call it up prefiguratively.

City-reading

Kevin Lynch's ground-breaking *Image of the City* of 1960 maintains that legibility is a vital component of all modern cities: the recognizable symbols in their accustomed and understandable grids, the apparent clarity, and the ease of detection of its parts in their own visibly coherent pattern (4) all contribute to a heightened sensation, quite like the sensation of reading poetry. (To make poetry out of the prose of our cities: is it, even now, near the end of the century, a possible one? The question remains. It is only, of course, as it is stated, an aesthetic exercise, as if one were to convert all suffering and exaltation into an image of art, ignoring or sublimating the practical and political issues—if we are to decide to make that conversion, we must at least know what we are doing.)

The city has been, in the far and near past, and in the recent and present present, deeply unvalued, desperately overdespaired-of, too little cared for, and decentered. A recent group of essays called *Visions of the Modern City: Essays in History, Art, and Literature* (5) runs through the schools of urban and city-history thought, from nineteenth-century London, with the examinations of the working class and the poor (Engels, Mayhew, Booth), to the German School at the turn of the century (Weber, Simmel, Spengler), down to the Chicago School of the second and third decades of this century, with their examination of the interrelations between physical structures and moral order, and sketches out various of the more significant theories of city-history history and urban perception. (For example, Schorske's division of the development: from the Enlightenment City of virtue, to the Victorian City of vice, and to the Modern city beyond either.) Yet never, claims Schorske, has American culture developed any positive image of itself—that in itself is worth dwelling upon. Such an image could not be projected by either the generations of Hawthorne and James, with their scorn on the non-civilised new world, or the apostles of anti-urbanism like Leo Marx and Leslie Fiedler.

But, having read them, is it not now, in some deeply bothersome sense, yet again, up to us to do our own readings? To that question, the authors collected in these pages give an answer in the affirmative; however qualified by the problematics of always coming-after, of addressing a thing much-addressed, thinking in the present has its own sure value.

Public problematics

One of the clearest of attacks on the morals of contemporary public thinking is that leveled by Richard Sennett, in his *Fall of Public Man*. (6) As with the Roman empire in decline after the death of Augustus, says Sennett, a passive spirit has taken us over; we, like the ancient Romans, are learning to invest "less and less passion in . . . . acts of conformity." Our self-absorption, our devotion to our single life-stories, our judging intimacy in all its tyrannical sway, and the "market exchange of confession" to be marks of authenticity, means that we are loath, even unable, to recognize the "reality and worth of the impersonal life" (FP, 340) which he chooses to present as the more valid one. In what we have made as a Dead Public Space, our social expressions become merely the *"presentation* to other people of feelings which signify in and of themselves, rather than as *representation* to other people of feeling present and real to each self." (FP,38) (7) That convincingly pessimistic view has its adherents and the advantages that forceful presentation suggests.

Yet we have wanted to present another aspect, in several modes. As for the kind of enlivening mode that would seem profitable for this public space of conformity even as confessional: it might well be best represented by Robert Harbison's brilliantly bizarre *Eccentric Spaces* (8), a disquisition on the museum and the map, on the catalogue and the garden; the strange uplift characteristic of this writing is a model of how we might learn to perceive, from the inside out and not the contrary: "If one takes architecture," he says, "as the expression of an individual life, one starts at the center rather than at the face, asking what space is created rather than what plot is filled" (ES,22) This may sound like the celebrated glass either half-empty or half-full, in that it tests the upbeat potential of our imagination: but is that not exactly what the history of the imagination needs? a test of our belief, if nothing else, of the "creative consciousness" of possibilities?

Our own presentation

Just so, the essays we have chosen to present here, collectively,
represent diverse literary, sociological, historical, and philosophical bents: the contributing authors come from several fields and
were asked to offer their individual perspectives, in their difference and their convergence. To make up, as it were, a reflective
grid for the general thinking through of the city as textual and
actual referent, and as idea. The essays move from the broad
scope and wide focus, where the idea of *city* is seen as trafficking
in its own thought, or dreaming its own fantasy, or presenting
itself as polis and philosophical project, to the more focussed and
work-specific studies of individual cities, their authors, and their
legacy.

In this second part, some cities and some figures stand out ob-
sessionally—the warning was given—as the foci of our collective
and individual passion: Baudelaire and Benjamin, difficult to by-
pass those so-present texts of our near past. (9) This book did not
want to ignore obsession or passion, dealing, as it does, not just
with *polis* and the idea of perfection, but with the everyday and
then, what takes that everyday into art and architecture—from
Sheeler to Venturi and Arman—a sort of "long-term parking" in
literature and thought.

Reading New York, as Alfred Kazin so lyrically does, as he
writes and rewrites it and himself, as did Melville, Crane, Wharton, James, Lorca (by such strange and sad contrast with Madrid
and Granada), Celine and Sartre (9), Auden and Marianne Moore
and James Merrill and Oppen, reading Chicago through Dreiser
or London through Dickens and Virginia Woolf and Alison Lurie,
Berlin through Benjamin and Rome through Marinetti, Dublin
through Joyce, or reading Paris, as many of the contributors do,
rewriting it, whether through Benjamin and Baudelaire (10) or
Henry James again, whether through Butor or Robbe-Grillet, and
always through themselves: these are figures and acts which
find themselves, I think rightly, juxtaposed. Whatever they expose, & whatever they hide even in their address, these *acts* of
the words and the imagination make a grid through which to
look at the literary, artistic, and philosophical seeing of the city,
always only on the way to knowing what that is.

Whether it be visible or invisible. It may well be that some of
us, however post-Utopian we may (perforce) be, still making our
own Last Manifesto, resemble Calvino's Marco Polo (11) in having a perfect and present city always in our minds. "And Polo
said: 'Every time I describe a city I am saying something about
Venice.'" About Venice something is said in these pages, lyrically. And yet, of course, some of us speak always of the same,

passionately-loved, place, which is never quite that of the other. It is probably not the same city, whatever city it is. ". . . I must locate myself within this mad geometry": So Alfred Kazin concludes his first sentence, about the Upper West Side of New York City. Whatever place we have, and wherever we keep it, we have somehow to find our place in it, always again.

Another figure: complicity in the city
In the *New York Times* of last year appeared an article, perturbed, on the topic of the amount of space men and women take up on the city street. The typical man, it was observed, walks along swinging his arms, affording himself the place he needs, whereas the typical woman walks with her arms held in toward her, in order to take up less space. Perhaps indeed so: but our essays, aimed as they are at the space in the mind, mean also to be about locating the self, of whatever gender, through—in some cases—other selves. "Now the heavens are as crowded as the earth," Kazin observes. Yes, and the question still concerns the room we have as our own. Having and using that room, as Virginia Woolf knew all too well, depends on material means; marginality in the many senses of the term threatens to cut off room altogether.

The eyes of the poor are hard to avoid, and the windows and gates up against which the separating pressures come to bear mark those obsessive texts we have, somehow, to deal with. Besides Benjamin and Baudelaire, there is another figure to be dealt with: that of the beggar, making a strangely alliterative and unforgettable trinity. Haunting not just the texts of our cities and of the cities of others, but our own city streets, the most obdurate consciousness, however it has been created, recognized, and sharpened. The things which cannot be, in cities, in prose, or in poetry, poeticized, are forcefully brought to our attention in whatever and whoseever room we find ourselves.

Not everyone has the space and the means to practice the arm-swinging art, and that is one of the principal reasons for which Baudelaire does haunt us, from this preface through many of the essays to the concluding one, which takes up again this issue, in its own place and with its own room.

The whole issue of distance and of presence, of theory and of practice, arises—in relation to the beggar and the figures of the poor—in the "discussion" of the perverse text called, roughly, "Let's Beat Up on The Poor," which tests out a practical and violent approach opposed to the contemplations of "The Toys of the Poor" and "The Eyes of the Poor." These texts, says Jonathan Monroe (12), set up, as often in Baudelaire, "an inescapable com-

plicity between author and reader, both producers of the contradictions and antagonisms of the social context and text itself."
(PO, p.116) What kind of irony it is a question of remains in
question, and warnings abound, in the text and out, about any
certainty of reading, and in particular of reading too easily as a
simple irony that "we" of the title with its invitation: "Let's Beat
Up . . . ":

> The "we" of "Assommons les pauvres!" should stant as a warning
> to all those intent on "rescuing" Baudelaire's motivations and in-
> tentions by assuming a Marxist or historical materialist perspec-
> tive. One of the problems with such a reading is its tendency to
> minimize or repress the antisocialist aspects of the poem along
> with that deep duplicity Benjamin rightly maintained as character-
> istic of Baudelaire. (PO, 116)

There is no easy reading of the city or its texts, no simple shuf-
fling about of ironies as covers of the situation. About city misery, physical and mental, about loneliness and loss and
powerlessness, we know: that consciousness we must not lose.
And yet it must not be, either, an excuse for yet more city-
despair, for yet less use of the imagination, political, textual, and
personal. If the imaginative result of yet more essays on the city,
more new-classical, new-romantic, or new-post-anything moments, modernist, Marxist or not, were ever to be, in public or
private space, a bit more arm-swinging, even if it were for the
moment, to be only in the mind where there is always room, at
least it would have been worthwhile. The city is there too.

Discourse between the cities

What is it to engage in an enterprise dealing with the representations of the city? We have wanted to offer a selection of
perspectives on this representation itself, playing the more traditional thematic readings: of images and figures, of styles, of city-
histories and historicizing, of perceptions themselves in their
urban mode, against a more theoretically reflective and, in some
cases, politically perceptive mode.

But the structuring of the volume itself is meant to move from
the idea of "mediating images" and historical consciousness to a
definite problematization about all such representation and their
power structures, via some city streets and byways with their
own modes and problems, to work from the specific and the historical both in and out, in towards what the representations
mean in terms of our own city-living, and out towards a question
about "lastness" and involvement of a necessarily collective sort.

Molesworth brings poetry to bear on theatre and market-place as the localizing emblems of city and citifying experience, taking us through history down to the present. The hopes for and impossibilities of the very idea of perfection applied to anything at all, including the urban and its literary associations, are ironically dealt with by Ross, who draws on Foucault for his aesthetic relation of things and notions.

Traversing urban places, mapping a poetics for reading and writing, representing the mazes of the mind and its dwelling by the notion and the notation of the labyrinth, Faris suggests a way of looking that opens into Joseph's reflections on labyrinth and library, on disorder and order, and into Winspur's patterings of streets into the known and the to-be-discovered, the short cut and cross-cuts. We have wanted here to focus on what is near *and* what is further off, what is comprehended and what remains still-to-be.

Character in the city: that's what it takes. So Jane Augustine reflects on the city-in-and-as-novel, by American writers, with its own characters evolving in general and specific senses. As the city becomes character in Augustine, its own poetry becomes as certain as the uncertain poetics Heller deals with, an exploratory poetics, reflecting the exploratory nature of modern American poetry with its tentative attitude. Others continue the reflection on poetry and its different ways of writing the city.

But these essays are meant to be in correspondence. Thus Weinstein's meditation on loss and the desires of recapturing, on the images used in this representation, leads from imaging to the idea of invisibility. It could be seen in correspondence with Garber's view of Blake's viewing of innocence, corruption, and the pastoral colors of edenic times lost in the greyness of London, as well as Esch's view of Benjamin's "figures of thought," and the conflicts of reading with the pragmatics of economic truths, one thread of which joins the reflections on poetry, via Wordsworth, linked to Baudelaire. (13) Baudelaire reappears as the essential figure in several of these essays, and in the picturing and problematizing of the city as it is mapped out, trafficked in, lost, found, traversed, remembered, and loved.

Godfrey's essay takes up the figure of the swan and the notions of loss and memory from the Weinstein essay, and joins to Diamond's view of Baudelaire and Benjamin, which leads to the Prendergast essay with its own Benjamin lighting.

A reflection on engagement and on problematics initiates this: the notion of a stroll down a city street—recalling that flaneur figure who so ubiquitously recurs in the nineteenth-century literature itself heavily figuring here, and associated with the many-windowed Jamesian dwelling, and with the Forsterian room with

a view. One of the principal ideological moves of our contemporary reflections on the urban is, says Prendergast, the "occlusion
of who is master of the house in favour of the idea of the city as
a 'free field of stimulus and aventure' for the relaxed and skillful
amateur."

Cities walked through and loved: Cingria's meditations and inscribing of his pedestrian traces take us to the Street-Haunting
Virginia Woolf did at such length and recounted so movingly:
Squier's Virginia's London is a memory of such haunting. Loving
a city: Kazin's intimate and evocative text takes us into the heart
of New York the city, his city in all its richness, with a personal
tone that is his only. Its very poetic quality sets it apart and keeps
it close to the heart.

The contemporary nowhere city with its traffic lots and films of
vacuity speeding alone is taken from various angles in Laura
Rice's "Trafficking" (like Ruskin's great essay "Traffic," on a building he so hated that he undid it by his very words) and Lewis'
essay on film and population—rushing by in confusion, stagnat-
ing in emptiness, pushing its power around and us with it.

And in spite of that, many of these essays reflect upon what it
is to picture and to philosophize about preservation. Kuhns'
deeply-thought essay comments on paintings as it comments on
the attempt to build a post-modern housing for what we would
keep. Le Corbusier and Kant meet here, in the discourse he constructs, to hold what we can of what we want most not to lose,
even now. This essay continues Weinstein's reflections on loss
and restoration, and brings the world of thought and the world
of art together in an imagination of aesthetic possibility, even
now, hoping for the lasting, even in lastness and lateness.

Indeed, this volume is not an essay in mastery or in nostalgia
in the opposing mode, a foggy invocation of mysterious city va-
pors. We have wanted to present an array of possible kinds of
reflection upon the notion of city in general, and city in specific,
so as to move from a philosophy or politics of city-writing and
city-thinking: city, text, and thought—to some modest display of
writing on writing of particular cities.

The essays are meant to respond, in their difference, to each
other as to the cities and the idea of city they concern. Just as the
discourses, the modes and contents, and the cities at issue themselves require each other for their own inter-questioning—so, ultimately, the considerations of certain topoi are enriched by their
convergence. Thus, the repeated focus on viewpoint, on the
place from which the landscape is seen. In what Josephs calls the
"optics of overview," the framing of sight from balconies and
windows (Kazin's New York from his upper West Side window,

Prendergast's Paris from Baudelaire's and Zola's windows) responds on the outer level to those notions of the gathering-in of information or material, the images and allegories of organisation and storage, as in the library and the archives, linking the city with narrative itself. The notion of linking and crossing is stressed in several essays, which return (Heller, Kazin, Kuhns) to Whitman's great poem about the Brooklyn Ferry; bridges and tunnels, crossroads, and labyrinth, avenues and streets, lanes and boulevards continue the linking theme, in varying degrees of complication. The essays of Weinstein, Godfrey, Winspur, Prendergast, deal with the latter, whereas the crossroad recurs in the essays of Faris, Joseph, and Esch, who interrogates—along with Wordsworth—the beggar at the intersection of reading and history. The theme of asking and and and that of demand were bound to recur, in the material and mental senses, in a place of emptiness and abundant possibility; making a terrible contrast with the figure of the *flâneur*. That of the blind beggar, like that of the dog in Kuhn's last summoning sentence, stands like some memento mori for us all, some constant recall of how intense an emptiness can exist in a "nowhere city"—of the sort Rice discusses—and even in the center of our own city. "Each city," says Calvino, "receives its form from the desert it opposes," and that opposition makes part of the cityscape.

To the concern about how we represent, with sufficient responsible involvement, a city at once material, and mental, Esch's own interrogation of the inadequacy of literary forms in response to "the demand of the moment" and in their failure to provide an image of adequate reading, is essentially on our minds. The beggar gives notice, in Benjamin's One-Way Street, that "things can't go on like this," and is both, as Esch says, readable and unreadable as a figure of "the urban sublime, the city's own resistance to interiorization and appropriation by the mind as a figure for the mind." The claims, Esch continues, of history and of fact cannot be settled—no more than can those of the beggar—easily. (Can it really be an impossible task for our own social ingenuity to imagine, even to work towards, a city beggarless and equitable?)

There is no way, either, of abandoning the almost impossible claims of representation, or of hoping to represent it all. If the conceptual city is, like the real one, difficult either to wander in or be at home, with its contradictory claims and promises, our representations double back on each other, promising nothing but problematics. Even that politics of display the first essay deals with has its own counterpart in a desire for reticence, however improbable; and in an odd way, the outside demands, even

in its impossibility, an effort at interiorization. By some circuitous
device, then, the narrative of the city and its wanderings brings
us, ironically yet again, back to the idea of labyrinth, linking the
ancient and the modern quest for happiness, or simply, some-
place to dwell secure. The idea of amazement with its own built-in
maze is never far from the consciousness of the city, of whatever
epoch. For among the other things it contains, and is, the city is
eternally a source of energy, empowered, empowering, and dis-
empowering, with desire eternally at its center. The high and
continuous erotic charge finds its concrete statement in the latter-
day futuristic vision (from which, alas, it may precisely prove impossible to erase all traces of Fascistic energy and its drastic
empowering), or just the actuality of Grand Central Station,
where the poetry of trains provides a momentum as useful as
that of the market and the stage themselves discussed in the initial essay. Long-term parking lots and the dream of power captured in celluloid (as in Rice and Lewis) play the same role of
gathering as the library and the archive for long-term storage of
information, and the labyrinth for long-term wandering: these
are all possibilities of the mind as of the instruments the mind
employs and uses for the embodiments of its desire.

Desire and viewing, and the telling of presence and the past,
on the street to the future: along with its speed, its orgiastic longing, and its potential for narrative understanding, the city is
manifest in its own frequent emptiness, its own enforced exile
from some other place. Weinstein introduces John Berger's obsessional empty space, and many of the essays invoke the strong
sentiment of exile, of loss, and of homelessness—Baudelaire's
swan haunts these pages as does Whitman's ferry—in some
strange pattern of strength dependent on otherness. Heller,
Godfrey, Weinstein, all invoke this same sad remaining figure,
holding over into the twentieth century a nineteenth-century
nostalgia, and even despair. Lorca's city of New York has all the
geometry, terror, horror, and anguish the lyric modern could desire . . . What we have lost is partially the sense of making sense
of our own narrative: the labyrinth must remain, in some sense,
legible as it is our city space. As New York and our other cities,
are increasingly torn down, the same old impulse to read what
was never written or never-yet-written (like the surrealist desire
for the never-thought with its energizing impulse) comes over us.
Yet we find ourselves telling the same tale with the same despair,
in the same eternally temporary place, our discourses responding
to each other more—perhaps—than to the surroundings, as if we
were to recreate some lost paradise of narrative, or then some
future utopia, even here, telling tales of our own disorientation

and our own hope. Kuhns' final reflection on possible exchange between the writers and readers we are holds out, finally, some modicum of hope. As if we could, indeed, "name what has no name," make legible our story, delay the lastness of the last manifesto, and salvage some overview. Whatever the genre of telling our own and others' cities: film, novel, poem, essay, staging, or journal—all these genres enter into discourse here, as if for a combination of display and quietness, external and internal city-dwelling, in some long-term parking of life and some possibility of love as of longing, even in exile.

> . . . seek and learn to recognize who and what, in the midst of the inferno, are not inferno, then make them endure, give them space.
>
> Italo Calvino, *Invisible Cities*

Mary Ann Caws
New York, 1990

NOTES

1. Raymond Williams, *Writing in Society*. London: Verso Editions, p. 19.
2. A chapter in *Ibid*, pp. 259–268. His discussion of the future tense of the imaginatio, of what he calls a future fiction, is particularly valuable in focussing on the city and its possibilities. We may just conceive of a negative present as the possible future, from which everything to be opposed in the current situation is absent; when we read cities in the future, this may well be our standard of legibility.
3. Raymond Williams, *The Country and the City*. New York: Oxford University Press, 1973.
4. Kevin Lynch, *The Image of the City*. Cambridge: M.I.T., 1960. Of course seeing the pattern may depend on a certain distance taken from both detail and problem—some observations depend on stance.
5. Edited by William Sharpe and Leonard Wallock, 1983, at Columbia University's Heyman Center for the Humanities. Subsequently, Baltimore: Johns Hopkins University Press, 1987.
6. Richard Sennett. *The Fall of Public Man*. New York: Alfred Knopf, 1977. See also Sennett's group of essays assembled in *Classic Essays on the Culture of Cities*; Englewood Cliffs, N.J.: 1969.
7. Sennett attacks here the most evident (the genial and much regretted) presenter of presentation in the sociological sense: Erving Goffman, *The Presentation of Self in Everyday Life*.
8. Robert Harbison. *Eccentric Spaces*. New York: Knopf, 1977.
9. See also Kazin's *An American Procession*. New York: Knopf, 1984.
10. Baudelaire's and Benjamin's Paris appears in the essays of Diamond, Godfrey, Prendergast, Weinstein, and Winsour.
11. Italo Calvino. *Invisible Cities*. New York: Harcourt Brace, 1974.
12. Jonathan Monroe. *The Prose Poem and the Politics of Genre*. Ithaca: Cornell University Press, 1987.
13. As is only fitting for the poet of the most famous text on "Correspondences," along with Forster's "Only connect."

SIPA/Art Resource. Disaster photo: Fires at the Waldorf Astoria, New York.

1

DISCOURSE AND THE CITY

Who ever believed in perfection? Moments question other moments, at their best, and ours. The power is built into the narrative of politeness, and cannot be undone, except by some conflicting text.

THE CITY: SOME CLASSICAL MOMENTS

Charles Molesworth

I start with the words of a Roman author; a characterization of cities, from *Scipio's Dream*, by Cicero: "You must know, my friends, that among all things done upon earth, nothing is more agreeable to the eyes of those who rule the universe than societies of men founded upon respect for laws, which we call cities." If we take this as our master text we can easily summarize the main significance of "the city" as the source of those qualities that we name with those city-born words, civility and civilization and urbanity. These are the hallmarks of a law-abiding society, a structure built upon a sense of respect and maintained by that respect. But also, while using this text, we must remain suspicious of its elevation, and be aware of how it speaks from "on high" and how it seeks to be definitive and exhaustive in what it describes. The fact that Cicero speaks from "on high" should also alert us to the sense of the city as a stage, in fact the place where a distinct sense of self undergoes a staging. We might even begin with a preliminary definition: the city is the stage where staging

13

itself occurs. If, as one critic has argued, the city is the place
where everything is both available and vanishing, then we can
also see it as the stage in which all prosceniums are unfolding
and disappearing.

Part of this unfolding and disappearing is due to what we
might call the aesthetic ecology of the city. For in the urban setting we constantly confront the intersection of private and public
spaces, as much of our urban experience allows public space to
become the stage for private experiences and private spaces to be
unfolded onto public experiences. This intersection of spaces results in large measure from the market aspect of the city, since it
is the market that is especially capable of mediating private desire and public activity. There are a number of places in modern
literature where this sense of the city is strikingly conveyed. Four
such places will frame the following discussion: a poem by
Baudelaire, a passage from Wordsworth's *Prelude,* a poem of
William Carlos Williams called "Perpetuum Mobile: The City,"
and John Ashbery's "Self-Portrait in a Convex Mirror." In each of
these passages there will be appeals to tropes of both stages and
markets, and we will see that the city is both market and stage,
those exemplary places where the available and the vanishing become virtually interchangeable.

The poem by Baudelaire is called "To a Red-Haired Beggar
Girl" and it is in the section called "Parisian Scenes," from *Les
Fleurs des Mal*. The poet, from circumstances equally "reduced"
(as he quaintly and ironically puts it) tells the beggar girl that her
vocation is not only beggary but beauty. He can make this claim
because he imagines her transformed through a comparison to a
queen, but a queen seen in dramatic terms:

> the frail and freckled body you display
> makes its own appeal-
>
> queens in velvet buskins take the stage
> less regally than you wade through the mud
> on your wooden clogs.[1]

Baudelaire goes on to imagine a most regal fate for the beggar-
girl, but it remains a most theatrical sort of fate, complete with
gentlemen sending their flunkeys to find out who owns the carriage that visits the queen, herself busy entertaining "a Bourbon
or two" in bedroom intrigues. But the poem ends with the poet
admitting he cannot even donate forty sous to the beggar, and
must content himself with urging her to go forth with no orna-
ment save that of her starving nakedness. The simplest way to
read the poem is as an ironic reversal of the cult of beauty, a

reversal which in fact can be read as a reaffirmation, since the cult of Beauty has always stressed the force of an ideal beauty that existed above and beyond mere physical details. But as we pursue the poem's irony, past Baudelaire's typical "nostalgie de la boue," past the aesthetics of decay, we find in the "stage" metaphor not only one of the organizing notions beneath the "Parisian Scenes" section but one of the poet's fundamental ways of appropriating urban experience. This experience is one of sudden revelations and concealments. In the poem immediately after "The Red-Haired Beggar Girl" Baudelaire tells us that "no human heart / changes half so fast as a city's face," and then goes on to see in his mind's eye the image of a poultry-market that used to be where now only a flea market, with its glittering junk, fills the "new" Place du Carrousel. Here it is the market rather than the stage that serves as the poem's controlling trope. But Baudelaire is constantly interweaving both tropes throughout his book, constantly showing us how all the forms of display are manifestations of desire, and as such are no sooner fully expressed than they are exhausted. Again, the available both hides and reveals the vanished, and eventually the city's buildings are turned to allegories and the poet's memories are felt to be heavier than stones, as the public and private realms are interchanged.

The enormous prestige of *Les Fleurs du Mal* might lead us to think that such an urban phenomenology as Baudelaire's is completely new, unlike anything that went before. But in fact a comparable sense of the city is available in the seventh book of Wordsworth's *Prelude*. It is in the *Prelude* that Wordsworth presents an extremely complex sense of city consciousness, and he does so in large measure by utilizing images of the market and the theater. These two sets of imagery might be seen as culminating and merging in the long passage on St. Bartholomew's Fair, where the availability of various phantasms becomes the norm, thus making the city the simulacrum of the entire world, catching up all the other places—such as Cairo and Babylon, which Wordsworth begins the book by placing in the context of London as the type of all cities. Part of the great energy of the city is reflected in its spectacles and markets, in both of which Wordsworth observes the presence of "imitations, fondly made in plain / Confession of man's weakness and his loves." The plain confession of appetite and imitation will return to haunt both Ashbery and Williams, and we can see how such confession is in part a staging of those human experiences. Wordsworth also remarks on the ethology of city life, and gives us pictures of Pitt the orator (adding Burke in the 1850 version) as well as the "comely bachelor / Fresh from a toilette of two hours" who delivers a most theatrical sermon. The poet nearly turns completely to satire in places, and even flirts with the tone of a jeremiad, as when he summarizes at one point:

> Folly, vice,
> Extravagance in gesture, mein, and dress,
> And all the strife of singularity,
> Lies to the ear, and lies to every sense—
> Of these, and of the living shapes they wear,
> There is no end.[2]
>
> (11.371-6)

I would offer "the strife of singularity" as one of the key phrases in this passage and in all of Book VII, for what Wordsworth finally ends with is a sort of nightmare vision of the city as the seat of nominalism, the place where singularity reigns as the only principle of value. This vision is made more clear in the passage where he comments on the description of the St. Bartholomew's Fair:

> Oh, blank confusion! and a type not false
> Of what the mighty City is itself
> To all except a straggler here and there.
> To the whole swarm of its inhabitants:
> An undistinguishable world to men,
> The slaves unrespited of low pursuits.
> Living amid the same perpetual flow
> Of trivial objects, melted and reduced
> To one identity, by differences
> That have no law, no meaning, and no end—
> Oppression, under which even highest minds
> Must labor, whence the strongest are not free.
> But though the picture weary out the eye,
> By nature an unmanageable sight,
> It is not solely so to him who looks
> In steadiness, who hath among least things
> An under-sense of greatest; sees the parts
> As parts, but with a feeling for the whole.
>
> (11.695-712)

Here the "same perpetual flow / Of trivial objects" presents what we might almost call an epistemological challenge, for it is an "unmanageable" sight which can only be properly perceived and understood by someone who keeps "an under-sense of greatest" things. But the trivial things themselves, despite the "strife for singularity", are always threatening to be "melted and reduced / To one identity", and thus by their lack of law and meaning to serve as the instruments of oppression. Of course Wordsworth's solution to this epistemological challenge is to rely on the forms of Nature and "converse with the works of God" where "appear / Most obviously simplicity and power," as he says a few lines later.[3] We can perhaps turn this formula around and say that what the city typifies is not simplicity and power, but rather complexity and the desire which can never be stilled. Indeed, two of the most curious moments in the book are those related to figures of complexity and baffled desire, namely the two "blind" men. Actually the first such figure is not precisely a blind man, but an actor on the stage who wears the sign "Invisible." He becomes the type of semantic confusion in the city, the marker of that which he cannot be, who must nevertheless declare himself in such a way as to answer a role, a social need. The other figure, an actual blind man, appears to Wordsworth like an admonishment "from another world." This blind beggar also carries a sign, a piece of paper on his chest which contains "the story of the man." This sight—the sightlessness proclaimed for all to see—becomes for Wordsworth "a type / Or emblem" of the "utmost that we know." These two figures are both the victims of city life and its emblems, since they together represent the threat of meaninglessness, as the ethos of display in urban existence turns everything into a realm of confused semantic claims. The particularity of individual human existence is distorted into an objectified world of display and proclamation whose rules are ultimately those of the market and the theatre.

The speaker in the poem[4] by William Carlos Williams begins by viewing the city from a distance, and is able to see it as "small / as a flower", but at night he knows that the city becomes dreamlike and "more / than a little / false." The poem proceeds by a series of cubist-like views of the city, a flow of contending and patterned energies that can range from the ironic invocation of the Postal Service motto ("neither the rain nor storm can keep them") to a whimsical image of armored car guards turned robbers. But in each instance Williams' refrain is "For love!", and he sees the city as the goal of all those who recognize that "There is no end / to desire—." But near the end of the poem Williams turns to an image of cloacal waste as he imagines an eel fattening in a water pipe by feeding on the waste products of the city. It is under the sign of this scavenging appetite that the speaker points over and over to the city, shouting "There!" three times in order to express his delight at the expanse of human effort, but also to convey a sense of discovery. However, this discovery is a demystifying one, for he claims that the city lights are "hiding / / the iron reason / and stone," and the "stars of matchless splendor" are able to bring only "silence." The poem ends with a "farewell!" while the city is imagined as dwindling in the hard grey rain of a summer's day. Williams' city is one where necessity has shown itself, and while the realms of *anake* and *eros* are interlocked, the elements of display and availability are set forth as the stars, the moon, and the bright-edged clouds. These natural "apparitions" dwarf the city and set it off, like a flower on a bush, and indeed the city itself disappears when the speaker and his anonymous lover enter it. In Williams we can see the dialectic of the available and vanishing shifting toward the latter term. The city can only be turned into an aesthetic object or faced as a market place of endless desire; it is a place of perpetual movement not only for those who live in it but for those who try to "view" it from some safe and significant distance. Of course, Williams does not have access to the heavenly viewpoint that provides Cicero with his perspective, so he must supply something like the time-worn Romantic naturalism of the stars and clouds and yet undercut this framework at the same time. By dramatizing and even enacting the very problem of viewpoints, Williams does more than bring a modern consciousness to bear on the city; he makes us aware of the city as a place where no coherent perspective is possible. Wordsworth and Baudelaire act as guides to the city by moving along on a street-level and there presenting the "strife of particularity," but when these poets take flight, as it were, for the higher view of the city they must resort to either a supposed divine framework or its inversion in a kind of satanism. In Williams we have the secular city in all its unceasing movement, but that movement must be thought of as taking place both in the city itself and in the consciousness of its ever mobile observers.

In John Ashbery's "Self-Portrait in a Convex Mirror," the ostensible subject is the Renaissance painting of the poem's title, but because of its powerful reflective energies the poem's real subject might more accurately be described as the problem of selfhood. Furthermore, the notions of selfhood embodied in the poem's complex structure are in part existential and in part a collection of decentered models of identity that are best described as profoundly post-modern. But what becomes apparent in the poem is that the notions of the self it advances and explores are even more profoundly urban in their texture and lineaments. At one point Ashbery names three cities: the Rome where the painting was executed, the Vienna where it is housed and where Ashbery first saw it, and the New York where the poem is being composed. It is New York that is called "a logarithm / Of other cities." The painting (and by extension the city) serves the poet as an emblem of how to live his life, or at least an emblem of how to conceive his own consciousness; this consciousness centers on the awareness that "the soul is not a soul," that we can never express it in words, and that "We see only postures of the dream." This search for the soul takes many forms, including the recognition that the search is fruitless, that it is condemned constantly to approach but never to take possession of the "here and now," that the surface of life may well contain all the meaning there is, and so forth. The city becomes an emblem of the painting, or the consciousness the painting is trying to teach the speaker, in many ways; but chiefly the city represents a form of what Ashbery calls "play," which has elements of the dramatic as well as the nominalistic, the acceptance that everything is both fully and undeniably itself, but that any attempt to represent this awareness inevitably betrays it. Here is the crucial passage:

> Today has no margins, the event arrives
> Flush with its edges, is of the same substance.
> Indistinguishable. "Play" is something else;
> It exists, in a society specifically
> Organized as a demonstration of itself.
> There is no other way, and those assholes
> Who would confuse everything with their mirror games
> Which seem to multiply stakes and possibilities, or
> At least confuse issues by means of an investing
> Aura that would corrode the architecture
> Of the whole in a haze of suppressed mockery,
> Are beside the point. . . .
> It seems like a very hostile universe
> But as the principle of each individual thing is
> Hostile to, exists at the expense of all the others
> As philosophers have often pointed out, at least
> *This* thing, the mute, undivided present,
> Has the justification of logic, which
> In this instance isn't a bad thing
> Or wouldn't be, if the way of telling
> Didn't somehow intrude, twisting the end result
> Into a caricature of itself.[5]

Here the "strife of particularity" seems to be resolved by the logic of the undeniability of the here and now, the "mute, undivided present." But the resolution is purchased at the price of unrepresentability.[6] The impulse to recreate simulacra of the world, an impulse explored in the seventh book of Wordsworth's *Prelude*, is doomed to frustration, since those "assholes" who believe in mirror games and "investing" auras fail to see that the surface *is* the meaning, just as the soul, by being an emptiness, is what allows for the wealth of consciousness. The city, too, is like the soul, everywhere available and vanishing, and since it allows us to see everything, it turns reality into a pageant, a pageant that dissolves the barrier between public and private space:

> We have seen the city; it is the gibbous
> Mirrored eye of an insect. All things happen
> On its balcony and are resumed within,
> But the action is the cold, syrupy flow
> Of a pageant. One feels too confined,
> Sifting the April sunlight for clues,
> In the mere stillness of the ease of its
> Parameter.

Here the poet turns into a would-be reader of oracular signs, condemned to operate on the static edges, observing life as if from a balcony. But in the meantime the city itself has become an optical instrument as well as a doubly visible surface; it is both eye and mirror, both how we see and what we see.[7] By re-presenting the world for our delectation and inspection, the city becomes both market and theatre, but it does so only at the cost of confinement and marginalization of the active subject.

One can see much of the literature that treats the city experience as not only reflecting anxiety about understanding signs, as in Wordsworth's case, but also anxiety about marginalization and confinement as the quintessential urban experiences of post-Romantic poetry. One way to measure this is to see the poetry of Whitman's urban experience as an anxiety-ridden attempt to conquer this condition. In "Crossing Brooklyn Ferry," for example, Whitman turns to a sort of mystical atomization of his ego which enables him to defeat the double threat of confinement and marginalization. But for those poets who don't possess Whitman's optimistic belief in progressive, democratic materialism, such a mystical solution is much more difficult, indeed virtually impossible.

Whitman's atomized self extends itself into an urban space and time, but not without a struggle. The desublimation that Whitman undergoes in Section 6 of the poem ("I am he who knew what it was to be evil") is stabilized by the end of the section by a resort to theatrical metaphor, as he tells us he "Played the part that still looks back on the actor and the actress, / The same old role, the role that is what we make it . . ." The concept here of the autochthonous self serving to master a threatening situation might be the watershed that marks off romanticism from modernism, for in the high modernist era—say 1910 to 1945—the idea of a self, (or the model of agency, that is, the paradigmatic way a self gains, preserves and expends its powers of selfhood) relies greatly on ironic dispersal rather than the mastering atomization of Whitman. Whitman's atomization, after all, his ability to claim to be watching not only all people in the urban space but those in future generations, could not proceed without an inordinate trust in the ultimate unity of one's ego. But Eliot's strategy in *The Waste Land*, for example is to "surrender" the poem's controlling ego by redrawing it in the figure of Tiresias, who is more a rhetorical construct that a psychological one. When Eliot tells us in a note that what Tiresisas sees is in essence the poem, we have at our disposal an ahistorical ironic observer for whom the city is fundamentally "unreal." Eliot's Tiresias has gone in a diametrically opposite direction from Whitman's speaker, who says, "I . . . had receive'd identity by my body / That I was I knew was of my body . . ." It is hard to have in the urban experience a strongly body-centered consciousness and not experience the sensations of marginalization and confinement.

There have been many attempts to discuss modernism and urbanization in the same framework. Some of the more conspicuous examples would include Marshall Berman's *All That is Solid Melts in the Air* and Richard Sennett's *The Uses of Disorder*, as well as the work of Deleuze and Guattari. I see these arguments as in some way trying to deal with the urban experience by revalorizing it, turning its perceptual chaos and disorienting simultaneity into a richness and multidimensionality of consciousness. The four poets I have chosen to illustrate my argument might be said to be operating in this large general framework. But what happens for these four poets, at least in these passages, is that the re-valorization of urban experience occurs in a way that allows them to mediate between the anxiety and the richness of that experience. Ashbery's image of the "cold, syrupy flow / Of a pageant" might be seen as the culmination of this mediating tradition. To deny that the city is like a pageant would be to cast oneself as hopelessly old-fashioned, something like a Luddite of urbanization. But at the same the unquestioning or unstinting acceptance of the city's pageant-like richness would require a disavowal of all irony. So to present it as a cold and syrupy flow is to mediate between its deterministic, entrapping qualities and its sweet and natural unfolding of desires and appetites.

What the market and the theatre do as mediating images is quite similar. Both of them are ways of emblematizing desire into something ineluctably bound up with narrative entrapment (the walker in the city observes a life that seems to him or her "staged" in its prizing of purposive activity and movement, whose overarching design is hidden even from the "actors") and commercial marginalization (everything available for sale is also vanishing, set before the walker but equally indifferent to his particular needs). Market and theatre are images that need the texture of spontaneity and even chaos in order to be fully energized, fully themselves, but both images also rely on an invisible control by forces that apparently transcend the power of individual agents.[8] In political terms this resembles what Hannah Arendt, in trying to characterize modern bureaucracy, has called "rule by nobody." The coming together of the general characteristics of the corrupt version of communism and the modern totalitarian state can be viewed—at least partially - as the culmination of an urban sense of the "proper" relationship between power and the self of modern mass man. Everything is promised as available in such political orders, as both forms trade on utopian desires, but everything is also subject to a power of conferral that can never be questioned, and so is always, in a real sense, vanishing. The brutal irony of such political forms is that they are likely to founder when they fail to supply their populations with the requisite consumer satisfactions, for despite their heroicizing, even myticizing of the principle of labor they often have contempt for material skills and appetites. The principles of the modern city and those of the workers' paradise may be inescapably opposed, as modern man-as-consumer will always outstrip modern man-as-maker.

So we can see where each poet "stages" the phenomenology of urban consciousness as itself a form of "staging", a form which causes the act of perception to take on a contested and yet patterned interlocking of awarenesses. From Baudelaire's claim that "no human heart / changes so fast as a city's face," to Wordsworth's blind man who reflects a higher vision, to Williams' perpetually changing viewpoints, to Ashbery's priestly decoder of a suspended vision, the poetry of the modern city often shows a scene in which the very notion of the scenic unsettles all our notions of singularity and totality. Many of our poets can envision the city as a comprehensive type, a "logarithm," which contains the structure and texture of all our individual urban experiences. Yet many of these poets also insist on the "strife of particularity" as the prototypical urban experience, since the city is the one place that hallows the "mute, undivided present." Because it is difficult for the modern poet to see the city from on high, the way to mediate this singularity and this typicality is to resort to tropes of the theatre and the market place. In these two tropes we can see the successful but also the unstable nature of such a mediation, for the market and the theatre are places where desire is always endlessly doubled, since the acts we perform there are both relentlessly particularized (because they are always in a bodily gesture) and inescapably signs of some higher order (either the aesthetic or the erotic). This unstable mediation, between a version of nominalism and the felt need for a transcendent but unavailable perspective, is the central philosophical "truth" of the urban experience.

NOTES

1. From *Les Fleurs du Mal*, translated by Richard Howard (Boston, Mass., 1982), p.88. This poem can also be read as a poem about "exchange relations," in which the failure to give the beggar any money is compensated for by the poet's idealizing of her. In turn, the beggar girl gives the poet a valuable "experience."
2. I cite here the 1805 version from *The Prelude: A Parallel Text*, ed. J. C. Maxwell (Harmondsworth, England, 1972), p.284. Subsequent citations are from the same text, with line numbers given in parentheses.
3. I have discussed Wordsworth's republican sentiments in "Wordsworth's 'Westminster Bridge' Sonnet: The Republican Structure of Time and Perception," *CLIO* VI:3(1977), 261–273. Also, the image of the "straggler" (1.697) can be read as that of the typical city-dweller, the Cain figure whose presence defines the urban space.
4. From *The Collected Earlier Poems* (New York, 1951), pp.384–390.
5. In *Self-Portrait in a Convex Mirror* (New York, 1975).
6. Speculation on sources (who are the philosophers who have often pointed this out?) is hard to resist here. I would suggest that Ashbery has in mind the Hegel of *Phenomenology of Mind*, specifically the passage on sense certainty.
7. Ashbery's insect eye is a very complex image, as is the meaning of the entire passage. However, since the city is shown metaphorically as both something to look into and something to see by, the passage may also be taken as a mediation of the notions of the city as both surface and container, as explored by Gerald Bruns.
8. We might have resort here to Kenneth Burke's dramatistic terms. The city is a place where agency threatens to overwhelm the agent, where the required tools of living replace the aims and intentions of life. Also, when the agent/agency ratio tips in favor of the second term, we have a theatrical experience close to melodrama: when a character says, speaking of the emotion that should be seen as issuing from (and thus subservient to) a human agent, "It's bigger than both of us." The city in modern poetry might also be an image of where the agent/scene ration becomes dominated by the second term. Nearly everyone has their favorite one-line characterization of the urban experience. I can't resist recording mine, which comes from Kurt Vonnegut. He once said New York is the place where you feel something exciting is happening even if you aren't doing anything.

DISCOURSE, POLIS, FINITENESS, PERFECTION

Stephen David Ross

One of the great textual traditions is that of the city. In many of its most powerful forms, it has echoed our expectations of heaven and hell. I want to argue that this glorious tradition rests on a fundamental error: that of the ideal perfectibility of human being. This is by now an old story. My excuse for discussing it is not so much to break new ground as to connect a variety of themes, largely by analogy.

My primary analogy is between the city and the novel, a specific application of a more general analogy between politics and literature. And it may be appropriate to begin with a brief discussion of the analogy, since it may seem farfetched. It is based on two major considerations: one the impossibility of disentangling the spheres of human life and understanding, the other the discursive nature of both politics and literature. I am referring to the ways in which discourse, power, understanding, and desire are interrelated.

> The central issue, then (at least in the first instance), is not to determine whether one says yes or no to sex, whether one formulates prohibitions or permissions, whether one asserts its importance or denies its effect, or whether one refines the words one uses to designate it; but to account for the fact that it is spoken about, to discover who does the speaking, the positions and viewpoints from which they speak, the institutions which prompt people to speak about it and which store and distribute the things that are said. What is at issue, briefly, is the over-all 'discursive fact,' the way in which sex is 'put into discourse.' Hence, too, my main concern will be to locate the forms of power, the channels it takes, and the discourses it permeates in order to reach the most tenuous and individual modes of behavior, the paths that give it access to the rare or scarcely perceived forms of desire, how it penetrates and controls everyday pleasure—all this entailing effects that may be those of refusal, blockage, and invalidation, but also incitement and intensification: in short, the 'polymorphous techniques of power.'[1]

Simply substitute the city, humanity, or truth for sexuality here to consider how these are put into discourse entangled with diverse forms of power and exclusion. What we must add is that the novel is one of the prominent forms of discourse just as the city is one of the prominent forms of human life, but reciprocally, that the novel is one of the prominent expressions of humanity while the city is one of the prominent symbols of humanity. Novel and city are large-scale images of truth and life. What is involved is understanding how the notions of the city, of justice, of truth, even of humanity, belong to discourse and are manifestations of power and desire.

> One must not suppose that there exists a certain sphere of sexuality that would be the legitimate concern of a free and disinterested scientific inquiry were it not the object of mechanisms of prohibition brought to bear by the economic or ideological requirements of power. If sexuality was constituted as an area of investigation, this was only because relations of power had established it as a possible object; and conversely, if power was able to take it as a target, this was because techniques of knowledge and procedures of discourse were capable of investing it.[2]

One must not suppose that there exists a certain sphere of literary discourse that freely employs linguistic and discursive resources independent of the relations of power that constitute any form of discourse, or that there exists a sphere of human life, the "city," that does not at the same time inhabit discursive formations.

> Power must be understood in the first instance as the multiplicity of force relations immanent in the sphere in which they operate and which constitute their own organization; as the process which, through ceaseless struggles and confrontations, transforms, strengthens, or reverses them; as the support which these force relations find in one another, thus forming a chain or a system, or on the contrary, the disjunctions and contradictions which isolate them from one another; and lastly, as the strategies in which they take effect, whose general design or institutional crystallization is embodied in the state apparatus, in the formulation of the law, in the various social hegemonies.[3]

Force relations and discursive relations are inseparable from each other as well as from desire. But we must add that desire is itself, as is humanity, something that belongs to discourse.

The question I wish to discuss, from the point of view of these manifold entanglements of discourse with knowledge, power, and desire, is that of perfectibility, primarily of human life as manifested in our view of politics, but drawing from our understanding of discourse. One assumption to be laid aside is that there is a perfectible discourse: a perfected discourse cannot belong to itself or to human experience. Discourses, along with cities, are major sites at which desire and power function.

We may add that the notion of a perfected discourse is rather like that of a perfected polis. I am arguing that this notion of ideal perfection is incoherent, in both cases, and that with its rejection, we must abandon as well the notion of a perfected human being, even of a perfect peace. What I mean here is not simply that we cannot achieve perfection, but that the notion itself in any of these applications is incoherent. The perfection I am rejecting is that of an ideal independent of history, an ideal that overcomes the inexhaustible surplus of discourse and being.

There cannot in this sense be a perfected discourse or an ideal language. Such a language would be one in which every expression had a preferred form and in which, given certain linguistic formations, we could not err. Yet if we can say whatever we want to say in language, and if what we say is a function of how we express it as well as of who expresses it and under what circumstances, then such perfectibility is unintelligible. In relation to the novel or poetry, there is no relevant notion of perfectibility. There is no perfect poetic form, no ideal novelistic style, no perfect novel. Perfection in works of art expresses not an ideal in terms of which works are comparable, but sovereignty and incomparability. This incomparability expresses not conformity to an ideal but an inexhaustible surplus in every work of art.

Moreover, the existence of poetic and literary discourse directly contravenes the perfectibility of any other form of discourse. We would have to hold that—for example—scientific or propositional discourse was perfectible while literary discourse was not, implying that the latter was defective, and *because* of its expressive powers, not in spite of them. Yet such perfectibility could at best be in certain respects, perfect for particular purposes and not for others; in addition, such a "perfect" discourse could not reflexively interrogate itself, for if we have learned anything from Derridian and Foucauldian discussions, it is that modes of discourse require each other for their own questioning. Modes of discourse require each other to establish the legitimacy of any. (I include the development of new forms.) The social and political entanglements of discourse, seen as intrinsic to discourse rather than ways in which it falls short of an ideal if external movement of thought, are incompatible with perfectibility.

There is another sense of perfection, quite different from one that rests on independent ideals, one far more appropriate to the finiteness of literary production and human life. This sense, based on the sovereignty of individual works and texts, emphasizes the impossibility of improvement of a perfect work, not because it adheres to ideal norms but because there is no external ideal against which to measure improvement. We have here a sense of perfection as completeness in a kind, but based on no antecedent limitation of kinds, inclusive therefore of novelty and incomparability. This sense, derived from literary texts as paradigms, I am arguing, is the only one appropriate as well to political judgments, the only one appropriate to human life.

The analogy I am pursuing becomes rather suggestive. The city belongs to story and to discourse, not simply in the Foucauldian sense that our understanding of the polis is the result of discursive strategies, but in the more powerful sense that a discursive strategy that includes the polis, that includes human moral and political life, is imperfect and imperfectible because every such strategy implies others necessary to its own legitimacy. Every political structure demands alternative structures; every discourse entails manifold discourses. Specifically, every society is divided within itself into subsocieties; political institutions and forms are divided within themselves by opposing forms. Foucault calls these "resistances."

> Should it be said that one is always "inside" power, there is no "escaping" it, there is no absolute outside where it is concerned, because one is subject to the law in any case? Or that, history being the ruse of reason, power is the ruse of history, always emerging the winner? This would be to misunderstand the strictly relational character of power relationships. Their existence depends on a multiplicity of points of resistance: these play the role of adversary, target, support, or handle in power relations. These points of resistance are present everywhere in the power network. Hence there is no single locus of great Refusal, no soul of revolt, source of all rebellions, or pure law of the revolutionary. Instead there is a plurality of resistances, each of them a special case: resistances that are possible, necessary, improbable; others that are spontaneous, savage, solitary, concerted, rampant, or violent; still others that are quick to compromise, interested, or sacrificial; by definition, they can only exist in the strategic field of power relations. . . . Resistances . . . are the odd term in relations of power; they are inscribed in the latter as an irreducible opposite.[4]

This notion of resistance expresses two important principles of power: that there is no discourse that is not a strategy of power, and that there is no such discourse that is not divided within itself by resistances; exclusions belong to both power and resistance. There is no monolithic form of domination, and, similarly, no monolithic form of human life, no monolithic form of discourse, and none is perfectible. This is an old story in relation to literary discourse. It is not, however, in relation to norms of justice and peace.

The subject to which we come is that of positive ideals, including that of a positive peace. What I mean by a positive ideal here rests on the form of argument, cosmological or transcendental, that holds that in order for us to have a coherent and defensible value, it must be based on an intelligible sense of ideal perfection. There is no implication that such perfection is realizable.

I have suggested that the notion of an ideal novel or poem, ideal work of literature or art, is unintelligible. I mean this in a very strong sense, not only that works of art and literature do not compete normatively, are not generally comparable in rank if they are sometimes comparable in kind, but in the sense expressed by Kant in his theory of genius, that the norms we employ in evaluating works of art are in large part defined by them, not antecedently. The paradigm is both strong and precise: we can evaluate works of art effectively even though the standards we employ must inevitably await the production of new works for their definition. Such a paradigm, however, calls any theory of rational evaluation into question that would establish norms prior to their application. In the case of politics, however, or of any major form of human life that has importance for great numbers of people and in manifold ways, we must add that every such norm collapses not only in virtue of time and novelty, but because of the compromises required where matters have such moment. What is involved is either a notion of norms that are inevitably imperfect or of perfections that are inevitably limited. It is the glory of the human city that it is imperfectible, an expression of its richness and importance, just as it is the glory of art that perfection is unintelligible for it.

With such an orientation, we may consider a number of contrasts and analogies involving politics and literature, the city and the text, that have importance in current discussions. One is the recurrent theme of death: the novel is always on the verge of exhaustion and abandonment; similarly, the contemporary city is overcrowded, dangerous, inhuman. Yet of all the literary forms that are still being read widely, the novel perseveres. And where people have a choice, and are not entirely susceptible to economic determinants, a great number choose to live in allegedly inhuman cities. To this we may add the recurrent theme of the death of the Western metaphysical tradition. All of these views contain within themselves, however modern or postmodern they would be, the assumption that there is a historical essence to thought and discourse, to life and the city, to our relationship to being, and that if these were changed radically, they would take on a new essence. Such a view is profoundly millenial. To the contrary, I am arguing, the "essence" of these major human forms is that wherever they are the same, they are divided within themselves, differentiated, and wherever they are different, they nevertheless are able to widen themselves, with history and the future, to include oppositions within themselves. These are all forms that contain within themselves their own forms of antagonism and criticism.

To this we may add that the city of God rests on the perfectibility of the city, just as the story of God rests on the perfectibility of both life and thought. But the story of God is a specific and dense form of discourse, and in that form is both imperfectible and inexhaustible. There is no one "true" story of God, but manifold stories and expressions. Yet it does not follow that every story is an acceptable or significant story. Similarly, there is no perfect city, not even in heaven. Yet it does not follow that every city is an acceptably human city. What does follow is that every city is human, acceptable or not, with all of the complexity of that humanity, discursive and political. It follows that humanity widens to include all its forms of life and discourse, both positively and negatively, by prohibition and restriction.

What we are speaking of, in part, is the nature of the future and our relationship to the past. Here city and text exhibit comparable relationships to time. Each is partly visible, partly invisible, encrusted with human forms that carry them into the future and characterize their importance for different futures. Here perfectibility, in discourse or life, assumes a certain relationship to the perilousness of the future: it does not suggest that the future may become less dangerous in the everyday risks of life and death, but that we will be able to think the future completely, even if we cannot live it. Finiteness here is imperfection. What I am arguing is that finiteness cannot be imperfection if ideal perfection is incoherent. The greatest novels and works of art are not "imperfect" because there is no ideal work, but are magnificent in ways that include no sense of ideality, especially in the respect that their natures and essences await their future. The greatest forms of human life are not "imperfect" because no perfect form has been realized, but are magnificent because they are open to transformations that ideality would forbid. Here the dangerousness of the future is in part that it transforms the past, transforms every being that that past brings before us. Texts are always partly indeterminate because they await a future that can transform them, and that they transform. Discourse and politics do not merely share in this perilousness, but are the sites at which the perils are realized.

Foucault speaks of the dangerousness of discourse, not merely that we cannot entirely control it, but that in it we find the voids and negativities that inhabit our own being. Similarly, the dangerousness of life is nowhere more apparent than in the city, although the dangers of life are far greater in the country. To this we must add that we find our own absences in the forms of power that inhabit not only our forms of life—urban and other— but in the discourses that inhabit those forms. In this profound sense, the city not only is in our texts, but is a text, a site at which meaning is formed, with exclusions and prohibitions. Curb your dog; fight graffiti; keep your words and syntax standard American. The battle over linguistic hegemony in the schools is inseparable from the battle over who will control the cities and human life.

The conclusion of this discussion is that there is no perfect peace as there is no perfect truth, no perfect city as there is no perfect language or discourse. It does not follow that the city is then hell on earth, any more than that every discourse falls short of an ideal understanding and every language falls short of a perfect form of communication. Cities, texts, discourses, along with other forms of human life, are the sites at which human being realizes itself, in the inexhaustible ways in which such realization is possible. What we must understand is that consequently there is no intelligible meaning to a utopian sense of such forms of life. The inadequacies of our realization that ideal perfection is impossible may be offset by the further realization that inexhaustibility manifests its own forms of greatness and transcendence, even of finite perfections, in the context of the unintelligibility and incoherence of any notion of ideality.

NOTES

1. Michel Foucault, *History of Sexuality, Vol. I*, Robert Hurley tr., New York, Random House, 1980, p. 11.
2. *Ibid.*, p. 98.
3. *Ibid.*, pp. 92–93.
4. *Ibid.*, pp. 95–96.

Art Resource. Gustave Doré, The Houses of the Poor are not the Palaces of the Rich, Engraving.

2

COGNITIVE MAPPING: LABYRINTHS, LIBRARIES AND CROSSROADS

What makes the polis legible, and does the reading leave its traces? Having read ourselves in, can we read ourselves out? The most intricate of modern writers: Dickens, Borges, Eco, Butor, Robbe-Grillet for fiction, and the great practitioners of the prose poem deal in the scopic as in the maze: from labyrinth to library, wandering and grouping and overviewing, crossing over and tunneling in. Their readings of spatiality, from the world to the book and back out, cannot but concern us crucially.

THE LABYRINTH AS SIGN OF CITY, TEXT, AND THOUGHT

Wendy B. Faris

The labyrinth has persisted from classical through contemporary literature as image and as structural design in urban writing, highlighting the interdependence of those two entities, the city and the text. In a continuously generative project, the labyrinthine city forms the labyrinthine mind and the traces its activity leaves as texts, so that questions of mimesis become curiously involuted. Verbal semiotic systems—including literature—are of course primarily symbolic, visual ones largely iconic. But where the building of cities and of texts interact, each modeling the other, the distinction becomes less clear. In addition, the literary

33

symbol and structure of the labyrinth comes clearly from the visual arts, so that it mediates conceptually between a symbolic mode of discourse and an iconic mode of representation. Though I will indicate how I have drawn my formulations from specific texts, I will present here on theoretical conclusions as to *why* the labyrinth is such a strong and persistent literary image associated with the city, with writing, and with thought.

What we see in following the ancient pattern of the labyrinth through the centuries is that as a literary image it serves an increasingly metaliterary function, commenting on the activity of writing itself. This tendency is reinforced by the capacity of the labyrinth to blur the distinctions between the physical qualities of cities and the natures of the texts and thoughts they engender. Early on, Ovid describes the twistings and turnings of the Cretan labyrinth, concluding that "so Daedalus made those innumerable winding passages, and was himself scarce able to find his way back to the place of entry, so deceptive was the enclosure he had built."[1] Ostensibly a visual description of the physical structure, Ovid's account already prefigures the metatextual pull of the labyrinth in his portrait of the fabricator entrapped in his own deceptive enclosure—an implicit warning about the dangers of artistry. Here it is clear that the labyrinth often serves to point up what a particular writer judges to be wrong with the metropolis. But what is wrong changes considerably through the years: earlier labyrinths bemoaned the chaos of cities, later ones their excessive—and no less bewildering—regularity. Not surprisingly, in medieval and Renaissance times this critical potential was realized with increasingly moralistic force. As always in such an architectural figure, the interaction between visual and verbal signs is important here; the labyrinths that serve as warnings against the intrigues of the worldly city and the overzealous mind build on resonances of the earliest Christian examples of inscriptions in stone—mosaic labyrinths on church floors which functioned as patterns for ritual processions. Labyrinth designs, some of them with captions, accompany religious texts, particularly those which speak of man's wanderings and temptations. A German translation of Boethius (ca. 1085) contains a design of a labyrinth whose center holds figures of the world and the devil—man's destination at the end of the labyrinth of the world unless he follows the chosen way.[2] John Comenius offers a particularly unappealing view of the city as labyrinth in his *The Labyrinth of the World and the Paradise of the Heart*. As he approaches the city, Comenius' traveller first sees it as "seemingly fine and beautiful"; but he then perceives it to be "crowded with people as if with insects," and notes that the streets are broken through in

many places, suggesting confusion and even decay.[4] On the one
hand, Comenius' work can be seen to duplicate structurally for
the reader his experience of a European city: the profane space
of the streets corresponds to the first part of the text, the labyrinth of the world, the sacred space of the cathedral to the second part, the labyrinth of the heart. The reader wanders in the
first and comes out upon the second. On the other hand, by locating urban labyrinth and interior paradise in two separate
domains, he underlines their difference. In the secular realm, the
labyrinth has frequently served as a sign for the entanglements
of plots and plotting as they duplicate the corridors of palaces
and their amorous intrigues. (Here I am thinking primarily of
plays, like those of Boccacio and Cervantes, both called *The Labyrinth of Love*.)

Recently, in addition to evoking the labyrinth as a symbol for
the city, the mind, and the text, novels like Joyce's *Ulysses*, Butor's *Passing Time*, and Robbe-Grillet's *In the Labyrinth* duplicate
the form of the labyrinth in the structural design of their prose,
so that in them besides the labyrinths *in* the texts we experience
the labyrinths *of* the texts. The labyrinthine experience of error
and backtracking, of dead ends and repetitions, is most clearly
developed in the structure of *In the Labyrinth*. There passages or
scenes identical to preceding ones suggest the trials and errors of
narrative discourse as it articulates a story. In following these
comings and goings, and in interpreting them, the reader constructs an accompanying labyrinth of interpretation, one which
will often include alternative pathways of explication. The same
situation characterizes *Passing Time*, though there the reader's
choices regarding events are fewer, and the narrator's backtrack-
ings do not appear as repetitions of entire passages or scenes
which would emphasize the construction of a labyrinthine discourse but rather as his remembering various events over and
over again, so that they exist primarily in the domain of story.
Butor's text is probably the most elaborate contemporary fictional
interweaving of the labyrinths of city, text, and thought, for in it
he exploits extensively both the iconic and the symbolic potential
of the pattern. The formal structure of the diary/novel activates
on the iconic level the repeated references to the myth of the labyrinth it contains. Reversed paths and impasses are less easily
recognized in *Ulysses* than in either of the French examples; they
consist principally of image or thought patterns that the reader
encounters throughout the novel. And though the process is less
formalized than in *In the Labyrinth* or *Passing Time*, the text of
Ulysses often suggests the need to pass a series of associated objects or ideas before emerging into a new branch of the labyrinth.

Bloom and Molly—like most of us—often think of objects or ideas as parts of a series, and when one reappears in their monologues, so do several of the others. Within this design, the reader also makes choices regarding syntax, and so language itself becomes a labyrinth. My conclusions about modern urban labyrinths of words are based both on the narratives of Joyce, Butor, and Robbe-Grillet—and Borges (of whom more in a moment) which specifically invoke the sign of the labyrinth either symbolically or iconically, and on the whole domain of fiction-as-labyrinth that they implicate by this invocation.

In *Of Grammatology* Jacques Derrida explores (after Rousseau) the phenomenon of "writing by furrows," that is, "writing by *the turning of the ox*—boustrophedon": proceeding "economically," the ploughman, "arrived at the end of the furrow, . . . does not return to the point of departure. He turns ox and ploughs around. And proceeds in the opposite direction." Derrida then asks why writing in similar fashion, from left to right and back again from right to left was abandoned. "Why did the economy of the writer break with that of the ploughman? Why is the space of the one not the space of the other?" Derrida, still folllowing Rousseau, explains this rupture by the fact that "it is more convenient to read than to write by furrows," and so script developed from left to right, in deference to the movement of the hand.[5] The turn of the ploughman that Derrida describes and the way he makes it question the identity of the two kinds of cultivation, of text and terrain, is conceptually similar to the impulse toward the conflation of terrestrial and scriptural itineraries made explicit in recent labyrinthine fictions. Could we consider these fictions as attempts to recover in part that original spatial coincidence of ground and text, reversing the original economic imperative in favor of an aesthetic and philosophical one? These textual labyrinths represent traces of exploration rather than cultivation, made not to bear fruits but to pose questions, their proliferation of linguistic possibilities contrasting with Flaubert's statement (as reported by de Maupassant) that "whatever you want to say, there is only one word to express it, one verb to animate it, and one adjective to qualify it."[6]

Continuing in this same vein—or furrow—we need to note briefly the existence of another kind of three dimensional labyrinth. Particularly in the cases of Butor and Robbe-Grillet—and in European literature generally since the Renaissance—the model of the hedge maze can be seen as an intermediary between the architecture of cities and the construction of verbal labyrinths. It cleverly combines both nature and art, abstracting its form from the paths in forest and town, similar to urban writing

in both reflecting and transforming its referent. Like cities themselves and the texts they engender, the formalized and avowedly
ludic form of living script that is the hedge maze continually
threatens to overflow its prescribed boundaries. Present in many
parks and grand gardens, it prefigures labyrinths constructed for
readers to wander in.

In ancient architecture and myth as in early church design and
Christian doctrine we can chart the movement of the labyrinth
from visual icon to verbal symbol. But as I have suggested, a significant recent innovation is that a number of novels exploit the
labyrinth's iconic verbal properties as well as its symbolic resonances, so that in them the shape of rhetoric, we might say, corresponds imaginatively to the grammar of cities. Butor has said
that he walks around in books as he does in houses—and (I add)
as he does in cities.[7] His statement encapsulates the sense in
which the cognitive maps of the walker in the city resemble the
decoding strategies of the reader in the text. They are both rep-
ertories for the competent traversal of a given space. This complex interdependence of urban and textual construction suggests
that we take seriously the calembour of "architexture" as a metaphorical description of much urban writing. In the end this
matching of the shapes of story and discourse or of visual and
verbal labyrinths blurs the distinction between subject and object. Bachelard's discussion of dream labyrinths helps to explain
the process. He imagines the dreamer as not only experiencing
labyrinths but as constituting labyrinthine matter: "in our
dreams, we are sometimes a labyrinthine substance, a substance
that lives by stretching itself, by losing itself in its own turnings. . . . The being in the labyrinth is at once subject and object
combined as a lost being" ("l'être dans le labyrinthe est à la fois
sujet et objet conglomérés en être perdu").[8] So it is with a text
which not only describes a labyrinthine trajectory through a city
but constitutes a labyrinthine discourse.

In a different, and largely symbolic way, the writing of Borges,
who is intimately aware of the topography of both ancient cities
and his own, constitutes another significant example of the labyrinth as it functions as a sign of the interdependence of cities,
texts, and thoughts. Borges persistently uses the labyrinth to suggest how the shapes of thought, and their print-out in writing
both inform and reflect the shapes of their worlds.[9] Over and
over again in his fiction, labyrinths of words or thoughts coexist
with labyrinthine itineraries, each variety implicating the other.
The best known example is the labyrinthine book of Ts'ui Pên in
"The Garden of Forking Paths." It hovers behind the labyrinthine
spy story enacted in the foreground by Ts'ui Pên's descendent Yu

Tsun and the decoder of his work Stephen Albert, and finally encompasses that story as Albert explains to Yu Tsun that "in the work of Ts'ui Pên, all possible outcomes occur; each one is the point of departure for other forkings. Sometimes, the paths of this labyrinth converge; for example, you arrive at this house, but in one of the possible pasts you are my enemy, in another, my friend."[10] Furthermore, and in reference to Borges' portraits of one particular city, it is possible to show how Borges' texts register—among other things—the transformation of Buenos Aires. As the city expands from the large town whose streets allow glimpses of the pampa to the metropolis whose paths become ever more intricate, Borges' texts change from poetry describing the still rather primitive city to prose works whose linguistic limpidity encloses labyrinthine convolutions of thought. (Strangely enough, in his later years, once blind, and no longer able to see the city—except in his mind's eye of course—Borges returns to poetry.)

Because the design of the labyrinth simultaneously represents a puzzle and a solution, a journey and an arrival, it embodies the way in which urban texts can be seen as both maps and routes, as descriptions and projects, portraits of streets and guides within them. Fictional urban labyrinths—symbolic or iconic—duplicate man's experience of the city as diachronic wandering and synchronic mapping. The labyrinth signals this duality well because it figures both time and space, becoming and being. A paradox that inheres in the traditional visual symbol of the labyrinth enables it to suggest this aspect of cities and their texts. This is the dichotomy between the confusion the labyrinth has come to symbolize and the formalized visual pattern the image calls up—as I have said, in human terms between the wanderer and the mapmaker. Nevertheless, unlike earlier uses of the labyrinth pattern, recent texts reflect the decentered configuration of the modern city. Thus they do not represent escapes from but rather affirmations of entrapment in the city and its languages. The labyrinth of the world does not open into the paradise of the heart just as Paris is no longer centered by Notre Dame and the textual enigmas of *Ulysses* are not unravelled at its end.

These modern labyrinths, reflecting the trajectories of wanderers in cities, thus illustrate the movement Burton Pike perceives in literature from the Renaissance city, which he imagines as consisting of "fixed spatial relationships embodying an ideal cosmic order," to the "dynamic modern city," which is "presented in terms of action in time."[11] Still, the image of the labyrinth, as it "schleps, trains, drags, trascines" its load of ancient symbolic resonances, can never be rid of that dream of cosmic order.[12] It gains in poetic force because it permits a glimpse of sacred space through the pervading profane. It is thus a nostalgic, not a futuristic image of the city, however many times we may see the labyrinth-as-computer-chip. This may be one reason why it appears so persistently in literary portraits of cities—a tribute to the archeology of thought.

In an indirect way, the narrators of *Ulysses, Passing Time,* and *In the Labyrinth* all express a fear that this mobile labyrinthine city will soon cover the world, just as city suburbs spread over the landscape. The narrator of *Passing Time* pictures the city of Bleston as interlocking with other similar cities so that he cannot reach clear countryside. *In the Labyrinth* ends when the narrator leaves the city, a city whose characteristics suggest those of Everycity. And it seems unlikely that Bloom will ever find his way permanently out of Dublin to relocate in the country cottage of his dreams. Thus in many modern cities, man becomes minotaur. Old labyrinthine city defenses were designed to keep out invaders; modern inhabitants are frequently trapped inside cities described as labyrinths. The convolutions have moved within and are threatening rather than protective.

In this context I would like to consider briefly the labyrinth as a problematic figure of desire in language. To recall very early uses of labyrinths in rituals of sexual initiation reinforces our sense of literary labyrinths as structures of desire, or of postponed gratification. And the many literary labyrinths of love where amorous intrigues are straightened out at the end of the text also implicitly associate the processes of desire and decoding. At first glance, however, the modern labyrinths of language I have been describing appear to serve as distancing mechanisms, as frustrations of desire carefully encoded in the text. They propose their own centers, or rather their own possibilities for gratified desire, embodied in the successful quest for linguistic meaning, only to subvert and annul them. Do they then only tempt us with a lost region of satisfaction and understanding we can never reach and explore? Are we, following their circlings, in the position of Gide's Theseus, who is able to conquer the labyrinth and to kill the minotaur but not to claim Oedipus' knowledge of the divine? Or like Borges' figure of Gracián, hopelessly lost in "labyrinths, quibbles, emblems"?[13] The convolutions of the discourse remove the quester/lover/reader from the object of his desire; they complicate penetration and definitive union leading to a climax of comprehension in the possession of meaning. On the other hand, if we continue with the metaphor of desire, in a labyrinthine narrative mode the erotic paradigm of penetration and satisfaction shifts in part to the act of reading, locates itself in the realm of discourse rather than in that of story. From this viewpoint the distancing effect is reduced, so that the labyrinths *of* the novels reinstate the expressive powers of language that they as well as the labyrinths *in* the novels have seemed to deny.

This process is similar to the one that Peter Smith describes in discussing what he terms the "maze factor" in cities. Smith maintains that "the labyrinth was a sign of citizenship in cities; to know its secret conferred both status and the freedom enjoyed by burghers." Furthermore, he maintains that "inscrutable urban space holds a fascination for people" and that "when the key to the labyrinth has been discovered, or, in psychological terms, a cognitive map or model has been constructed, the relationship between the individual and the environment aspires to a new level. Once a place has yielded its secrets it facilitates empathy between mind and artifact. Man and buildings become symbolically bound together."[14] This comprehension and subsequent appropriation of a form, the symbolic binding of man and his dwelling places, describes the reader's experience of labyrinthine urban fictions. Those fictions are verbal equivalents of Smith's cognitive maps and models, but they achieve their empathetic connection between mind and thought by not always yielding their own secrets or those of their places. In foregrounding the problematic nature of writing and reading, and in linking them symbolically and iconically to the designs of cities, they function as multivalent signs of the unity of city, text, and thought.

NOTES

1. Ovid, *Metamorphoses*, trans. Frank J. Miller, Loeb Classical Library (Cambridge, Mass.: Harvard University Press, 1951), I, Book VIII, 11. 165–8.
2. This labyrinth, along with many others, is described in Paolo Santarcangeli, *Il libro dei labirinti: Storia di un mito e di un simbolo* (Florence: Vallechi Editore, 1970), p. 248.
3. For an explanation of this use of the word, see María Rosa Lida de Malkiel, *Juan de Mena* (Mexico City: Publicaciones de la Nueva revista de filología hispánica, 1950), pp. 262–63.
4. John Amos Comenius, *The Labyrinth of the World and the Paradise of the Heart*, ed. and trans. Count Lutzow (London: Swan Sonnenschein & Co., 1901), p. 69.
5. Jacques Derrida, *Of Grammatology*, trans. Gayatri Chakravorty Spivak (Baltimore: Johns Hopkins University Press, 1976), p. 288.
6. Cited in Harry Levin, *The Gates of Horn: A Study of Five French Realists* (New York: Oxford University Press, 1966), p. 238.
7. Michel Butor, *Essais sur le roman* (Paris: Gallimard, 1969), p. 68.
8. Gaston Bachelard, *La Terre et les rêveries du repos* (Paris: Corti, 1948), p. 253.
9. For another discussion of this point, see Nicolás Rosa, "Borges o la ficción labiríntica," in Jorge Lafforgue, ed. *Nueva novela latinoamericana, II: La narrativa argentina actual* (Buenos Aires: Paidós, 1974), pp. 140–73.

10. Jorge Luis Borges, *Labyrinths: Selected Stories and Other Writings*, ed. Donald A. Yates and James E. Irby (New York: New Directions, 1964), p. 26.
11. Burton Pike, *The Image of the City in Modern Literature* (Princeton: Princeton University Press, 1981), p. 139.
12. James Joyce, *Ulysses* (New York: Random House, 1961), p. 47.
13. Jorge Luis Borges, *Antología personal* (Buenos Aires: Editorial Sur, 1961), p. 83.
14. Peter F. Smith, *The Syntax of Cities* (London: Hutchinson, 1977), p. 171.

[This material appears, in slightly different form, in Wendy Faris, *Labyrinths of Language: Symbolic Landscape and Narrative Design in Modern Fiction* (Baltimore: Johns Hopkins University Press, 1988).]

THE LABYRINTH AND THE LIBRARY *en abyme*:
ECO, BORGES, DICKENS . . .

Gerhard Joseph

The world is so full of a number of things,
I'm sure we should all be as happy as kings.
                                    Robert Louis Stevenson

Like other Victorian novelists Charles Dickens could hardly have
sympathized with the now-fashionable doctrine that a text mirrors not the world but other texts, often *en abyme*. Indeed, Dickens regularly affirms the representational character of his art
when its basis in life seems most precarious. "I have never
touched a character precisely from life," he says in the Preface to
the "Charles Dickens Edition" of *Martin Chuzzlewit*, "but some
counterpart of that character has incredulously asked me: 'Now
really, did I ever really see one like it?' " Particularly with respect
to *Chuzzlewit's* pre-eminent example of imputed caricature, Seth
Pecksniff, "All the Pecksniff family upon earth are quite agreed, I
believe, that Mr. Pecksniff is an exaggeration, and that no such
character ever existed."[1] Thus insisting upon the verisimilitude of
his portrayals, Dickens claims membership in the tradition of
nineteenth-century realism more centrally occupied by Thack-
eray, Trollope, and George Eliot. But Victorian "realism" is not a
simple matter of representation and lifelikeness, as recent criticism of the Victorian novel—notably John Romano's *Dickens and
Reality* and George Levine's *The Limits of Realism*—has emphasized. In fact, Dickens' novels—and especially *Chuzzlewit*[2]—so often refer to the act of their composition and allude to earlier texts
that they seem adaptations of the Book as well as responses to
the World, moments in a self-reflexive discourse about the nature
of writing as well as a discourse about the phenomenal universe
that writing professes to copy.

Whatever the case for the creator, today's critic can have little
doubt about the textuality—or rather the "intertextuality"—of his
enterprize. He may hark back nostalgically to a Victorian objectivist ideal, to an Arnoldian belief that the critic's function is to
see each independent aesthetic object distinctly "as in itself it really is"; he may at least proclaim such a critical version of mimesis as a necessary fiction that may help to curb within himself
some of the more self-indulgent gestures of recent theory when it

equates the critical and creative act. But a fiction that ideal nevertheless is—or so I am forced to acknowledge as a preamble to the reading of *Martin Chuzzlewit* that follows. For my reading is no more shaped by a single book than was that book by a single perspective on the world. Just before sitting down to read *Chuzzlewit*, I happened upon Umberto Eco's *The Name of the Rose*, with its central trope of the world as a labyrinthine library. The metonymical dialectic of labyrinth and library within *Martin Chuzzlewit* that I posit below has consequently been shaped by that encounter with Eco—and with the figure of Jorge Luis Borges who hovers behind *Eco's* novel.

The Name of the Rose[3] is a delightful detective story set in the fourteenth century that comes down hard on the side of an ancient nominalism, in support of the notion that the world is a mysterious book or set of books (i.e., a library) whose structure must be deciphered by the world's detective-inquisitors, critical and otherwise. As the novel's concluding sentence affirms (in the only allusion to its title—and that in Latin), we experience in this life only the *name* of the rose, not its essence, the signifier but not the transcendental signified (to jump momentarily to the linguistic context that the semiotician Eco must surely have had in mind). What seemed to me most puzzling about Eco's book was its various allusions to Borges, that blind Hispanic inventor of fictions and director of the National Library of Argentina during the Péron regime. In its bibliophilia, in the pertinence to its detective plot of a labyrinth and a library, in the ingenuity of its epistemological games, Eco's fiction seemed to be paying a sly homage to the Borges of, say, "The Babylon Lottery" or "The Library of Babel," as at least one of the book's earliest American reviewers noted.[4] But if so, why does the *murderer* turn out to be a highly unattractive, rigidly dogmatic blind Spanish former librarian named Jorge of Burgos? For me that question was partially answered when—again, accidentally—I recently ran across the following epigraph from Borges on the opening page of Gabriel Josipovici's *The World and the Book*, a passage that affirms Borges' philosophical realism against which Eco's nominalism with respect to the ontological status of the rose seems to be directed.

> Then came the revelation. Marini saw the rose as Adam might have seen it in the Garden of Eden, and he understood that it had existed in its eternity, and not in his words, and that we can refer to or evoke, but never express, and that the high and splendid volumes which in the shadows of his chamber gave out a golden glow, were not (as his vanity had dreamed) a mirror of the world,

but one more object added to the world. This revelation came to
Marini on the day of his death. It is possible that Homer and
Dante experienced it too.[5]

Whether Dickens experienced it as well, i.e. whether *Martin
Chuzzlewit* puts him closer to the ancient nominalist or realist
camp, is one way of reframing the question of Dickensian—and
Victorian—representational realism. Medieval philosophical realism and Victorian literary realism are of course different con-
cepts, but they do intersect in their common claim of mastering
by representation the relationship of *verba* and *res*, words and
things. The juxtaposition of *The Name of the Rose* and *Martin Chuzzlewit* can thus highlight certain metaphorical continuities among
medieval, Victorian, and modern discussions of the World/Book
nexus. For like such modernist medievalizers as Eco and Borges,
Dickens now fuses, now opposes the world as a labyrinth of
things to be mastered and a library of words to be arranged. Or
so I would like to argue in the following pages.

As readers have been wont to point out, the greatness of *Martin Chuzzlewit* arises from its fecundity of character and scene (it
is arguably the funniest of Dickens' novels) rather than from the
tight coherence of its comic, melodramatic, and romantic plots.
For better or worse, it lacks what Coleridge called unity of feeling; the qualities we admire are rather its energy and variety, its
sharp discontinuities—the newspaper virtues of Dickens' early
years. The novelist, that is, harks back to—as he will never entirely escape—the tendencies of the sketch collector as he piles
up memorable portrait after portrait to generate the impression of
a dense but ungraspable urban world. The very randomness, the
leisurely, nine-hundred-plus page accumulation of intermittently
related, repetitive detail, the imperfect coherence itself are the index of a verisimilitude for the reader who can immerse himself in
the chaos, in a mirror for the incomprehensible universe. And to
the spatial dispersion of the sketch gallery was added—for the
earliest readers of *Chuzzlewit* at any rate—the temporal distraction of serial publication: both writer and reader had to keep in
mind a rich array of character and incident over a nineteen-
month period.

Well aware of the diffusionary impulses within himself which
were reinforced by the conditions under which he worked, Dickens from *Sketches by Boz* onward moved to counter them in the
unification that followed loose serial publication. Indeed, as he
tells us in his first Preface of 1844 to *Chuzzlewit*, he has tried "to
resist the temptation of the current Monthly Number, and to

keep a steadier eye upon the general purpose and design" of this
burgeoning work than he had over the parts publication of earlier
novels (p. lxix). His main object was "to exhibit in a variety of
aspects the commonest of all vices; to show how Selfishness
propagates itself; and to what a giant it may grow, from small
beginnings" (Preface to the "Cheap Edition," p. 846). But we are
not entirely convinced by the insistence of the retrospective eye.
What is most striking about the backward glance of the Preface—
or, for that matter, about synoptic views that subsequent commentators have been tempted to substitute for Dickens' own—is
the inadequacy of generalization to the rambling, baggy monster
under inspection. For as Steven Marcus has rightly said, "*Martin
Chuzzlewit* is the first of Dickens' novels in respect to which criticism, if it is to remain reasonable, must settle for suggestive commentary and fragmentary analysis." Because it shares with all of
Dickens' mature work a combination of expansiveness and com-
pactness, it does not open itself to any single vantage point; like
the world it professes to mirror, the book cannot be seen steadily
and whole but vertiginously and in part. Precisely because we
are given the God's plenty of a Shakespeare or a Chaucer, no
description of *Chuzzlewit* is likely to strike us as comprehensive,
since, in this first novel of Dickens' maturity, "scarcely a page
goes by which does not in some way further the central course of
development; no detail is too small or by-the-way for it not to be
discovered as elaborating some larger organic theme—even as it
stands by itself, as a locally justified detail."[6]

The task of the artist and the commentator, of the creator and
his interpreter, are thus arguably analogous as they try for a to-
talizing comprehension. Both the imaginative and the discursive
writer are driven by the need to record completely a prolixity of
place, character, and idea, while at the same time imposing a design over that prolixity so as not to be overwhelmed by it. And
that dilemma becomes acute in a nineteenth century of proliferating things and books. Do we not, thus, in the prefatory anxiety
betrayed by the heavily insistent "unifying motif of Selfishness"
for *Chuzzlewit* sense a Dickensian foreshadowing of Matthew Arnold, who tells us that Keats and Browning (and by implication
all modern writers) "must begin with an Idea of the world in
order not to be prevailed over by the world's multitudinousness"? Better yet, with respect to the spatial figure that seems to
attract nineteenth-century theoreticians of intellectual catalogu-
ing and cartography, we might take as a jumping off point relevant to *Chuzzlewit* John Henry Newman's assertion of the need
for an aerial perspective, for intellectual ascent. "If we would im-
prove the intellect," says Newman in *The Idea of a University,*

first of all we must ascend; we cannot gain real knowledge on a
level; we must generalize; we must reduce to method, we must
have a grasp of principles, and group and shape our acquisitions
by means of them. It matters not whether our field of operations
be wide or limited; in every case, to command it, is to mount
above it. Who has not felt the irritation of mind and impatience
created by a deep, rich country, visited for the first time, with
winding lanes, and high hedges, and green steeps, and tangled
woods, and everything smiling indeed, but in a maze? The same
feeling comes upon us in a strange city, when we have no map of
the streets. Hence you hear of practiced travellers, when they first
come into a place, mounting some high hill or church tower, by
way of reconnoitring its neighborhood. In like manner, you must
be above your knowledge, not under it, or it will oppress you; and
the more you have of it, the greater will be the load.[7]

The movement to an imperial intellectual height, which Newman undoubtedly learned from Coleridge's *Treatise on Method* and
passed on to Arnold, while hardly unique to the nineteenth century, is nevertheless a characteristic procedure for those whose
field of inspection is the modern metropolis, whether that
"strange city" for which "we have no map" be Dickens' London
or Ruskin's Venice.[8] To cite a final preparatory analogue to the
specifics of *Chuzzlewit*, Wordsworth in order to do justice to the
anarchy of London in Book VII of *The Prelude* must, for once, "the
Muse's help" implore so that she will lodge him "wafted on her
wings, / Above the press and danger of the crowd, / Upon some
showman's platform," from which elevated vantage Wordsworth
can describe St. Bartholemew Fair, that single, jumbled "Parliament of Monsters" which for him becomes the "true epitome" of
a chaotic urban landscape.[9]

For if we content ourselves with remaining on the ground level
of the world's phenomena, we may be energized by the jostle—
but, to move on to Dickens, we finally experience a "resigned
distraction," the paralysis of failing to master Dickens' version of
the city's "true epitome," the area around Todgers' Commercial
Boarding House in *Martin Chuzzlewit*. To reach Todgers',

you groped your way for an hour through lanes and bye-ways, and
court-yards and passages; and never once emerged upon anything
that might be reasonably called a street. A kind of resigned distraction came over the stranger as he trod those devious mazes, and,
giving himself up for lost, went in and out and round about, and
quietly turned back again when he came to a dead wall or was
stopped by an iron railing, and felt that the means of escape might
possibly present themselves in their own good time, but that to
anticipate them was hopeless. (p. 129)

Such a description of the Todgers' neighborhood as "devious maze," as "a labyrinth, whereof the mystery was known but to a chosen few" may be taken as an example of what Albert Guérard some years ago defined as a fiction's "illuminating distortion," one of those metonymical or synecdochic passages that call attention to themselves as the key to a book's widest meaning.[10] To be sure, one can never be certain that any given part does illuminate the whole, that any fragment does have a legitimate microcosmic force. For that matter, after Dorothy van Ghent's influential essay, "The Dickens World: A View from Todgers's," the description of Todgers' has achieved the status of synecdoche with an even wider reach, as an emblem not only for the world of *Martin Chuzzlewit* but for the entire Dickens universe. Todgers' is for her all of London, as London is the whole world. "It is impossible," says van Ghent, "for the reader to dissociate these mazes of a squalid metropolitan district" from other equally maze-like places in the works of Dickens—from Coketown's "labyrinth of narrow courts upon courts, and close streets upon streets" in *Hard Times;* from the "wildernesses" of Park Lane, with their crumbling tenements "that looked like the last result of the great mansions' breeding in-and-in" where Arthur Clennam goes searching for Miss Wade in *Little Dorrit*, or from the corridors of the Circumlocution Office in the same novel; and from the mephitic honeycomb of Tom-All-Alone's in *Bleak House*.[11]

I have suggested that a typical nineteenth-century method for coming to terms with the urban labyrinth is to rise above it to achieve an aerial perspective, a perspective of overview that is a strategy of Dickens no less than of Wordsworth, Newman, Ruskin, and Arnold. Thus, after describing the frustration of the stranger who attempts to walk mapless through the Todgers' neighborhood, Dickens presents us with the attempt at a clarifying overview from the roof of Todgers'. But that perspective soon becomes worse than no compensation at all as it merely multiplies "wilderness upon wilderness":

> . . . the revolving chimney-pots on one great stack of buildings, seemed to be turning gravely to each other every now and then, and whispering the result of their separate observation of what was going on below. Others, of a crook-backed shape, appeared to be maliciously holding themselves askew, that they might shut the prospect out and baffle Todgers's. The man who was mending a pen at an upper window over the way, became of paramount importance in the scene, and made a blank in it, ridiculously disproportionate in its extent, when he retired. The gambols of a piece of cloth upon the dyer's pole had far more interest for the moment than all the changing motion of the crowd. Yet even while the

looker-on felt angry with himself for this, and wondered how it
was, the tumult swelled into a roar; the host of objects seemed to
thicken and expand a hundredfold; and after gazing round him,
quite scared, he turned into Todgers's again, much more rapidly
than he came out; and ten to one he told M. Todgers afterwards
that if he hadn't done so, he would certainly have come into the
street by the shortest cut: that is to say, head-foremost. (p. 132)

Whatever the character of synoptic vision in Dickens' later
mature work, in *Martin Chuzzlewit* the "resigned distraction" of
failing to master the labyrinth at ground level, far from being alleviated by an optics of overview, gives rise to an even more vertiginous distraction at the height. Pace Newman and Arnold, the
mapping that the stranger seeks is likewise impossible from the
ground and from the height (though, as we shall see below, it is
a possibility for an omniscient narrator). If anything, the prospect
from the roof of Todgers' intensifies a sense of the world's whirling multitudinousness: the ability to determine the relative significance of objects has completely broken down, and the
observer is consequently seized with a death-threatening nausea
at the momentary vision of a world in which focused meaning
has been replaced by random order, by the naked aggressiveness
of things moving at their own dangerous will. The point of view,
as van Ghent suggests, is hallucinatory and fearful; everything
has to be mentioned because nothing is significant, for,

> assuming that there is coherence in a world visibly disintegrated
> into things, one way to find it is to mention everything. Hence the
> indefatigable attention to detail. No thing must be lost, as it is
> doubtless essential to the mysterious organization of the system.
> The system itself is assumed to be a nervous one, and for this rea-
> son Dickens's language has its almost inexhaustible vitality and vi-
> vacity, inasmuch as its predications about persons or objects tend
> to be statements of metabolic conversion of one into the other.[12]

For the basic lesson of the "View from Todgers's" is the tendency
of "things," demonically possessed as they are in Dickens, to im-
itate the human, just as the course of human possession and obsession is to take on the aspect of the mechanical and the
inorganic. It is the constant fluctuation of the two states which is
Dickens' true subject—in *Chuzzlewit*, to begin with, the transpositions of the human and the architectural.

The labyrinth surrounding Todgers', having come into existence piecemeal, expresses the arbitrary nature of the human
city's expansion, the way each individual builder has pursued his
private design in the establishment of a house. While that architectural theme has its local manifestations, it is more importantly

built into the novel's basic structure. *Chuzzlewit's* full title engraved on the wrapper for the monthly parts makes the centrality clear: *The Life and Adventures of Martin Chuzzlewit—his Relatives, Friends, and Enemies. Comprising All his Wills and Ways: With an Historical Record of What he Did and What he Didn't: Showing, Moreover, Who Inherited the Family Plate, Who Came in for the Silver Spoons, and Who for the Wooden Ladles. The Whole Forming a Complete Key to the House of Chuzzlewit.* The dynastic sense of the corruption of a House accounts for the opening chapter's genealogical frame, as well as for the mythic resonances of Old Chuzzlewit's final verdict upon the entire race of Chuzzlewits: "The curse of our house . . . has been the love of self; has ever been the love of self" (p. 800). It is in Pecksniff's professional deceit that the novel launches its initial, and perhaps its most blatant, attack upon the corruption of actual buildings, for his barely disguised thefts of his students' architectural plans show him to be the first of the novel's dishonest builders. That English corruption has its American correlative in Mr. Scadder's description of the factitious Eden as a flourishing "architectural city," a thriving community of "banks, churches, cathedrals, market-places, factories, hotels, stores, mansions, wharves" and other public and private edifices (p. 353). The naive Martin discovers the reality beneath the verbal façade, the "paper city" of Phiz's illustration, soon enough in the fetid wilderness that is all but the death of him; and of course his cocky belief that he can make his fortune in America through the application of "ornamental architecture" to "domestic American purposes" is shown to be a ludicrous pipe dream when exposed to the enterprising schemes of America's false builders.

Finally, back in England, Tom Pinch's disillusionment with Pecksniff takes a comparable architectural guise, as he also discovers that the impressive façade of man's creations may conceal a shoddiness of spirit beneath. Arriving in London after his departure from an idyllic retreat in Wiltshire which has proven as illusory as the Edenic myth that has receded for Martin in the swamps of mid-America, Tom loses his way while trying to find Furnival's Inn:

> So on he went, looking up all the streets he came near, and going up half of them; and thus by dint of not being true to Goswell Street, and filing off into Aldermanbury, and bewildering himself in Barbican, and being constant to the wrong point of the compass in London Wall, and then getting himself crosswise into Thames Street, by an instinct that would have been marvellous if he had had the least desire or reason to go there, he found himself, at last, hard by the Monument. (p. 577)

The passage, to begin with, generates a useful qualification for van Ghent's notion that the View from Todgers' offers *the* paradigmatic Dickens perspective. For the care with which an overviewing narrator charts Tom's wandering within a London maze suggests that if there is a maze it has a plan that the narrator, as distinct from the visiting stranger, knows—just as that narrator understands the design of a rambling plot that he at one point calls "this maze of difficulty" (p. 740). Better, if one side of Dickens gives himself over to the bewildering View from Todgers', to the perspective of the visitor wandering through or hovering above the labyrinth of city and plot, another side is that of the native, all-knowing cartographer of the London maze, the painstaking cataloguer of person and incident. Tom may be lost, but the omniscient narrator knows precisely where he is and can identify the streets down which he wanders. The novel's patina of realism, such as it is, comes in some measure from such topographical exactitude, from the scrupulous recording of street name and locale.

The View from Todgers' is then an important expression of Dickens' perspective upon the true and false "architectural cities" of man, but that perspective is partial (as synecdoches by definition are). For if nineteenth-century London was a labyrinth in which it was easy for the mapless stranger to lose his way, it was at least an endlessly fascinating city—certainly more so than the city projected in Phiz's conception of Eden, a place of planned and predictable angularities. For if the overview of the London labyrinth generates a "resigned distraction" in the stranger, the visitor to America is distracted in a converse fashion: Dickens generally found American cities "distractingly regular." After walking about Philadelphia for an hour or two, for instance, he says that he "would have given the world for a crooked street."[13] Furthermore, London—and Dickens' London—was hardly one vast maze without a plan but a city of neighborhoods dotted with a plethora of green retreats, as it is for the wanderer in that city today. It therefore seems appropriate that if the earlier London sections of *Chuzzlewit* takes place in the uncomprehendable labyrinth around Todgers' dominated by a hollow architectural structure, the Monument, the resolution of the novel has as its setting one of London's carefully gardened cases, a Temple Inn that affirms the civilized and civilizing nature of London after all—and of the human city East of Eden that is finally preferable to the deceiving pastorals of Wiltshire and America.

For Tom's disenchantment with Pecksniffian monumentality in Wiltshire is reenforced by his discovery that the Man in the London Monument, which casts its sinister shadow over the roof of

Todgers', is nothing but a Cynic who sneers at gullible visitors eager to pay a shilling to climb a lot of stairs. Thus thoroughly disillusioned with the outward show of the world's phenomena, with the lying structures of the architectural city, Tom asks the question that has great resonance for all of Dickens' work: "If Truth didn't live in the base of the Monument . . . where in London . . . was she likely to be found" (p. 577)? A potential topographical answer that the later pages of *Chuzzlewit* gives, I would suggest, is in Temple Inn—or, more specifically, as a counter to the thesis implied by Dorothy van Ghent's title, in "A View from the Temple." If the Todgers' neighborhood is dominated by the false public Monument; if the elaborate pretensions of the American Eden center, absurdly enough, on a water pump, the focal point of the Temple is its lovely and functional Fountain, an architectural conduit for the natural flow of water and for the love that springs up between John Westin and Ruth Pinch.

Even more significant for purposes of answering Tom's questions is the perspective from within the Temple room in which much of the novel's climactic action occurs, an enclosed space which also provides an alternative to the open view from Todgers'. Todgers' overview, we have seen, seems beyond redemption: from the death-dealing vantage of Todgers' roof the world is a hodge-podge, a wilderness of sprawling, breeding, unmanageable, unmappable disorder, and *Martin Chuzzlewit* faithfully captures a sense of phenomenal multitudinousness to the extent that it generates an impression of the discontinuous, the uncloseable, the unnarratable—in short, the labyrinthine—quality of human existence. In this respect, Dickens' most obsessive, most rambling, most grandiloquent characters, those who seem most out of verbal control are the apt inhabitants of the labyrinth. While the "round" characters of Martin or Merry or Tom Pinch may change and learn, such "flat" ones as Pecksniff and Mrs. Gamp are comically trapped within their respective verbal gestures, and this very self-containment of character makes for the glorious explosions of comic energy. It is indeed such latter figures who make us most readily aware that they *are* the twists and turns of their eloquence, for our attempt to sum them up by an allusion to their name or to so inadequate a tag as, say, "hypocrite" seems as beside the point as an attempt to straighten out the labyrinth at Todgers' would be. And on his most important side Dickens is perfectly willing to thrust himself and his reader into the distraction of the labyrinth without any searching, with Tom, after "Truth."

But there is of course the other side of Dickens, that of the moralist unwilling to rest content in uncertainties, mysteries, doubts without any irritable reaching after ethical closure. That side emerges most fully, I would suggest, through the central function of Tom Pinch in the novel as a whole but especially through his role in the Temple. In order to alleviate Tom's jobless condition in London, an unknown benefactor, acting through the agent Fips, installs Tom in a windowless Temple room whose essential function turns out to be that of a library: as Tom first enters the room, he learns that his task will be that of straightening out "piles of books, to the amount perhaps of some thousands of volumes; these tied in bales: those, wrapped in paper, as they had been purchased: others scattered singly or in heaps: not one upon the shelves which lined the walls (p. 612). Tom is told that his benefactor wishes him to put the books in order, arrange them on the surrounding shelves, and catalogue them—an occupation that, as Tom says, is congenial to his taste and temperament, is full of "interest" for him. When we see the restored room later in the novel, Tom has arranged the books "in *perfect* order," has mended the torn leaves, pasted the broken backs, "substituted *neat* labels for the worn-out letterings," and he is busily at work draughting the fair copy of a catalogue upon which he concentrates "with all the ingenious and laborious neatness he had ever expended on map or plan in Mr. Pecksniff's workroom" (p. 766; italics added). In the view from Todgers' roof, the mind's ability to classify the relative significance of phenomena—of chimney pots, the blank upper window, the dyer's cloth, etc.—had broken down, and the viewer's vertigo had been generated by an overriding sense of randomness, of the terrifying disconnectedness of objects. But if the world of deceiving things and architectural structures will not render up its mysteries, will not allow Tom an intimation of the Truth he seeks in public places, the words that refer to those things, especially as arranged in books which are themselves susceptible to a further ordering, may offer a compensatory comfort. We may not be able to straighten out the spatial labyrinths of this world and only the most percipient of us can master their plan through overview, but we can all order our books in a space set aside for such a purpose. Thus, as Walter Benjamin says in an essay describing the unpacking of his extensive library, the arrangement of one's books serves a deep human—and, more precisely, aesthetic— need.[14] For the specifics of Todgers' momentarily aside, if the creator of a labyrinth is a certain kind of artist (Daedalus, after all, forged the initial one), the assembler of a library, as the careers of Benjamin and Borges make clear, may be seen as a different kind; if the artist is both a perceiver and a shaper, the viewing of the labyrinth and the ordering of the library in *Chuzzlewit* are tropes for these aesthetic functions.

Thus, because the labyrinth at Todgers' is only recordable rather than subject to rearrangement, it suggests the imperviousness of the world to manipulation, whether experienced at ground level or from the viewer's speculative height. The fact that it has no center, that its chaos seems beyond human control, is the source both of its fascination for and of its threat to the imagination. The enclosed library offers a relief to that threat because, perhaps more than any other institution, it satisfies the human passion for method, for system, for totally coherent pattern. And to the extent that even the library is a kind of labyrinth (as in *The Name of the Rose*), to the extent that it contains residual intimations of the world's multitudinousness, its catalogue serves as the final hedge against disorder: "if there is a counterpart to the confusion of the library," says Benjamin, "it is the order of the catalogue," the true epitome of the world as a series of interrelated books.[15] For as Borges suggests in "The Library of Babel," still another parable behind this meditation on the View from the Temple, at the center of the universe conceived of as a system of words rather than of things, is "the faithful catalogue of the Library"—and, of course, as we might expect from Borges, "thousands and thousands of false catalogues, a demonstration of the fallacy of these catalogues," and "a demonstration of the fallacy of the true catalogue."[16]

To be sure, if the chaos of the urban labyrinth threatens to draw its spectator to a precipitous death, the library has some polar deficiencies. For one thing, as a phenomenologist of the catalogue, Robert Harbison, has put it, bibliographies (or "bibliographies of bibliographies") "can offer no way of getting in immediate touch with reality. Indeed, for the cataloguer objects exist to be transcended or at least bypassed."[17] For another, his rigid taxonomies, his passion for correctness courts the dangers of tedium and dessication—even such a bibliophile as Benjamin acknowledges the "mild boredom" to be associated with the library's ordering. It is therefore perhaps no accident that Tom, who is thirty-five and a mover of books rather than of women, looks like sixty. Of course, such an observation hardly does the complexity of Tom's inner nature full justice, especially in scanting his role as lyrical dream organist at book's end, a position accentuated by Dickens and Phiz in the Frontispiece. Perhaps Tom's double nature as artist-figure is best captured in the detail that at the novel's close he moves between a select library that Ruth and John have purchased and an organ that they have had built for him (p. 815). Nevertheless, we are surely meant to feel that there is something slightly enervating and pallid, something limited, something "pinched" about Tom's rectitude, about the neatness and perfection that he prizes. And also something arbitrary: from the perspective of those who prefer labyrinths to libraries, most ordering seems factitious—something akin to the sham of Tom's functionless task, an insignificant piece of make-work on the literal level of the plot.

In citing Benjamin's "Unpacking my Library" as a frame for Tom's action, I have thus far ignored a distinction: Benjamin shelves his own library (and indeed glories in the idea of owner-ship), while Tom works for someone else as befits his self-deny-ing nature, a cataloguer of other people's books: (" . . . burying their conclusion as well as concealing their maker, catalogues aim to be incontestable, by being selfless to become a virtuous form. Making one satisfies someone else, produces something neces-sary that others will use. . . . ")[18] If the Temple library thus ex-presses an important aspect of a Tom who values a self-effacing spatialization of the idea of order, it more obliquely embodies the values of Old Martin Chuzzlewit, the secret source of that order-ing and the arch manipulator of the plot's central motion. For to the extent that the plot moves according to a method and a plan, Old Chuzzlewit is the master of its complex ceremonies. Whereas the later Dickens will explore the darkest side of the expectations aroused by old calculating exploiters of the young for selfish pur-poses (preeminently in Abel Magwitch and Miss Havisham), Old Martin's maneuverings, while selfish in their origin, seem rela-tively benign, at least in their outcome: we are apparently meant to applaud the system of distributive justice he metes out at nov-el's end, rewarding Tom and Young Martin, exposing Pecksniff, and censuring Sairy Gamp—in short, rewarding Virtue and pun-ishing Vice. Such categorical determination, I would suggest, is the moral equivalent of the organization of his Temple library in which the final confrontation scene appropriately enough takes place, the ordering of the world of books now neatly arranged and catalogued by Tom. When Cecily Cardew in *The Importance of Being Earnest* discovers that Miss Prism had written a novel, she asks whether that book ends happily. Miss Prism replies that "The good ended happily and the bad unhappily. That is what Fiction means." In at least one passage in *his* novel Dickens sug-gests that he is as aware as Miss Prism of the bookish quality of the categorically just ending. "You think of me, Ruth," says Tom Pinch to his sister in resigning all claim to Mary Graham,

> and it is very natural that you should, as if I were a character in a book; and you make it a sort of poetical justice that I should, by some impossible means or other, come, at last, to marry the per-son I love. But there is a much higher justice than poetical justice my dear, and it does not order events upon the same principle.

Accordingly people who read about heroes in books, and choose
to make heroes of themselves out of books, consider it a very fine
thing to be discontented and gloomy, and misanthropical, and perhaps a little blasphemous, because they cannot have everything ordered for their accommodation. (p. 763)

Of the novel's many passages of authorial self-consciousness
that one might linger over in stressing the non-representational,
non-mimetic element in Dickens' art, Tom's speech seems the
most subtle. Precisely by insisting that he is not merely a character in a book, he most surely reminds us that he, like the other
characters among whom he moves, is—and that "what we had
taken to be [the] world is only a book. The real world is that
which the book is not."[19] Precisely by asserting that a bookish
system of poetic justice does not apply to him, he points to the
ways that it does at the very least to the characters that surround
him: he is merely the exception proving the rule that in the
world as universal library "poetic justice" and the "higher justice" he privileges come to about the same thing. For that matter,
except for the fact that Martin rather than he ends up with Mary
Graham in the romantic plot, Tom is not even a very convincing
exception to the fictional convention of the comic novel that Miss
Prism defines.

Of course that categorizing system that I have characterized as
the order of the Temple is constantly being undermined by the
labyrinthine impulse within the novel—by all that is uncontrolled, rambling, saturnalian, grandiloquent—in short, by the
subversive power of a Pecksniff. Phiz's illustration of the confrontation scene in which Pecksniff's villainy is fully exposed contains at least one detail that seems rather odd. Everything in the
picture seems to conform to the ideal of mimesis that, as we have
seen, Dickens affirmed for his novel: Phiz's details correspond
quite directly to the sentences that have generated them in Dickens' text—except that in the left corner of the picture Tom Pinch
seems to have opened the glass door of one of the bookshelves
he had arranged and is either trying to keep books from tumbling out or, more bizarrely still, is actually tossing them onto the
floor. Or, if we are to let them illustrate van Ghent's thesis, the
books, like other inanimate objects in Dickens' world, are demonically possessed and move through an agency that has nothing to do with human will. In any event, the motion of the books
makes little sense on the literal level of the plot, although Dickens' who, as Sylvère Monod has shown, carefully controlled the
design of Phiz's illustrations, must have approved of, even
though he didn't suggest this detail.[20] The very strangeness and

ambiguity of Tom's act call our attention to it, however we read it: if Tom is trying to hold the books back, the scene would seem to argue that the imposition of order is always subject to the return of a repressed disorder. Alternatively, if Tom is himself throwing the books to the floor, we understand that the character who has ordered the library is now the proper agent for—accidentally or intentionally—choosing the books that will most suitably comment upon the action of the scene they are flying through: *Tartuffe* and *Paradise Lost* (though one wishes that Phiz had added Shakespeare's *Measure for Measure*).

The correspondences between the hypocrites Tartuffe and Pecksniff hardly require comment, and several readers have discussed the relevancy of Milton's epic to the story of Martin's fortunate fall in America and Tom's parallel expulsion from the false Pecksniffian Eden of Wiltshire.[21] But the Miltonic connection that makes the most sense in light of the present argument concerns the exposure and humiliation of a Satanic vice figure, Pecksniff, by an Old Martin Chuzzlewit reminiscent of Milton's God, or at least the Romantic version of that God. All along Old Martin has understood the malign principle that has opposed him, but he has not intervened to foil its operation. The force behind the arrangement of the books in the Temple is now also revealed as the designer of the action as a whole. His indictment of Pecksniff has essentially two prongs: "If he [Pecksniff] had offered me one word of remonstrance, in favor of a grandson whom he had supposed I had disinherited; if he had pleaded with me . . . I think I could have borne with him ever afterwards. But not a word, not a word." Secondly, he repeatedly calls upon Pecksniff to remember that "he [Old Martin] had not trapped him to do evil, but that he had done it of his own free will and agency." In his trial of Pecksniff, Old Martin has been ever so careful to allow for a redemptive irruption of virtue: "He cannot say I have not left him freely to himself in all things; or that I have not been a passive instrument in his hands, which he might have used for good as easily as evil. Or if he can, he Lies! And that is his nature too." But the very repetitions of these protestations of Pecksniff's free agency and Martin's passivity arouse our suspicion. If only because of the volume of *Paradise Lost* flying through Phiz's illustration, we cannot help but entertain reservations as to Old Martin's excessive reserve, as to the theatrical willingness of an omniscient authority which allows evil to flourish for such a long time merely to "test" a grandson. Do we not at any rate sense the partial justice of Pecksniff's rejoinder accusing Old Martin of entrapment: "Whether it was worthy of you to partake of my hospitality, and to act the part you did in my house; that, sir, is a question which I leave to your own conscience" (pp. 801–807).

That is, despite Pecksniff's undeniable villainy and stone-walling propensities in the scene, we hear the echo, in a comic register, of a metaphysical rebellion against God that has an ancient history in Judeo-Christian apologetics. God tests, while Satan tempts, the Fathers from St. Augustine onward have insisted in their books. But that is a fine distinction that escapes the Satan of *Paradise Lost*, who in Book II accuses an omnipotent and omniscient God of using him in a grand universal design and then punishing him for that agency. Romantic Satanism from Blake to the Shelleys repeats that accusation, and in Pecksniff's defense against Old Martin's coercive, role-playing overview, self-interested though the indictment may be, we hear an echo of the old Romantic charge. Certainly the relentlessness and sheer brutality of Old Martin cannot but create a secret—or not so secret—sympathy within the reader for Pecksniff. To adapt Blake in the matter, Dickens was of Pecksniff's party without knowing it, although it is hard to believe that he did *not* know it.

Such a charge against Old Martin may finally be seen as evidence of Dickens' own uneasiness about the stance of overview, and I would like to conclude with some tentative generalizations about that authorial self-questioning. Relying upon the work of Foucault and others, Jonathan Arac has convincingly argued that overview as a narrative strategy accompanied the new techniques of inspection and observation worked out by a post-Benthamite interventionist bureaucracy and that Dickensian overview may be seen as an expression of that reformist social tradition.[22] In the mature Dickens, we seem to experience the thrust toward redemptive omniscience: the expansive novelist strives for a disciplined, magisterial sensibility; he would become a kind of god, freely creating and controlling experience as his strategy of overview manages an ever-widening focus while moving toward comprehensive vision. But however urgent the desire, the later Dickens serves to explode the progressivist myth that totalized vision is either feasible or that its mimicry in the novelist's "omniscience" would supply a redemptive vantage point above a corrupt society. As David A. Miller has aptly put the matter with respect to the paradigmatic situation of *Bleak House*, "If Chancery . . . names an organization of power that is total but not totalizable, total *because* it is not totalizable, then what is most radically the matter with being in Chancery is not that there may be no way out of it (a dilemma belonging to the problematic of the carceral) but, more seriously, that the binarisms of inside/outside, here/elsewhere become meaningless and the ideological effects they ground impossible."[23] All perspectives, including that of the author, are flawed by the condition of Chancery nor are we ever out of it.

To be sure, Dickens will suggest that long perspectives are not inevitably tainted by occasionally presenting them in characters who are more sympathetic than their overviewing forerunners in *Chuzzlewit*: Inspector Bucket, the all-knowing detective of *Bleak House*, while a version of *Chuzzlewit's* Nadgett, is no mere spy in the employ of a con-artist, while Boffin's manipulation of Bella to cure her of greed in *Our Mutual Friend* is a wholly benign version of Old Martin's more suspect maneuverings. But however fervent the later Dickens may have been for largeness of scale and breadth of vision, he is also, like Yeats, aware of the dark side of a power that would be put on with totalized knowledge, even were such knowledge possible. The obsessive hand-washing of Jaggers in *Great Expectations* conveys clearly enough the guilt attendant upon knowing everything. If partial vision is thus one form of blindness, omniscience brings its own kind of damnation, whether one uses it like Old Martin to further one's ends or dispassionately refrains from intervention like Jaggers. With or without action, after such knowledge, what forgiveness?

Among its other virtues, *Martin Chuzzlewit* thus prepares for one of the major emphases of the mature Dickens, his disillusioned sense of man's (and the artist's) cognitive limits. For the comprehensive order affirmed by Old Martin and Tom in a Temple library full of books is finally as insubstantial, as much a source of readerly "distraction" as the sprawling disorder of an unredeemable world of things associated with the Todgers' labyrinth.[24]

NOTES

1. Charles Dickens, *Martin Chuzzlewit*, ed. Margaret Cardwell (Oxford: Clarendon Press, 1982), p. 846. Further references to the novel, its illustrations, and its prefatory materials are from this text and will be cited parenthetically.
2. In her introduction to the Clarendon *Chuzzlewit*, p. xlv, Margaret Cardwell attributes the novel's high degree of authorial self-consciousness to "Dickens's difficulties in starting without a thoroughly conceived plan," which John Forster described in his *Life of Charles Dickens*.
3. trans. from the Italian by William Weaver (New York: Harcourt Brace Jovanovich, 1983).
4. David Lehman, *Newsweek*, July 4, 1983, pp. 72–73.
5. Gabriel Josipovici, *The World and the Book: A Study of Modern Fiction* (London: Macmillan, 1971), page following title page. The passage comes from Borges' "A Yellow Rose" in *Dreamtigers* (Austin, University of Texas Press, 1964), p. 38, a translation of *El Hacedor* (The Maker).
6. Steven Marcus, *From Pickwick to Dombey* (New York: Basic Books, 1965), pp. 213–14.
7. John Henry Newman, *The Idea of a University* (Garden City, N.Y.: Image Books, 1959) Discourse VI, Section 7, pp. 160–61.

8. For a widely ranging discussion of nineteenth-century "textual eminence" and particularly of the way in which the tower of Saint Mark's provides the potential for observational control of Venice in Ruskin's *Stones of Venice*, see Jay Fellows' "The Vantage Point of the True Centre: Problems in the Transcendental Altitude of the Self" in *Ruskin's Maze: Mastery and Madness in his Art* (Princeton: Princeton University Press, 1981), pp. 45–59. My sense of the overview that attempts to master the Victorian urban maze is generally indebted to Fellows' book and to Jonathan Arac's *Commissioned Spirits: The Shaping of Social Motion in Dickens, Carlyle, Melville, and Hawthorne* (New Brunswick: Rutgers University Press, 1979). See also Gerhard Joseph, "Tennyson's Optics: The Eagle's Gaze," *PMLA*, 92(1977), 420–28.

9. William Wordsworth, *The Prelude*, Book VII, ll. 681–717, in *Selected Poems and Prefaces*, ed. Jack Stillinger (Boston: Riverside Press, 1965).

10. "The Illuminating Distortion," *Novel*, 5(1972), 101. See also Richard J. Dunn, " 'Illuminating Distortions' and the Dickens Critics," in *Review*, ed. James O. Hogue and James L. West III (Charlottesville: University Press of Virginia, 1979), pp. 92–104.

11. Dorothy van Ghent, "The Dickens World: A View from Todgers'," *Sewanee Review*, 58(1950), 419–38; reprt. in *The Dickens Critics*, ed. George H. Ford and Lauriat Lane, Jr. (Ithaca: Cornell University Press, 1961), pp. 213–32.

12. Van Ghent, pp. 220–21.

13. *American Notes*, The New Oxford Illustrated Dickens (London: Oxford University Press, 1948–58), Chapt. 7.

14. "Unpacking My Library," in *Illuminations* (New York: Schocken Books, 1969), pp. 59–67.

15. Benjamin, p. 60.

16. *Ficciones* (New York: Grove Press. 1962), p. 83.

17. "Contracted World: Museums and Catalogues," in *Eccentric Spaces* (New York: Alfred A. Knopf, 1977), p. 153.

18. Harbison, p. 154.

19. Josipovici, *The World and the Book*, p. 307.

20. *Dickens the Novelist* (Norman: U. of Oklahoma Press, 1968), p. 253 and note. Dickens' instructions to Phiz for plate 37 (in the Huntington Library), which do not mention the falling books, appear on p. 844 of the Clarendon *Chuzzlewit*. For the argument that Phiz contributed the touch of the falling books on his own authority, see Michael Steig, "*Martin Chuzzlewit's* Progress by Dickens and Phiz," in *Dickens Studies Annual* 2, ed. Robert Partlow, Jr. (Carbondale: Southern Illinois Press, 1972), pp. 139–40.

21. See especially Stuart Curran, "The Lost Paradises of *Martin Chuzzlewit*," *Nineteenth-Century Fiction*, 25(1970), 51–67; and Alexander Welsh, *The City in Dickens* (Oxford: Clarendon Press, 1971), pp. 122–23.

22. *Commissioned Spirits*, pp. 13–31.

23. "Discipline in Different Voices: Bureaucracy, Police, Family, and *Bleak House*," *Representations*, 1(1983), 59–89. The quotation appears on p. 61.

24. I wish to thank Jay Fellows, Anne Humpherys, George Levine, and especially Stuart Davis for their generous help at various stages in the composition of this essay.

ON CITY STREETS AND NARRATIVE LOGIC

Steven Winspur

The initial hypothesis behind this essay is that, from the heyday of the nineteenth-century novel onwards, city streets function not only as an element of verisimilitude in the overall decor of the modern novel but that they are also a metaphor for narrative itself. The street on which a fictional character walks leads in a certain direction and points to a certain end—both of which are either already known or else tentatively postulated by the novel's reader. Streets that lead nowhere in particular and which characters walk along aimlessly herald the appearance in nineteenth-century France of the new prose-poem genre—a genre that has a curious relationship to narrative and to which I shall return shortly. But if we put aside for a moment those avenues leading nowhere, and consider the typical frequenters of the side-walk that novels usually offer us in their opening pages, it is clear that the direction in which these characters walk is towards the novel's plot, that is, towards the disclosure of certain problems of human action and thence towards their eventual dissolution or closure. Here, for example, is the opening sentence of Dostoevsky's *Crime and Punishment:*

> Towards the end of a sultry afternoon early in June a young man came out of his little room in Stolyarny Lane and turned slowly and somewhat irresolutely in the direction of Kamenny Bridge.[1]

On reading these lines the reader's attention is immediately drawn to three questions: Why has this man come out of his room? Why is he heading in the direction mentioned? And why is he walking so hesitantly? The one answer to all of these questions—and it surfaces in the next five pages of the book—constitutes the ethical problem at the center of the novel's plot. This young man, whose name we find out to be Raskolnikov, was on his way to murder an old lady.

Not every novel, of course, opens with someone going off to knife senior citizens (indeed, because this motif has been taken over by the popular press its literary shock-value has been virtually eliminated). And yet, because so many novels (and their contemporary counterparts—movies) begin with mentions of people *going somewhere*—think of Balzac novels that invariably begin with a character leaving or entering a building, or of the start of

Zola's *Germinal* with its description of a solitary man walking along a desolate highway—we can see how the fictional street or roadway often acts as a conduit that leads both its fictional frequenter and its real reader to the locus of the plot. What is of more interest, however, are instances where the plot of the novel is itself generated by the narrative possibilities inherent in the crisscrossing of its fictional pathways. For if, as I have argued, a novel's city streets are in fact rails that draw its characters *and* readers towards important actions and significant consequences, then the intersection of these different rails will constitute the core of the plot. Zola's novel *La Bête humaine* is perhaps the best illustration of this point for by moving his characters around not on streets but in trains that go only in one predetermined direction—namely that of the track on which the locomotive is running—Zola lays bare the logic of narrative: actions unfolding in time and space. This is especially clear when he describes in his preparatory notes to the novel the Paris train station towards which most of the novel's characters gravitate: "A large station in which ten lines will cross, and on each line one episode will take place and all of them will come together at the main station."[2] *La Bête humaine* then, is a sort of marshalling yard for the various railway lines of narrative that together make up the book. In an earlier entry to his notebook, Zola had stressed the importance of narrative in his projected novel: "I would like, after *Le Rêve*, to do a totally different sort of novel [. . .]," he wrote, "without description and without any visible artistry [. . .] just pure narration [*du récit simplement*]" (Zola, pp. 16–17).

Zola was, of course, not the first writer to attach so much importance to the pathways on which his fictional characters passed. In *Crime and Punishment*, whose French translation Zola had read in 1885, around the time he began writing *La Bête humaine*, we find that crossroads play an important role in the development of plot: in Part 2, chapter VI of the book Raskolnikov is distracted from his decision to confess his crime to the police when he sees a crowd gathered at a crossroads and then, near the end of the novel, Raskolnikov eventually makes a public confession by falling to his knees at another crossroads and kissing the mud. In both these instances the crossroads metaphorically designate the new direction taken by the book's plot: the chance encounter between Raskolnikov and the crowd in Part 2 effectively represses, until the end of the book, the hero's decision to confess his murdering the old lady, while the act of kissing the ground at the crossroads in Part 6 signals Raskolnikov's rebirth as a cleansed sinner—the figure of the cross in the crossroads is no mere accident—who is ready to follow a new path and thus make the novel fill out a new intertext—namely the Christian intertext of man's ascension to God through a recognition of sin.

We find the same crossroads metaphor for narrative shifts in *Don Quixote* where the hero's quests for adventure (along with Cervantes' quest for narrative) invariably begin with Quixote leading his horse to a crossroads and then letting it decide which of the three paths to follow. Even if we go way back to the model of classical tragedy singled out by Aristotle—namely, Sophocles' *Oedipus the King*—again we find that it's at a crossroads that the hero's tragic narrative is set in motion—the crossroads where Oedipus runs into a stranger, kills him, and then takes the path from whence the stranger came.

All the crossroad examples that I have given so far (including Zola's "high-tech" locomotive version) function as generators that push forward the plot of the book in question. In other words, the figure of the crossroad in these works does not bring into question the supremacy of narrative continuity in fiction; it merely perpetuates this supremacy. A Zola or a Dostoevsky looking at the intersecting streets of Paris or St. Petersburg is therefore very much akin to Sherlock Holmes scanning the comings and goings on Baker Street from the window of his flat and speculating on the possible interactions between the passers-by, as well as on the hidden motivations behind these interactions. Cross-streets provide the nineteenth-century novelist with the ideal of *hidden narratives* brought about by chance encounters and forming the stuff of crime dramas—not only in Conan Doyle but also in *La Bête humaine* and *Crime and Punishment*.

There are, however, some cross-streets in nineteenth-century French literature that do bring about a radical upturning of the notion of a linear narrative. These are the cross-streets that appear in prose poems. Writing about this new genre in his dedicatory preface to *Le Spleen de Paris*, Baudelaire comments, "It is especially from the frequenting of enormous cities, from the intersecting of their innumerable connections, that this ideal [of a 'poetic prose'] arises."[3] Much important work has been done recently on French prose poems, and especially on those of Baudelaire: for instance, Barbara Johnson's 1979 book *Défigurations du langage poétique* (Paris: Flammarion), Sima Godfrey's 1982 article entitled "Baudelaire's Windows" (*L'Esprit créateur*, vol. XXII, no. 4, pp. 83–100) and the useful collection of essays edited by Mary Ann Caws and Hermine Riffaterre, entitled *The Prose Poem in France: Theory and Practice*, that appeared in 1983 (New York: Columbia University Press). Amongst these studies, crucial arguments have been put forward about the nature of poetic language in the prose poem (principally by Barbara Johnson and Michael

Riffaterre) and also about the affinities between the aims of early prose poem writers such as Bertrand and Baudelaire and those of painters and illustrators of the time (the articles by Sima Godfrey and Michel Beaujour are of particular relevance here). What all these studies have in common, however, is an attempt to define what is poetic in the prose poem by downplaying what is prosaic in it—arguing, for instance, that its prosaic side is to be found in the *topoi* of the texts (banal incidents or scenes from modern city life) rather than in their structure which, according to this view, betrays an essentially poetic nature.[4]

In the pages that follow I shall take the opposite approach and, continuing my initial hypothesis on the metaphoric function of city streets, argue that the narrative structure of prose poems (and particularly those of more than one page in length) cannot be explained away by invoking various, and increasingly sophisticated, definitions of what is "poetic". I shall be using the work of the contemporary French writer Yves Bonnefoy to support my argument and, in particular, his collection of texts entitled, significantly, *Rue Traversière* (or "Cross Street").

Bonnefoy begins his earlier book *L'Arrière-pays* with the following sentence:

> I have often had a feeling of anxiety at crossroads. It seems to me that in those moments, at that place or close by, there, a couple of steps down the path that I didn't take and which I'm already leaving behind, yes, it's there that a land of a higher essence was opening up, where I could have gone to live but which I lost from that moment on.[5]

In many ways, the short prose pieces in *Rue Traversière* are rewrites, albeit with different characters and different locations, of this kernel crossroads metaphor for narrative. The text that gives its title to the collection, "Rue Traversière", tells of how the narrator rediscovers a street called simply "Cross-street" in the town where he grew up as a child. What is special about this particular cross-street is its effect on the narrator: at one end of the street, he tells us, "it was the ordinary world, while at the other, over there . . ." (and the sentence ends with these three suspension points[6]). A few lines later we are told that the other end of the street opens out into a botanical garden, described as an otherworldly, Edenic "jardin des essences" (p. 96) or "garden of essences." The brief story ends with the narrator concluding that "the Cross-street hadn't changed", and that it still led him out of the world of poor dwellings and old women knitting at their windowsills (the spatio-temporal world in which the street actually was situated) to another world. Six pages later in the book, however, we find another story entitled "Seconde rue Traversière" ("Second Cross-street") in which someone tells the narrator of the first story that he knows the cross-street referred to in the first story but that the narrator was wrong to situate it in a working-class neighbourhood since in fact the cross-street was in an archetypal upper middle-class neighborhood—highlighted in the story by a description of the calm bourgeois complacency that reigns over the neighbourhood and that is interrupted only by the sound of some well-bred child tapping out scales on the piano. The narrator protests: "Bourgeois? No. It's one of the poorest of streets" (p. 105) and then proceeds to disagree with all the details of the street offered by his interlocutor. Hoping to solve the dispute, the narrator goes home and pulls out an old map of the town, only to find to his amazement that the Cross-street *is* in a rich part of town after all. Where then was the original Cross-street the narrator remembers so distinctly? The story ends with this question unanswered.

This story contains all the elements of what I call the kernel crossroads narrative from *L'Arrière-pays* and that I quoted a few moments ago. First, there is the path that is now lost and yet a while ago was still within reach. Second, this path leads its fictional narrator and real reader not only to another place but to an altogether different *kind* of place, an a-temporal "land of a higher essence" according to the passage I quoted from *L'Arrière-pays*. Finally, in both stories the lost path does not continue straight on from the road the narrator was on and that, presumably, he is still on, but instead it cuts across this path, pointing neither forward nor back in time but rather sideways. It is this special sideways shift in the Cross-street that the narrator of the "Second Cross-street" story searches for vainly in his map: "I look," writes Bonnefoy, "and find nothing. For indeed here are several streets that go towards the sunset [. . .] and yet I seem to know them all down to the smallest detail, and none of them is the one that I see so distinctly whenever I close my eyelids [. . .]." (p. 107) None of these streets on the map has the special trait that is called a few lines later in Bonnefoy's text "la qualité 'traversière' ", or the crossover quality of his lost path. And the reason for this is quite obvious: the crossover quality of this path was precisely its ability to shift the narrator sideways, to move him out of the spatio-temporal maze of streets that led him to that point and to take him to an a-temporal realm. The map, on the other hand, deals only in spatio-temporal streets; it is a map of another type of world. It is now that certain metaphors in the first "Cross-street" story begin to take on significance: the old la-

dies, for instance, whom the narrator had seen on his approach
to the cross-street, and who were sitting at their window sills
sewing, were not just darning their husbands' socks but rather,
and I quote, "sewing infinity into faded sheets." The ungrammat-
ical word "infinity" in this most unmetaphysical context points to
the fact that these old ladies are not just functioning literally but
rather figuratively. And their figurative meaning becomes clear
when we read the description of the Botanical Garden that the
Cross-street opens on to. "Once I arrived at the garden, which
has names inscribed under each tree [. . .], I would run off,
suddenly awoken.[. . .] Oh what good that name Cross-street
did for me; and that garden of essences; and that plant-like Latin
on sultry evenings!" (p. 96) The botanical names written on little
plaques beside each tree function here not just as arbitrary labels
for the natural realm; on the contrary, the foreignness of their
Latin form guarantees for the narrator that these are the proper,
original names for the flora in question, designating the essence
of each tree and bush. They are the names that these objects of
Creation received at the very dawn of Creation, in that other botanical garden—Eden. Eden is precisely the "other world" of "essences" that the cross-street opens on to since its otherness
comes from its existence *outside* time—prior to Man's fall there
was no temporality, and therefore no change to damage the im-
mutable essence of each object. The infinity that the old women
at their windows are weaving into the banal fabric of their faded
sheets is, therefore, on a first reading, a figure for the realm un-
bounded by time and space that the narrator has discovered. But
on a second reading it becomes clear that the opposition between
the finite dimensions of the womens' faded sheets and the infinity of their thread turns these old sewers into modern versions of
Clotho, Lachesis and Atropos—the three Greek goddesses who
spun out the narrative of each mortal. Not only is Bonnefoy's
narrator seemingly fated to have found, then have lost and then
constantly search for, his lost paradise, but, more importantly for
my argument in this paper, the lost paradise is a paradise of narrative, woven into, and hence grounded in, the linearity and fin-
itude of basic, prosaic narration.

    Let me say what I mean by a "paradise of narrative". It is com-
mon to point out about prose poems that they give artistic monumentality, and hence an a-temporal eternity, to brief events that
take place in time, or that, to adapt Baudelaire's phrase about
Daumier, that the prose poem "extracts the poetical [. . .] from
the historical." (Godfrey, p. 84) Sima Godfrey has shown very
convincingly in her article "Baudelaire's Windows" how the
Baudelairean prose poem narrator "glimpses moments of the

'eternal' in the elusive rhythms of the city and frames them into
tableaux of modern life" (p. 83). And others have pointed out how
many of Baudelaire's prose poems offer, what Peter Demetz calls
in reference to Benjamin's city-writings, "ontological thresholds"
that open on to a higher-level view of city-being.[7] What I want to
argue, however, is that this so-called "poetic" or "ontological"
effect of certain prose poems is produced by *narrative* techniques.
For the eternity that prose poems give us a glimpse of takes on
meaning only through its opposition to narrative time which is
not an eternal present but rather a continuous roadway pointing
backwards into the past and forwards towards plot resolution.
This narrative time expresses itself through movement in time
and space and is an essential frame on which the prose poem can
construct its illusion of another, non-temporal realm. It is therefore crucial that *Le Spleen de Paris*, for instance, be framed (as
many have shown) by the gaze of the wandering narrator, for
without this initial framework of movement through time and
space, borrowed, as I showed at the beginning of my essay, from
the nineteenth-century novel, the illusion of another world, both
inside and outside the everyday world of narrations, cannot be
fleshed out. This interdependence between the streets of narrative and the cross-streets of prose-poems, shifting us sideways to
an extra-narrative realm where nothing happens since all is already inscribed and waiting to be read off like a hieroglyph (as in
a Baudelaire or Benjamin "reading" of the city), is clearly visible
in the other texts collected in Bonnefoy's volume *Rue Traversière*.
In a story called "Rome, les flèches" we read of how an art amateur comes to the amazing discovery that apart from the spatio-
temporal Rome whose streets he knows so well there is another
Rome, not situated in time and space but everywhere, all around
him and visible when he looks carefully at certain paintings by
Giotto, Duccio and others. "You are in Rome, of course," says a
friend to the narrator. "Did you think that there is only one of
them? Haven't you understood the lesson of the arrows [in the
paintings] that come from God knows where and attach themselves here or there on the target? Rome is the center, she is
therefore everywhere." (p. 39) But to get access to this *other* Rome
we have to know the spatial Rome, know its streets, which is to
say, know its stories, its past. The friend continues: "Rome is
one, she is therefore multiple. And since she has a history . . .
Ah, don't you see, it's all in that! In fact, *the Popes never did leave
Rome. There was no Avignon.* Art, the great art that the West was
waiting for, the art of the place and the formula, took place, yes,
[. . .] here." (p. 39)

Cross-streets, then, generate two sorts of cities: first, the city here and now, and second its Baudelairean counterpart that is the "elsewhere" in such prose poems as "La Chambre double" or "Les Fenêtres." Other examples of these dual cities are Léon-Paul Fargue's Paris in his prose-poems entitled *Poèmes*, or Claudel's Tokyo in the piece "La Muraille intérieure de Tokyo" in *Connaissance de l'Est*, or Saint-John Perse's Bordeaux in his collection of short prose pieces *Images à Crusoé*, where the cross-street's role as signal for a crossing-over to the "elsewhere" is taken up by "l'obscure croisée" ("the obscure casement window" with intersecting joinery work) and where the elsewhere is not a paradise version of Bordeaux—which would be somewhat of a contradiction in terms in the French sociolect—but rather Robinson Crusoe's Edenic island beyond all civilisation and city confines.[8]

It is not only in prose poems, however, that we find cross-streets generating such other-worldly cities. The same role is taken over by the fashionable passageways pointing sideways (towards dreams) rather than forward (towards the completion of actions), that were the Parisian arcades of the 1820s and onwards. The arcades in their heyday made tangible the wishful fantasies of the strolling consumer, lifting him or her into a dreamworld of commodities and exchange.[9] Even when the arcades had ceased being fashionable, a hundred years on, their poetic value still remained, as we can see in the opening chapter of Aragon's *Le Paysan de Paris*. By extending the arcades' dreamworld beyond the realm of the merchandise displayed and out into the space of the consumer, so that passer-by *and* merchandise both become an object of desire (as in the classy malls of the 1980s), Aragon's description of the famous Opera Arcade fully exploits the poeticity of the arcade-cross-street. This "poetic divinity," as Aragon calls it,[10] comes from the fact that the arcade forms a world apart, with its own dimensions, colours, and tone formed by the glass roof that lets in a special submarine type of light, as if all the shops, objects and inhabitants were moving around inside a fish tank solely for the contemplation of others.[11] It is a world different from that of the outside, for inside the arcade where narrative time (i.e. pathways leading *somewhere*) is suspended a new temporality of instantaneous ephemeral pleasure is opened up:

[Modern city planning] is soon going to destroy the upkeep of these human aquaria that are already dying, detached from their primitive life, and yet which deserve to be seen as the receivers of several modern myths, since it's only today, when they are

threatened by the pickaxe, that they have in fact become the sanc-
tuaries of a cult of the ephemeral, the ghostly landscape of ma-
ligned pleasures and professions (Aragon, p. 21)

Surrealism's exploitation of these side-streets of pleasure illus-
trates exactly the same strategy that we saw at work in *Rue Traversière*. The "paradise temporality" (p. 12) that Aragon's arcade
opens up demands for its effect on a prior rejection of the narrative temporality of actions-leading-to-conclusions. Thus, just
as Bonnefoy puts spinners of narrative time inside his poem to
indicate the shift to a new sort of temporality (see pp. 10–11
above), so Aragon uses exactly the same metaphor for an identical purpose:

> The doorway of building no. 2, which gives access to the staircase
> of the furnished apartments, allows one to catch a glimpse of the
> glassed-in porter's office set back from the staircase.[. . .] For
> years and years the porter and his wife have remained in this
> mole-hill watching skirt bottoms and trousers pass by as they as-
> cend to their rendez-vous. For years they have been constricted to
> the dimensions of this absurd place, on the fringes of the arcades,
> these two old people that one catches a glimpse of, wearing out
> their lives, he by smoking she by knitting, by knitting again, tire-
> lessly knitting, as if the destiny of the universe hung on this knit-
> ting. (p. 27)

The endless, prosaic knitting that accompanies the passage of
narrative time (the endless procession of people going up and
down the staircase) lies at the "fringes" of another world (the
arcade) where, instead of the absurdity of time spun out, we find
the *suspended* time of amorous encounters, passion and poetry.

What I've argued in these pages comes down to two basic
points. First, by reading streets and crossroads as *figures of narrativity*, we can better explain certain features of prose poems or of
novels, such as *Le Paysan de Paris*, that deliberately flaunt the poetic quality of their subject. For this reason we should not dismiss
the relevance of narrative in prose poetry—a point touched on by
Bonnefoy in his inaugural address to the Collège de France when
he remarked casually that "Every poem harbours a story or a
piece of fiction in its depths."[12] This is because the opposition
between narrative and poetry is not really a formal opposition at
all but has rather become during the last century and a quarter a
thematic contrast within certain novels and prose poems themselves. The goal of writing a "pure" poem is as illusory an ideal as
Zola's professed aim in writing *La Bête humaine:* "to do a totally
different sort of novel [. . .] without description [. . .] just pure

narration." Poetry and narrativity seem to be inextricably bound together. So when Mary Ann Caws remarks in the preface to the collection *The Prose Poem in France* that the prose poem is a genre "so clearly situated at the crossroads" (p. vii), her metaphor is by no means a casual one since it points to a fundamental truth about prose poetry's relation to narrative and about narrative's relation to roadways.

My second point concerns cities themselves. The Bonnefoy and Aragon texts discussed earlier are in fact using city streets (and the narrative temporality that these metaphorically designate) to posit an ideal Arcardian realm.[13] Whereas French poetry up until the later Romantics (such as Gautier and Baudelaire) followed the classical tradition of depicting Arcadia according to pastoral conventions (as, for instance, in Ronsard), it seems that French writers of the past century and a quarter have resurrected the Arcadian myth within the city itself. The title of Aragon's novel—"The Paris Peasant"—is but one instance of this curious juxtaposition of literary conventions. By situating Arcadia *within* the city (not in its grandiose avenues but rather in the half-hidden vistas of its cross-streets) these writers have underlined a fundamental truth about the Arcadian myth itself. The "natural," a-temporal world of immediate sense and presence designated by Arcadia (or by the botanical garden in Bonnefoy's first "Rue Traversière" text) is not, in fact, a natural "Eden" from which we have all fallen. Arcadia derives its meaning only from its opposition to a temporal world of comings and goings, of human actions and their consequences—in short, the world of the city. Only in contrast to this world (and in contrast to its pathways of linear narrativity) can the poetic other-world of Aragon and Bonnefoy begin to take on meaning as an escape from all-pervasive narrative time. The ideal of a timeless countryside beyond the city streets always was a city ideal.

NOTES

1. Feodor Dostoevsky, *Crime and Punishment*, trans. by George Gibian (New York: W. W. Norton and Company, 1975), p. 1.
2. Emile Zola, *La Bête humaine* (Paris: Garnier-Flammarion, 1972), "Introduction", p. 11. This and all subsequent translations from French are my own.
3. Charles Baudelaire, *Oeuvres complètes I* (Paris: Gallimard, Pléiade, 1975), p. 276.
4. See Tzvetan Todorov, "Poetry Without Verse," and Barbara Johnson, "Disfiguring Poetic Language," in *The Prose Poem in France*, pp. 60–78 and 79–97, respectively.
5. Yves Bonnefoy, *L'Arrière-pays* (Genéve: Skira, 1972), p. 9.

6. Yves Bonnefoy, *Rue Traversière* (Paris: Mercure de France, 1977), p. 95. Subsequent page references to this edition will be included in the body of my text.

7. Peter Demetz, "Introduction" to Walter Benjamin's *Reflections* (New York: HBJ, 1978), p.xviii.

8. Saint-John Perse, "Le Livre," *Images à Crusoé* in his *Oeuvres complètes* (Paris: Gallimard, Pléiade, 1972), p. 20: "Mais sous l'obscure croisée, devant le pan de mur d'en face, lorsque tu n'avais pu ressusciter l'éblouissement perdu [. . .]" ("But sitting by the obscure casement window opposite the stretch of wall across the way, having failed to resuscitate the lost splendor [. . .]").

9. Walter Benjamin, "Paris, Capital of the Nineteenth Century," in *Reflections*, pp. 146–148.

10. Louis Aragon, *Le Paysan de Paris* (Paris: Gallimard, 1926), p. 19.

11. Aragon, p. 21. Cf. Benjamin's characterization of this submarine space of gazes in Baudelaire's work: "The Paris of his poems is a submerged city, more submarine than subterranean [with dream images such as] the prostitute, who is saleswoman and wares in one." (Benjamin, p. 157)

12. Yves Bonnefoy, *La Présence et l'image* (Paris: Mercure de France, 1983), p. 35.

13. For a sustained reading of Bonnefoy's debt to the painting by Nicholas Poussin entitled "Et in Arcadia ego," see John T. Naughton, *The Poetics of Yves Bonnefoy* (Chicago: Univ. of Chicago Press, 1984), pp. 115–118.

Martin/Scala/Art Resource. Interior of an English Inn.

3

CHARACTER AND POETRY IN
THE CITY

*What becomes a city most? The characters who inhabit it,
through the years, uncertain as they are. As we are.*

FROM *TOPOS* TO ANTHROPOID: THE CITY AS
CHARACTER IN TWENTIETH-CENTURY TEXTS

Jane Augustine

The city in pre-twentieth-century novels written in English is almost wholly *topos*, a place, a locale which is the backdrop for realistic dramas of individual consciences making choices in order
to solve personal dilemmas of love, marriage, work, war, parental origins, psychic identity—the themes are familiar. City as *topos* and background still remains a stock feature of much
contemporary 'realism.' But that mode looks backwards to the
nineteenth-century tradition, not to say fantasy, of the individual's freedom to act and to dominate situations. As the twentieth
century opens, however, a reinterpretation of the city begins to
emerge in the novels of certain American writers who are particularly sensitive social observers of the influence of urbanization
upon the individual psyche. In the minds of Theodore Dreiser
and Henry James, and—later—of Saul Bellow and Alison Lurie,
'the real' is complex, built out of interactive values; it is not reflected by the crude 'naturalism' of many proletarian novels in

which city life is wholly evil. In these writers, who are psychologically as well as sociologically conscious and alert to the shifting values of this century, the city takes on the mixed qualities and functions of a human character. The city becomes less a *topos* and more anthropoid—'man-like,' 'resembling the human being,' more organic and seemingly capable of choice. It becomes quasi-human.

The cause of this change lies outside of literature. Through technological developments—highspeed transportation, mass communication, hydroelectric power—American cities in the twentieth century have grown unplanned with great rapidity into enormous multi-faceted entities, dwarfing individuals and forcing new kinds of decisions upon them. Correspondingly, in the novel, with its inherent bent toward verisimilitude, the city becomes a larger and more active agent standing in a new literary relationship to the individual human beings who are actors in the plot. What precisely is this new relationship? Before citing specific novels, I would like to offer five general observations as a guide to my analysis.

First, the city as character is present when the human characters, especially the protagonists, are travelling, in transit, rootless, not fixed in a domestic environment, urban or rural—that is, they are in physical and cultural flux. Second, the city as character is present when the human characters are confused, unformed or weak, out of touch with their prescribed set of values, thus shaky and uncertain in personal identity and consciousness—that is, they are in mental flux. Third, the city as character is present when the particular features of a particular city are perceived by a human character as a will or force or pressure bearing upon him or her, producing a decision or reaction which would not have occurred otherwise. Human characters then even develop into manifestations of the stronger force, the city, instead of developing into selves divergent from or opposed to it.

Fourth, the city as character is also a city which is a fact in 'real life,' a great city actually existing on this planet—Paris, New York, London. Such a city is not only large in size but rich in history and idiosyncratic style—rich because it calls forth from individual citydwellers' lives unpredictable elements which arbitrarily, inexplicably, shape that style and augment it, in the same way that individuals' personal qualities provoke decisions which shape their personal style—a process which is mirrored in the novel. Fifth, the city as character is present, acutely present, when the human characters in the novel discover the erotic—the power of sexuality. Is there a causal link here? I think there is, and the implications are manifold both for art and life.

Now for the evidence in novels to support these generalizations. At the turn of the century, the city as character manifests virtually simultaneously in the work of Dreiser and James, novelists who differ vastly in almost every other respect. The ground-breaking *Sister Carrie* was published in 1900, *The Ambassadors* in 1902. Carrie, 18 years old in 1899, is emotionally unformed, in transit between childhood and adulthood as well as physically in transit on a train from her small home town in Chicago. She thinks ahead: "There was the great city, bound more closely by these very trains." The train, with its theretofore inconceivable speed and power, behaves like an organism. It is intimately linked to the quantum leap in the city's power which occurred at the turn of the century, a power seen as not merely mechanical. Not by accident did Cornelius Vanderbilt plan Grand Central Station as the concentrated gathering-point for those incarnations of power, as a *locus* of a veritably spiritual grandeur, a building larger than any cathedral on this continent. Moving out, moving on, moving 'up' is America's religion. Cities are hubs from which and to which one travels not only physically but also psychically.

Sister Carrie opens with a significant description of Chicago which is applicable, in Dreiser's mind, to all cities:

> The city has its cunning wiles, no less than the infinitely smaller and more human tempter. There are large forces which allure with all the soulfulness of expression possible in the most cultured human. The gleam of a thousand lights is often as effective as the persuasive light in a wooing and fascinating eye.

This passage is not mere personification, a gimmick of style, but a statement of the analogy between the "more human" being and the quasi-human city. The simile is sexual, foreshadowing the seduction of Carrie by Drouet, the 'drummer,' but Carrie's individual fate is perhaps of less interest to Dreiser than his understanding that the city, with its "forces wholly superhuman" is the actual seducer of naïve persons. Its manifold phenomena "appeal to the astonished senses in equivocal terms" which mislead anyone who has no "counselor at hand to whisper cautious interpretations."

Although Dreiser labels the city "superhuman," his metaphor suggests that the city is nevertheless like a person. It has a human voice which whispers in the ear but which offers no clue as to how properly to interpret and comprehend what it is saying. It is an extra-literary fact that the great city of the twentieth century has no system of meanings or values. Instead it presents endless sensory stimuli which dazzle the individual, especially the new-comer to the city who, out of touch with prior values, is left only with naked perception.

And hope. As much as the great city exists in fact, it exists as a projection in the mind of the individual dwarfed by its immensi-ties. It is seen as the site of larger life and more opportunity for pleasure. Chicago seen as a source of hope holds personal fluc-tuating power over the unformed, rootless Carrie as she contem-plates restaurants, theatres and the colorful nightlife which constitute that city's style of pleasures. In this period Chicago was sustaining an influx of 50,000 people a year to work in its burgeoning businesses and industries. For this suddenly large group of toilers, the nature of work itself was different from what most of them, rural folk, had known. Factories with machinery changed work into labor (Hannah Arendt's distinction). Assembly-line methods were invented; workers then found themselves to be little more than handles on the machines they operated, so new compensations for this deadening routine toil had to be invented too.

Carrie is overwhelmed by sense impressions from all sides; the streets are jampacked with people, noises, smells, strange man-ners and modes of dress. None of these are codified or judged in familiar ways, and all are enticing, suggestive of something richer and more brilliant to come. As she sensuously encounters the city, she discovers herself sexually—a discovery which leads to the affair with Hurstwood, his theft of money to elope with her, and their going to New York where Carrie becomes an ac-tress and a success. She does well in a career which means con-stantly changing identities. She becomes the city, as it were, fitting into and manifesting "New-York-ness" in her career-mindedness, her pursuit of pleasure and her lack of familial and domestic virtues.

Sexually sinful Carrie is not punished in the novel's end by death or disgrace; she continues to live, dissatisfied, under the city's pressures for 'more.' But her life mirrors 'real life.' Among the anonymous crowds of strangers who are thrown together in the modern city, religion is conspicuously missing. There are no sins—no one insignificant individual's peccadillos have enough consequence to warrant the heavy label of 'sin.' There are also no final satisfactions but, in this scintillating flux, only phenomena and "astonished senses."

Certainly when Lambert Strether, the central character in Henry James' *The Ambassadors*, arrives in Paris, his senses are as-tonished. He too is in transit, having been sent to Europe to res-cue from an 'evil' woman Chad Newsome, his fiancée's son, and bring the young man back to Woollett, Massachusetts. Slowly Strether realizes that his physical uprootedness has seeded cultural uprootedness, resulting in his severance from Woollett's narrow and unquestioned verities.

The force producing this realization in Paris, the city, more than any individual in it—Paris in contrast to Woollett. Paris is "the city of consciousness itself," of art, of culture, of heightened and delighted senses. When Strether encounters Paris, he is unknowingly discovering the erotic along with the aesthetic. Paris ultimately manifests for him in the person of Mme. de Vionnet, Chad's beautiful, refined and generously loving mistress. Strether had hints of this link from his very first day in Paris, as its glowing sensuousness descends upon him in the Luxembourg gardens:

> His greatest uneasiness seemed to peep at him out of the possible impression that almost any acceptance of Paris might give one's authority away. It hung before him this morning, the vast bright Babylon, like some huge iridescent object, a jewel brilliant and hard. . . . It was a place of which, unmistakenly, Chad was fond; wherefore, if he, Strether, were to like it too much, what on earth, with such a bond, would become of either of them?

After he meets Chad's friends, all facets of that brilliant jewel, Paris, Strether knows he must act quickly to 'save' Chad,

> to advance, to overwhelm with a rush. This was how he would anticipate—by a night-attack, as might be—any forced maturity that a crammed consciousness of Paris was likely to take upon itself to assert on behalf of the boy.

Of course Strether, mere fallible individual, does end up liking Paris "too much"—its consciousness becomes his consciousness, obscuring the dimly-remembered fixed values and loyalties inculcated by his home town. Simultaneously and ironically, Chad's consciousness becomes Woollett, which is after all an expanding American industrial city; he will return there and take up the career of advertising man. Strether, stranded in Paris, cannot even accept an alliance with his proven friend, the Europeanized and therefore 'free' woman, Maria Gostrey. The moral basis of this rejection is detestation of the American profit motive; he feels obliged, as he says, "Not out of the whole affair, to have got anything for myself."

This 'tale of two cities' ends with the human protagonist overpowered by both of them. It is also a tale of two centuries, whose values paralyzingly conflict in Strether. He cannot completely abandon a nineteenth-century individual ethic—revulsion from the act of manipulating others for one's personal gain—nor can he wholly accept, despite its inroads upon him, the twentieth century's freedom of response to the erotic. He sees that response as selfish, getting something for oneself, a kind of 'profiteering' he now abhors. He is therefore left with the one thing he has gotten: "wonderful impressions" of a great city and its many allures, impressions, uninterpreted and for him uninterpretable, neither moral nor immoral, such as, in another place, met the "astonished eyes" of Sister Carrie.

A leap of fifty years brings us to Saul Bellow's *Seize the Day,* published in 1958, whose human protagonist, Tommy Wilhelm, is far more formless and malleable than Lambert Strether. He also confronts a more formidable opponent, New York city, which radiates such a multiplicity of powerful and violently active forces that it virtually becomes the central character, with Wilhelm a pathetically feeble and ineffectual antagonist.

Tommy Wilhelm is in transit in every way. He is weaker than the adolescent Carrie because he has her same naivete but is a man in his early forties. Wilhelm wants money. He yearns and longs for money the way Strether longed for beauty and emotional responsiveness and Carrie for indulgence in pleasure—in short, money perversely possesses erotic qualities for him. The New York city whose towers dwarf him is quintessentially the city of money-making—not by working for it, which is stupid and lowbrow, but by investing cleverly to get it without earning it. New York is therefore a city teeming with rumors, 'inside' information, 'hot tips' and serious discourses on the 'psychology' of the market, a city of words, words, words.

The city manifests to Wilhelm in the figure of Dr. Tamkin, the "psychologist" who is in fact a conman, who has a "scientific" approach to making killings in the market. So Wilhelm, conned before, gives a check—his last money—to Tamkin. As Strether on his garden bench grew aware of Paris soliciting him and of trouble to come yet could not resist the seduction, Wilhelm too lets himself be taken in. While watching stock market figures, he realizes that Tamkin is untrustworthy, possibly crazy. Yet New York is the city of craziness, an inevitable consequence of its contradictory and high-density stimuli which bombard the individual who has no reference point from which to interpret them. This lack breeds so much confusion that even words no longer communicate. Wilhelm meditates:

> Every other man spoke a language entirely his own, which he had figured out by private thinking. If you wanted to talk about a glass

of water, you had to start back with God creating the heavens and earth; the apple; Abraham; Moses and Jesus; Rome; the Middle Ages; gunpowder; the Revolution; back to Newton; up to Einstein; then war and Lenin and Hitler. After reviewing this and getting it all straight again you could proceed to talk about a glass of water. "I'm fainting, please get me a little water."

By the middle of the twentieth century, we see a citydweller even more stunted, paralyzed and helpless to make choices governing his or her life. In Wilhelm's impotence and confusion, New York appears as a titantic maniacal god who has created a world of miscommunication and madness. It creates and is addicted to language contortions isolated from referent; words are no guide to appropriate action, so the individual cannot act. Like the Chicago worker who seems an extension of a lathe or sewing machine, so the New Yorker becomes a cog in a mechanism manufacturing deceptive appearances and verbalized imaginings, because the city is too complex for the senses to surround. The mind, exhausted by stimuli, resorts instead to constructing projections of it. Once the city has thus invaded the mind and becomes internalized, its power over the individual is monumentally increased. The individual, enormously weakened, cannot even see, as Strether at least could, which choices the door is closing upon.

Wilhelm, defeated and cheated of his last cent, wanders out onto Broadway, where an apocalyptic vision of "the great, great crowd" dizzies him. He sees in every face

> the refinement of one particular motive or essence—*I labor, I spend, I strive, I design, I love, I cling, I uphold, I give away, I envy, I long, I scorn, I die, I hide, I want.* Faster, much faster than any man could make the tally. The sidewalks were wider than any causeway; the street itself was immense, and it quaked and gleamed and it seemed to Wilhelm to throb at the last limit of endurance. (104)

It is a vision of obsession, and the obsessed Wilhelm has become New York, himself throbbing at the last limit of endurance. Caught up in a knot of mourners on the sidewalk, he is accidentally swept into a funeral parlor. There, beside an unknown corpse, he bursts into uncontrollable, heartfelt tears. New York City has left him with nothing—with far less than Woollett and Paris left Lambert Strether. No money, no pleasure, no "wonderful impressions," no compensatory touch of the erotic. The city has even twisted away the words for his thoughts. He only retains enough humanity to realize loss. He can only mourn—and even that in such deprivation of individual capacity that he does not know who or what he mourns for. The city as character is revealed as energetic and vital, but also as a mad dictator, a monomaniac, offering too many possibilities while stamping out the remnants of the individual thought and strength needed to realize them.

Now, by a shorter leap of seven years, we come to the more extreme case of the particular contemporary American novelist whose overt agenda is to make the city the principal character in her work: Alison Lurie. In her 1965 novel, *The Nowhere City*, Los Angeles, America's *other* great city, becomes, like New York, a kind of arbitrary, obsessed, living, thinking being, while the human characters are reduced to pawns and semblances of inorganic materials poured by builders into pre-shaped molds. In addition to the title, the very structure of this novel makes clear that the city is the protagonist. There is no one human character who can be called central, but omniscient authorship brings together two couples, with a few hangers-on, who engage in various copulations in semi-tropical sun. When one lands on the opposite coast of America, Eros replaces Midas, but, as in New York, no one can tell the crazy from the sane, the young from the old, the men from the women, the animate from the inanimate.

One couple, Katherine and Paul Cattlemen, are in transit, their New England academic values in disarray. Paul's response to culture change is to find it liberating; he starts an affair with a beatnik waitress named Ceci. Katherine's response is to have headaches out of sheer rage at the "nowhere city," where everything is trying to be something else or at least *look* like something else, which now in this place amounts to the same thing. As New York manifested as a hydra-headed monster of noisy mouths pouring out noncommunicative languages, so Los Angeles is a holocaust of visual impressions exhausting the capacity for judgment in the deluged Angelenos. Like Tamkin, who conned Wilhelm by talking gently and persuasively as a philosopher and serious person, each spectacle in Los Angeles 'speaks,' insisting that its perceivers take it seriously and succumb to its purported beneficences.

The inanimate aspects of the city, thus adorned and promulgated, become living beings. Paul, for example, observes the life of the automobile in California:

> In Los Angeles cars were a race apart, almost alive. The city was full of their hotels and beauty shops, their restaurants and nursing homes—immense, expensive structures where they could be parked or polished, fed or cured of their injuries. They spoke, and had pets—stuffed dogs and monkeys looked out of their rear windows. . . . Their horns sang in varied voices . . .

Outshone by these glittering phenomena, human beings appear drained of their living passions. The inanimate is what Paul notices and admires in his wife: "something in her manner which recalled the unsophisticated, almost mute spirit of a tree or stream." A movie starlet looks like a wall: "Her face, including the mouth, was painted chalky brown all over, as if with Kemtone."

Even inanimate structures must not have any appearance which suggests function or mundane 'reality.' Houses are built not to look like houses but like French chateaux, Spanish haciendas, whatever. Paul is pleased by this inventiveness; Katherine, however, hates the fifteen-foot-high plaster cow on the roof of the drive-in milk bar. The gigantic rotating cement donut above a donut stand especially riles her. She sees only the gigantic hole: "That's what this city is! That's what it is, a great big advertisement for *nothing*."

Lurie has also learned a few lessons from Henry James about couples at odds and ironic transpositions. (We should recall that the interpairings of two couples is the structural basis of *The Golden Bowl*.) As in *The Ambassadors* Chad Newsome and Lambert Strether had by the novel's end reversed their initial positions, so Katherine, at first far more resistant than her husband, maintaining, like Strether, a mission on behalf of Massachusetts, finally turns into a pure manifestation of Los Angeles. She realizes that its very emptiness of meaning and values leaves everything open. She can, like Carrie, engage in any pleasure she wishes—dye her hair, sleep around. Neither a god nor an ethic survives in the Golden State. As she picks up a goodlooking stranger and goes off to have sex with him, she thinks:

> Nobody was watching her; she was in Los Angeles . . . where nobody saw or cared what she did. And at this thought, as always recently, came a little burst of giddy euphoria. . . . It didn't *matter*, nothing mattered here."

The transformation is complete when Paul observes across the room at a party "a pretty girl in tight yellow pants, with a smooth California tan and ash-blonde hair . . . an obvious Los Angeles type" who turns out, on closer inspection, to be his wife. Instantaneous belief in sense impressions is now religion. Sense impressions therefore can obliterate history—the fact of longterm intimate relations—and even preclude simple recognition. What has become of Wittgenstein's "seeing *as?*" The process of seeing something *as* something is now wholly controlled by the city, but a city without a motive, not knowing why anything should be seen as what it is not, or, for that matter, as what it is. An image is an image is an image. This obsession of course derives from Los Angeles' dominant and progenitive activity: movie-making. Los Angeles is always manufacturing poses before a camera, constructing itself as the star of an endless movie. It is "nowhere" looking at itself infinitely regressing in a house of mirrors, witlessly flashing lights and colors in a continuing effort to excite the by-now-unastonished and weary eye.

Lurie's novel *Foreign Affairs* (published in 1984) puts the city of London on stage as central character and protagonist. The *New York Review of Books* rightly pointed out that this novel's main purpose is to enable the author to describe London and reveal comic details of its *mores;* again therefore the human characters are merely manifestations of, or victims of, the distinctive style and 'personality' of that great city.

The human characters, again two couples, meet the five criteria described earlier. The Americans, Vinnie Miner, Chuck Mumpson and Fred Turner, transport themselves to old England not merely to tour but to discover alternatives to felt lacks in themselves. The city bears down upon their weaknesses and uncertainties, pressuring them into uncharacteristic decisions and postures, particularly in their erotic involvements. The fourth member of this quartet, Lady Rosemary Radley, incarnates contemporary London as Mme. de Vionnet had embodied Paris.

Lurie, student not only of Jamesian entanglements but also of Jamesian humor, permits to priggish Vinnie Miner a comic and Strether-like loosening of inhibitions under the influence of the city she had planned not to let intrude. Not unlike Strether, Vinnie discovers someone to love too late. Her paralysis, however, results not from personal ethics but from inherent bad timing. Paradoxically, as perhaps with Strether too, the very forces of the city which undermined her old habits distracted her from forming new ones in time.

These distractions—that is, those quasi-personal forces of London which override and mold individual consciences—play an even more decisive role in the case of Fred Turner. An American professor in London to write a book on John Gay, he falls in love with Rosemary, a British actress, who plays 'Lady Emma Talley' in an historical drama currently running as a popular TV series. Unlike Vinnie, Fred does not let London shake his prior conceptions. He is more like Tommy Wilhelm, unable to resist the city's spell because it, like Tamkin, tells him what he wants to hear through the lips of the beautiful actress. He loves her the way Paul Cattleman loved Los Angeles in the person of Ceci, the free-loving beatnik waitress.

Rosemary is quixotic, however, and deserts Fred for long periods. During one of these, he goes to find her at her house in Chelsea but, entering by the unlocked front door, instead in the kitchen finds only the cockney charwoman, Mrs. Harris, of whom Rosemary has often spoken. Mrs. Harris is obscenely filthy and very drunk. Fred is thoroughly repelled by her, but after a few minutes' conversation, to his horror she makes advances to him. "Let go of me, you dirty old cow!" he yells as he knocks her down and runs out of the house. Later, much too much later, the truth penetrates: that drunken harridan is one and the same as

> his false true love, the star of stage and screen, Lady Rosemary Radley. . . . Why hadn't he known? Because Rosemary had fixed in his head the idea of herself as beautiful and graceful and refined and aristocratically English . . . All these months he's loved somebody who was as much a theatrical construct as Lady Emma Talley.

Even then he does not understand that Rosemary *is* London—the insecure, confused, undermined London of today which, in a weak alcoholic haze, puts on the mask of the valiant, confident traditional England of Scott's romantic novels—an England with noble aristocrats and sturdy commoners accepting of the class system. Fred saw the London he wanted to see in 'Lady Emma Talley.' In Rosemary's descriptions of her unseen charwoman, Mrs. Harris, he failed, as a literary man, to see "Mrs. 'Arris," the fictional friend of Sairy Gamp in *Martin Chuzzlewit*. When he encountered "Mrs. Harris," he also saw but did not recognize the true ugly filthy London of the eighteenth century, locale of John Gay's *Beggar's Opera* and Hogarth's Gin Lane, the designated object of his intellectual study. Like Paul Cattleman, who never wrote the book on southern California which he was hired to write, Fred could not write his book for the same reasons that he failed to recognize his beloved—appearances blinded him. The modern city, then, conquers in two ways. One is by complete takeover, or 'body-snatching,' of sensitive but malleable persons like Katherine and Rosemary; they internalize the city. The other is by reinforcing the conventionality of rigid but shallow persons like Paul and Fred; they play by the city's rules but imagine it is still external to them.

As a finale let us turn to another Lurie city, as real as Chicago, Paris, New York, Los Angeles or London. In her 1975 novel, *The War Between the Tates*, Brian Tate, the principal male human character, broods on this place:

> Brian had known for some time that he and his colleagues were not living in the America they had grown up in; it was only recently

though that he had realized that they were also not living in present-day America, but in another country or city-state with somewhat different characteristics. The important fact about this state, which can for convenience' sake be called "University," is that the great majority of its population is aged eighteen to twenty-two. Naturally the physical appearance, interests, activities, preferences and prejudices of this majority are the norm in University. Cultural and political life is geared to their standards, and any deviation from them is a social handicap.

This city, like Paris or London, puts its own peculiar pressure on individuals. Brian realizes that "in University, he has the experience of being among a depressed minority. Like a Chinaman in New York, he looks different; he speaks differently . . ."

The significant fact here is that the city, heretofore seen as physical and geographical, has made another quantum leap. It is now a metaphysical City, a universal state of mind evolved from that same combination of technological progress and spiritual belief that built Grand Central Station. This City is the world. Brian Tate finds no comfort in that understanding:

> he can see quite well that the "real world" is growing to resemble University more every year, as the youth culture becomes more dominant; and he is aware that all he has to look forward to is the prospect of joining the most depressed minority group of all, the Old.

In this metaphysical City devoted to youth, there is an official religion: The Children with a capital C, but of course no ethics. The *Realpolitik* of University sinks under the weight of the majority young. Brian's colleagues try to project individual self-images strong enough to offset minority status. He sees them masking themselves as figures from past history, when individuals appeared to have strength and influence—the department head as Cordell Hull, the bearded dissident as Castro and so on down to his best friend, Hank Andrews, who

> long ago adopted for himself the role of Machiavelli. . . . he is as likely to be motivated by cynical amusement as by either interest or principle. Today . . . he has finally come out in favor of the Pass-Fail Option—largely, Brian suspects, in order to cause trouble.

To be an individual in relation to a collectivity is inherently to be a minority person and consequently to suffer a sense of diminishment and helplessness. What is the use of holding to personal ethics or of being rationally motivated? The collective—that is, the city—generates a complex network of interactions which generally come between any cause and what was once thought to be its predictable effect. But tremendous power circulates along this network, building and destroying. Not the individual machinator but this great contemporary supra-geographical city incarnates the characteristics of Machiavelli, of a person who magnetizes and manipulates power, dealing wholly in power terms, not in terms of any other value—not rationality nor love nor truth nor justice. Brian Tate's friend Andrews merely mimics the prevalent mode of power-brokerage in the city. The grossest, surest way to secure power over other people is to make trouble for them.

This final portrait of the city as character dishearteningly implies that the 'real life' city, if quasi-human, is no longer the individual's benefactor by facilitating enlargement of his or her consciousness, as Dreiser and James saw it, if somewhat ambivalently, at the turn of the century. Now it manifests as an oppressor, capricious and anti-individual, displaying the more brutal, irrational and aggressive aspects of human beings. It makes war upon individuals; it overpowers them, disregards their desires and nullifies the consequences of their efforts, driving them crazy. A large number of crazed individuals amounts to a crazed city, completing a vicious circle.

But does it need to be vicious? Must the citydweller always be diminished by the city? The evidence we have examined is mixed. Physical transition, mental flux and malleability in individuals make them vulnerable to domination by the massive congeries of appearances which is now the contemporary, possibly worldwide, city. When the city forces atypical decisions upon the individual, the result, however, is not always negative. One set of possibilities—the ingrained, familiar—is closed down, but others—new and therefore problematic—open up.

This paradox of opening up is particularly clear in relation to the erotic. As has been noted, cities engender many opportunities for sexual activity. They provide anonymity, pluralistic standards of behavior and plenty of potential partners densely packed into a small area. The erotic itself, however, comes from within. It is inherently anarchic, ungovernable and private. It arouses subjectivity, concentrating the attention of individuals upon themselves and their emotions, qualities which the city views as anti-social and subversive of its own efforts to control people by keeping them involved in public power struggles.

So a kind of 'self-destruct' mechanism begins to function. Cities work hard to stamp out the erotic activity they themselves, by their very nature, generate. The more they threaten the erotic, the more individuals take refuge in it. Sex, after all, is still linked not only with pleasure but with love, friendship, kindness, cooperation—qualities which are the only true antidote to war. Through the loophole of this paradox, the individual may emerge triumphant over the collective.

While the city increasingly assumes the role of protagonist in novels like those just discussed, modifying our assumptions about 'realism,' one 'realistic' element remains. In the final analysis, the human characters are inherently the ones through whose eyes we human readers see. Through the mediation of their minds—projections of the authors' minds, to be sure—we construe meaning. An individual erotic act, an act of love and pleasure, has created the novel. It mirrors the dilemma of American life, in which unpredictable appearances—gaudy, seductive, appalling—and disturbing identity-shifts now take the place of the essences once attributed to religion and personal ethics. Miscommunication and non-recognition are rife when appearances are all we have. Where shall we turn, detached as we are from faith and absolute values? Fiction remains an important antidote—even an elixir. As Marianne Moore said of poetry, it emits "a piercing glance into the life of things." With the help of this interpretive light, we come perhaps as close as we can to constructing substance out of appearances.

THE COSMOPOLIS OF POETICS: URBAN WORLD, UNCERTAIN POETRY

Michael Heller

"Does my telephone call to New York strengthen my conviction that the earth exists?"
—Ludwig Wittgenstein, *On Certainty*

My topic is American poetry as it is connected to our urban world, and while, in a way, I must write of the 'image of the city' in the poem, my true subject is the poem in the city. I will treat of this vast subject through three periods and three poets because I am attracted to the importance and elegance of their solutions. I will conclude with the briefest of notes on the present. In the process of writing this paper, I will have excluded a great many poets, not because they don't fit into my argument but because they fit in all too well and would make this paper ten times as long as it is. I hope that my reader's response will be something like, "but what about X or Y or Z, aren't they part of this demonstration?"

I start with an assumption or two, that by the 19th century, the city had firmly become the central mental environment of Western if not of nearly all culture, and that, at present, in literature and poetry, even of the most pastoral or nature-inspired, the city is a presence, a foil, an entity to resist.

Assuming that you have tentatively granted the above, I will move on briefly to an obvious, grander, more inclusive, hence more banal truism: The dreams of mankind are inevitably dreams of harmony. Whatever mankind has constructed by which to live, aspiration or image, a structure of the mind or of materials, the harmonious interaction of its parts, of a man or woman communally bound with others, and the community bound in orderly fashion to the rest of the world, such harmony permeates every one of these constructs. The natural history of paradise, to borrow the words of Frank and Fritzie Manuel, is a history of harmonies, of melliflous images and sounds, of orderly commerce between man and God or man and man, man and woman, woman and woman, man and beast, man and nature. The structure of the world, in these dreams and visions, whether of the wilds, the rural or of the urban, is that of, at the least, pleasant grids on which events occur. The harmony is there because it has been believed that the harmony is in mankind or in nature or in the divine rule of Gods and kings. Thus in our oldest imaginings, such as Gassire's Lute, a fifth century B.C. folk tale of the African Solinikas, the city of Wagadu "is not of stone, not of wood, not of earth. Wagadu is the strength which lives in the hearts of men and is sometimes visible because eyes see her . . ." What are our utopias, Republics, Cities of God, and even of the Devil, but finely tuned designs ruled by proportion and degree (and by decree as well).

Old hat. Old story! Yet, up until the end of the 18th century, when that urban world begins in oppressive fashion to take center stage in the thought of men and women, the possibility or imagination of harmony is all-pervasive. With respect to the city, as Joyce Carol Oates suggests in her essay "Imaginary Cities: America" the city is nearly always read as "utopian" and its failures, then, are thought of as a kind of "hell." Let me put this another way. The utopian idealization allows a critique of dystopia; harmony is the highest good, and mankind's fall as evidenced in the contemporary city is an infernal fall away from the good. Indeed, looking back a little to Romantic literature, the city is acceptable provided it is actually a pastoral, characterized by cyclical rhythms, seasons, sufficient respites from noise and filth. Let us consider, for example, Wordsworth's vision on Westminster Bridge which views sleeping London as it were panoramically "open unto the fields and to the sky". Here is a London depicted without its street life, its grimy slums, its teeming confusion, an unimpeachable image of the longed for harmony. Blake, at approximately the same time, supplies the dystopia to Wordsworth in his poem "London", with its "mind-forged manacles". "London" is a poem that today is as exacting in its understanding as when it was first written. For "London" makes explicit the nearly contemporary equation we seem to labor under, that perceived orders of harmonies are often concommitant with perceived orders of Authority.

Now, up until the nineteenth century, harmony has been the poet's ally. The pastoral version of reality whether it is as image, seemly metaphor, regular metres and sonorities in one's verse, is the poet's recourse against disorder. Where we get disharmony, as in Blake, still we get right analysis, symmetries of cause and effect. Where these are unavailable, the poet makes use of the epiphanic memory. Thus, in Baudelaire's "Le Cygne", the operative trope employed against the failed reality of the 19th century city, with its quick changes, its contradictions, its distraught "negress stamping her feet in the mud" seeking her lost Africa, is not a sense of the forces at work (as in Blake's "London") but a mind which reaches into history to exclaim: "everything becomes an allegory". We see here that allegory can structure not only hope or vision but also loss. Such loss, a Golden Age or Utopia of the Gods, is as idealized as Wordsworth's depiction of London.

As we approach the present, we see a shift in the strategies of poetry, in how the poem will deal with the ubiquitous presence of the urban. Consider the effects on the use of allegory. To the extent that allegory depends on the exemplary authority of the past, on the spiritual, mythological or historical figure, it is increasingly weakened because it cannot find parallel structures to relate to. The urban world is a welter, a swirl, a maelstrom of phenomena. Only an emerging science offers serious critical competition to existing religious views, and while it is an order, it is profoundly resistant to the clarifying lineaments of allegorical treatment. As the Manuels put it: "The biological and anthropological discoveries of the nineteenth and twentieth centuries completed the subversion of the Edenic myth—the further back one went the more bestial man appeared, and the idea of a heavenly paradise could no longer have a prototype on earth . . . "

Still, with the Utopian role model in disrepute, another strategy presents itself. Like many of the urban painters of the 18th and 19th centuries, the poet, determined to enact a mimesis of his or her world, now proceeds to seek the long, the inclusive view, the broad perspectival or aerial vantage that we find in such a diversity of artists of the period. Whatever the painterly or literary ambitions involved, it strikes me that both poet and artist have as a *sub rosa* purpose, inclusivity, totality of high and low, of sacred and secular, of simultaneously rendering order and chaos. The incredible detail of so much of this work, both in pictures and in poems, coupled with broad compositional ideas suggests this purpose. You shall have, all at once, these works seem to say, a secular version of the entire Divine Comedy. You will have states of being, conditions of individuals, Kings on thrones and beggars around the corner, immensities and ruins. This is like having it both ways, and to the extent that Authority is becoming as suspect as anarchy, the view from inclusivity alone cannot be maintained.

Let me parse, for a moment, a line of discussion developed by Jackson I. Cope in his remarkable little book *Joyce's Cities*. Jackson Cope, while looking for the sources of Joyce's imagery, surveys the poetry of James Thomson, in particular, the poem entitled "Doom of a City", a precursor to Thomson's more well-known "The City of Dreadful Night". What is of interest here is the activity which the poem depicts. The narrator of the poem, like many of the Romantic poets before him, flees "the mighty City" sleeping "in vast silence"; he flees because he is "accurst" with "hopeless doubt which gnaws the brain." His voyage is undertaken to relieve that doubt, a doubt attributable to the loss of older hierarchies and orderings, by finding a new vantage, a place to begin a re-vision of the city. On this voyage, the narrator's boat is beset by a storm and he lands upon the shores of a vast city. This city is an immensity of stone buildings and stone inhabitants, like statuary frozen in the various poses of their daily lives. It is, as Cope demonstrates, actually another metaphor for the one the narrator has left. Here we find conflated the frozen landscape of Dante's lowest *malbolgia* and Blake's "mind-forged manacles". The European city of the 19th Century is rendered in summative fashion; the tendencies of Western thought have moved toward this locus where utopic and dystopic visions are end-stopped, "coffined in eternal stone".

Enter America. Perforce, an American city cannot entirely be a European one. The European city is an archeological vertigo, history's barnacles on the urban ship of state, accretions and erasures of stone which make the cityscapes of Paris or London cultural as well as architectural palimpsests. America's oldest cities, New York or Boston, where they are not distinctly imitative of the European manner either through the importation of architectural style of the bald fakery of plaster and metal *appliqué*, tend to be thinned out or functional urbanscapes. After Madrid or Granada, New York to Federico Garcia Lorca is "geometry and anguish". While Paris seems a city made for humans, in New York, the urbanite looks as shockingly out of place as a fly on a wedding cake. Certainly part of that anguish is a human rootlessness desiring and not finding roots, the absence of the city version, to paraphrase William Carlos Williams, of a "peasant tradition" to give place character.

As with so much else concerning American poetry, the American urban poem has its true beginning with Whitman. This is a critical cliche, of course. However, the dystopian vision of the city, as I have suggested above, depends on the utopian possibility that some agency, human or divine, one which more than likely came before has the power to uplift the fallen. When that vision fails, as in Thomson, all we have is an entropic view of the city, barren, inert, decreative. But the American city of the early and mid-nineteenth century is in a sense, too young or new to have become a fallen place. Populated by, or in contact with diverse and displaced populations, by strange and threatening frontiers, the old world ethical or religious structures have gained no hegemony. And Whitman, the oracular agency of what he witnesses, the great refuser of the old inheritances, is so to speak the right voice in the right place.

If we look, for example, at Whitman's "Crossing Brooklyn Ferry," a poem nearly contemporary with Thomson's "Doom of the City," we see that like Thomson's, the vantage is panoramic: the city is seen across the water and the poet is attempting to make sense of what he sees by some attempt at inclusiveness. Everything else about the two poems is strikingly different. In Whitman, there is immense buoyancy of tone, partially due to the way Whitman dissolves barriers between what he witnesses and himself ("The impalpable sustenance of me from all things . . . myself disintegrated, everyone disintegrated", he exclaims) and the omnivorous syntax of his long free flowing lines, lines which seem to appropriate freely the contents of his vision. The line is, if you will, only a minor unit of a larger, democratic vista in which there are, to quote from the poem, "The similitudes of the past and those of the future/The glories strung like beads on my smallest sights, and hearings". Among these things, Whitman says, is one "which fuses me into you now, and pours my meaning into you".

Whitman's line involves a democratization of vision. It is nearly the first Western poetry after that of certain passages of the Bible which attempts to abolish hierarchical determinations. Its catalogs and lists aim not only for inclusivity but for a refusal to subordinate. The only thing which we are meant to consider higher or superior is the poet's archemedian lever of sight. Whitman's eyeball moves and reshapes the world in the strangest way; it desacralizes the sacred and consecrates the secular; it levels and uplifts. The holy of holies is the poet's mind, which like an amniotic sac holds everything in life-giving fluid. In the ninth section of "Crossing Brooklyn Ferry" the mind of the poet moves with a supple fluidity from the river to the sky, to the "tall masts of Mannahatta!" to, finally, the brain which expunges "questions and answers." The poet, no longer consumed by doubts, can "Suspend here and everywhere, eternal float of solution! / Gaze, loving and thirsty eyes, in the house or street or public assembly!" Whitman, in this poem seems to establish, not so much an image of the city, but, as I have suggested my true topic is, some of the major features by which the city poem (and by implication, its poet) might survive in the city. I note two things, at least, which must mark this poetry; one, the willed desire for inclusivity; the other, a kind of Keatsian negative capability, one capable of suspending "here and everywhere," an "eternal float of solution."

Let me indulge in some historical shorthand. As a glance at any anthology of American poetry will show, not much happens with this Whitmanian capability in the intervening years between Whitman's work and the Modernist period. Poetry, what there is of it, remains for the most part gentlemanly agrarian or reverts to pastoral allegorical gentility. It is only with Williams, and with Eliot and Pound, that the modern city again enters the poem and the poem again enters the modern city. Now I put both Eliot and Pound to one side in this discussion because by their "return" to Europe, by their search for authoritative and hierarchic realms of spiritual and political order, they most properly address the nature of the European city.

During this very same interval, roughly 1880 to the twenties, the American city, however, is radically transformed. There are the immense waves of immigration, of industrialization, of the building of skylines and suburbs. As profound as these are, the to-be-modern city exhibits something even more dramatically disturbing: a loss of that optimism concerning democracy which seemed so powerfully exhibited in Whitman. Instead there is a growing despair, a commercial optimism concurrent with the growth of greed and incivility. Whitman's idea that it all might work out is laid low by economic catastrophes, by competition for jobs, by the rapacity of landlords, by the shameful messages found in the work of Jacob Reis and Jack London, finally by the futile carnage of the Great War itself.

It is this failed city which Williams addresses in one of his earliest poems, "The Wanderer: A Rococo Study"; the narrator of the poem, like the Whitman of "Crossing Brooklyn Ferry" is also on a ferry boat, gazing across at the skyscrapers, and is moved to exclaim "How shall I be a mirror to this modernity?" Now this characteristic trope of many of Williams' poems about the city. The urban landscape, as with Whitman, is confronted *en face;* rather than looking upon the city with nostalgia or disgust, the stance is somewhat combative and the confrontation must be dealt with. Neither poet nor city stand alone but form the poles of a dialectical occasion. Like the mountain climber gazing at the mountain, Williams must write of the city because it is there.

This occasion is of particular interest. The English poet, Charles Tomlinson, surveying Williams' work has suggested that we can look at Williams' poems as attempts to find a language by which an identity, in particular an American cultural identity, can be created, to "name" Tomlinson says "what possesses no name". To put this another way, in the confrontation between Williams and the city, the city is not yet real for Williams, not because it is no longer true to its past (this being the European dystopia—utopia equation), but because there is no adequate name or definition for its present reality. If for Whitman, the city represented one of democracy's proving grounds, for Williams, it represents a realm of uncertainty, fueled by his own love-hate relationship with it.

In another of Williams' city poems, "The Flower", the poet-narrator is standing on the Jersey Flats looking toward New York City which he imagines as: "A petal, colorless and without form / the oblong towers lie / beyond the low hills . . ." Startling in its freshness, the image does not prepare us for the perceptions of the next few lines: "It is the city, / approaching over the river. Nothing / of it is mine, but visibly / for all that is petal of a flower—my own." The imaginative act, the city *cum* petal, enables a kind of partial possession i.e. if what belongs to the city belongs to the city, yet the city is also the poet's if inventively transfigured. Still, the way the word "Nothing" hangs at the line ending, and the qualification of "but visibly" carefully delineate the terms of this possession. "Real" possession is transposed to a literary one, reminding us, as Ibab Hassan has pointed out, that the city is a form of desire as well as a trope.

In still another poem, "Perpetuum Mobile: The City", Williams is speaking to a woman about the city: "a dream / we dreamed / each separately / we two / of love / and of / desire—". This is the dream "toward which we love", a dream Williams says "a little false", yet of such power that: "there is no end / to desire— / let us break / through / and go there— / in vain". The counterpoint of these lines, the force of desire and the hopelessness of attaining its object becomes the repeated motif of the poem. A litany of brutal factuality, of meaningless work, crime and gluttony is punctuated throughout the poem by the choral refrain of "for love". The poem is constructed, as Williams once defined his poetics, out of "inimitable particles of dissimilarity" a means by which the traces of a thing can imply what is left out as well as what is included. This is similar in effect to Williams' "obsolete" image of the rose in *Spring and All*, the visual datum "becomes a geometry" which "penetrates / the Milky Way".

The spatiality of "Perpetuum Mobile," its disjunctive deployment of images, far from giving us a picture of the city, present us with the ganglia of emotions the modern city might induce. Whitman's poetic line rolls across the page gathering all equally into its recursive movements, again, as I have suggested above, holding things 'democratically'. Williams, in contrast, seems, in his city poems, to create this spatio-linguistic web of criss-crossing vectors in which nodules of images, discrete kernels of rhetoric and sightings are barely held together. The city, which in

Whitman was a visionary's catalog, is now, in Williams, a constellation of opposed and contradictory forces. It is a net, to use Lorca's term, made up of "geometry and anguish". All its inbetweens are so much uncertainty.

Now the city is also an intellectual and artistic environment. A receiver of the new century's brickbats, it was also (and never more so than in Williams's formative years) the melting pot of the arts. In the modern city, particularly since the beginnings of the Modernist phase, a myriad of literary forms arises, an immense profusion of poetic experiments, genres and perspectives. For the contemporary city is not only physically different from the non-urban world, it is no longer governed by the countryside's cyclical and recurrent rhythms, its pastoral images, its allegorical modes of thought. Rather, the contemporary city can be characterized as a realm of continually generative, open-ended and accumulating traditions. For the poet, this means the city houses a plethora of poetics; the library and the bookstore comprise a warehouse of experiments, of poetic beginnings and endings. Here, contemporary *gestalts*, world-views, systems of totality, lose their standing under the implosive pressures of the urban environment. Each poem, each painting, will get to be a one-time only. The city will have now only one tradition, that of non-tradition.

After Williams, the Objectivist poets such as George Oppen and Charles Reznikoff (poets barely known in some academic circles) again address the problem of the poem in the city. The tangled and haphazard roots of Objectivist poetics begin in an attack on the naivete of the Imagists, on the transforming of the visual datum into a literary conceit, but the major thrust of their work is to discover how, amid the shopping centers of tradition (as the poet Armand Schwerner has called the contemporary poetry world), one can find an authentic voice.

Here I want to discuss the significance of Oppen's work. By the time Oppen began to write his major poetry, the late fifties and early sixties, the Modernist assumptions about language were being contested, in particular, the notion that poetry was a hieratic language capable of presenting the human condition. Williams's sense of "no ideas but in things", Pound's insistence on the ideogrammatic method and on the "natural symbol" as the adequate symbol seemed to represent outdated forms of mimesis; these ideas failed to take into account, so later critics would maintain, a necessary and appropriate suspiciousness towards language itself. Put in terms of urban poetry, the problem now would be one of not only finding adequate technical means by which to convey the disparate nature of the city, but also one of having a language tainted, indeed corrupted by political abuse, media debasement and the increasingly powerful notions among the academic community that language is best viewed as a self-enclosed, only accidentally referential, system.

Oppen's poetry, in its consistent focus on the urban, is also an attempt at relating to these new sets of forces. In "A Language of New York", the city "Glassed / In dreams / and images—" is contrasted with "the pure joy / of the mineral fact / Tho it is impenetrable / As the world, if it is matter / Is impenetrable". The poem's concerns are epistemological, i.e., how to give "truth' " in a realm of dreams and images, the status of the "mineral fact". Oppen, as also Wittgenstein, is wary of the bewitchments of language, the way our talk of reality, cities or nature, is more metaphysical than descriptive. "Possible / to use / words" he tells the reader "provided one treat them as enemies. / Not enemies— Ghosts which have run mad / In the subways / And, of course, the institutions / And the banks".

It is precisely this ghostly nature of language which makes poetry so uncertain. The city dweller, at once everyman and no one, is constantly, to use Goffman's term, presenting himself. City life demands one adapt role playing mechanisms at work, while shopping, while entertaining, including knowing when to keep one's mouth shut.

To modify Wittgenstein, in the city, an utterance is not so much an image of reality as a desire, simply to create an image, an image which may be so freighted with hopes and fears that beyond the grossest level it will barely suffice as an intercommunicative act. Such utterances are, as Oppen remarks in his booklength poem *Of Being Numerous*, "A ferocious mumbling, in public / Of rootless speech."

Of Being Numerous is one of contemporary poetry's most sustained investigations of rootless speech, an attempt to determine if the very concept of humanity as it has evolved into urban humanity can be maintained. Perhaps the most unique characteristic of Oppen's poem is its sustained singular voice. The poem shuns the multi-vocal effects of Pound and Eliot (effects which were meant to key in various strata of time) because it seems also to want to shun the nostalgia of history. For if, as I maintain, (and here I echo Eliot in "Tradition and the Individual Talent") the city represents the accumulation of traditions and genres, then, at any moment, the very weight of these traditions denies Pound's dictum that all ages are contemporaneous. This is how Oppen puts it in one of the prose passages of *Of Being Numerous:*

It is difficult now to speak of poetry—

. . . I would want to talk of rooms and of what they look out on
and of the basements, the rough walls bearing the marks of the
forms, the old marks of wood in the concrete, such solitude as we
know.

> One must not come to feel that he has a thousand threads
>   in his hands.
> He must somehow see the one thing;
> This is the level of art
> There are other levels
> But there is no other level of art

Curiously Oppen's poem strikes one as having intentions con-
sonant with Whitman's. For Whitman, the democratic vision
was, in a sense, a given, a principle by which to order the diversity of life, of city life before him on the ferry. For Oppen, humanity as a concept is yet to be proven; yet Oppen's poem, more
severe in its knowledge of the fictions of humanity, still ends
with a quote from Whitman; indeed, its last word is Whitman's
"curious".

I would suggest that curiosity, in the sense that Oppen uses it,
may well be the antithesis of harmony, a willingness to shun
easy reference points and conventions. And, if I were to try to
characterize in a word or two what is the most salient feature of
the contemporary urban poem it would be this admixture of curiosity and uncertainty. If the old orderings have come down,
come down around our heads, still the poem is a kind of clearing
house of knowledge, of systemized modes of thoughts. In the
poem, such modes of thought are felt and tested by an incarnate
poet, one sensitive to the pressures, to the accumulation of surrounding traditions and histories. The city poem is no longer expressive of steadfast and eternal values but of momentary
convictions, instances of tension and uncertainty. How else but
by the nearly untenable aspects of the city can we account for the
multivalent texts of Ashbery or O'Hara, or, in the work of Igna-
tow, the urge to give every urban artifact the status of mythos.
Even the *déjà vu* dadaism of the language poets, as they attempt
to move outside or circumvent meaning, seems predicated on the
city's potential infinity of contents.

Art Resource. Emil Nolde. Schiefer Turm in Soest, etching. 1906. New York. Sothebys.

4

THE CITY AS LANDSCAPE

Where could we go from the here we were already in? New York may be that the perfect place to get over things, romance or life, or even over the Stones of Venice. But it only shows that our places for the Street-Haunting Virginia Woolf did of London have, now, to be our own.

VIRGINIA WOOLF'S LONDON AND THE FEMINIST REVISION OF MODERNISM

Susan M. Squier

"Why do I dramatise London perpetually?" Virginia Woolf wondered in the last year of her life (L, VI: 434). To echo that question is to consider how the real bricks and mortar of the urban realm figure in a woman writer's imaginative constructions, to assess the city's role *in representation*.[1] The meaning of Virginia Woolf's representation of London in her fiction and non-fiction was the topic of my 1985 study, *Virginia Woolf and London: The Sexual Politics of the City*.[2] There, I argued that Woolf turned to the city in her writings to reflect on and to work through her experiences as a woman in a patriarchal society. My study of Woolf's London writings revealed a shift in her figuration of both self and city, as she moved from a position of anxious marginality in relation to its envied realm of intellectual and cultural centrality to, in her mature work, an embrace of the political and aesthetic possibilities for a woman in the modern city. Crucial to the

changed figuration of London in Woolf's works was her use of
the strategy of feminist revision—the realignment *in representation*
of the city's cultural and intellectual relations.

Since the publication of my study in 1985, a vigorous rethinking of modernism has been catalyzed by increasing interest in the
works of modern women writers, Virginia Woolf among them.
Susan Stanford Friedman's pioneering work on H.D. and modernism, Rachel Blau DuPlessis' major study of modern women
writers' treatment of the problem of narrative closure, the work
of Marianne DeKoven and Catharine R. Stimpson on Gertrude
Stein, Shari Benstock's study of *Women of the Left Bank*, Sandra
Gilbert and Susan Gubar's massive study, *No Man's Land: The
Place of the Woman Writer in the Twentieth Century*, Mary Lynn Broe
and Angela Ingram's edited collection treating *Women's Writing in
Exile* and Bonnie Kime Scott's superb anthology *The Gender of
Modernism*, have been or are being joined by feminist studies of
male modernists (sometimes in relation to their female colleagues)—Carolyn Burke on Ezra Pound, Elizabeth Abel on
Woolf, Freud and Klein, Ann Ardis on Wyndham Lewis, my own
work on H. G. Wells and Elizabeth Robins among others—to
produce a challenging reassessment of the critical construction of
the modern condition.[3]

The new reevaluations of modernism are likely to produce a
better understanding of both male and female writers of the
modern era. As Carolyn Burke points out, the lengthy list "of
female modernists whose writing does not quite fit traditional
definitions [may suggest in] their syntactical and rhetorical solutions to gender issues . . . more flexible and imaginative ways of
reading, offering new perspectives on the work of their male
contemporaries."[4] This is not to say, however, that feminist critics
are replacing high male modernism with a unitary, homogeneous
female modernism. "Tempting as it might be . . . to oppose
women Modernists to a parent culture defined as monolithic or
to argue that a collective female experience resulted in a homogeneous women's literature, such arguments force the delicate
network of female relationships and individual achievements . . .
into preconceived patterns."[5] Instead of replacing one unitary
critical construct with a parallel opposed one, criticism now problematizes the very categories with which we have approached
modern writers, demonstrating that the category of modernism
when applied to women often provides not an explanatory grid,
but a straight jacket.

Accompanying this rethinking of the modern period has been a
reconsideration of the conventional notion of the modernist city,
in the new awareness that the city often meant very different

things to women writers than to men, because of their different embodiment and social positioning.[6] My study of Woolf's representation of London can now be placed in a broader theoretical and critical context, for the London that Woolf contended with had significant links to, and differences from, the city of high male modernism, differences related to her particular position as a woman writer in the modern era. These differences had ideological as well as formalist aesthetic implications, for Woolf—like Stein and other female modernists—embedded a politics and poetics of gender within the more obvious formalist aspects of her urban writings.[7]

In this essay I have chosen examples drawn from the great variety of Woolf's urban works (from her first published London essay through the urban novels of her maturity to the London diary entries of her last years) to show how Woolf's representation of the city expresses many of the concerns characteristic of the varieties of female modernism as they are currently being formulated by feminist critics: attention to the problem of speech and silence and to the experience of marginality; a concern with gender politics and poetics, which complicates and deepens the formalist agenda; the strategic use of a decentered perspective; and a split focus or doubled gaze resulting from conflicted identification.

Woolf most succinctly expresses the difference of a woman's urban experience in the invented story of Shakespeare's sister, in *A Room of One's Own.* An aspiring poet like her brother William, Judith Shakespeare escapes provincial life for the stimulation of the city. William Shakespeare moved easily from Latin lessons in the country to acting in London, "practicing his art on the boards, exercising his wits in the streets, and even getting access to the palace of the queen." Yet such is not the case for Judith, whose literary pilgrimage to London ends not with fame and fortune as a playwright, but with mockery, pregnancy, and suicide.[8]

Judith's struggle to create a place for herself as a writer in the capital city fails because her "poet's heart" is "caught and tangled in a woman's body." (AROO, 49–50) While her brother finds the intellectual and cultural spaces of the city open to him—the stage, the streets, the queen's rooms—Judith finds no access route to the spaces of intellectual, professional, social or political power. Instead, because she is a woman, Judith meets many barriers to the development of her "gift, like her brother's, for the tune of words," and Judith falls silent. (AROO, 49) Inadequate education, the limitations imposed by her father's protective love, the social restrictions placed on her both within and beyond the family; all of these inner and outer obstacles to the writer's life make her ill prepared for her encounter with the city. Woolf explains, "[to] have lived a free life in London in the sixteenth century would have meant for a woman who was a poet and a playwright a nervous stress and dilemma which might well have killed her." (AROO, 52)

Indeed, after enduring ridicule, exclusion, and finally exploitation, Judith Shakespeare finds herself with child by the actor-manager who "[has taken] pity on her and . . . [she kills] herself one winter's night and lies buried at some cross-roads where the omnibuses now stop outside the Elephant and Castle." (AROO, 50) With consummate dramatic irony, Woolf reports that Judith ends her days as a physical part of the very city that scorned and excluded her, her unmarked cross-roads grave emblematic of the position of women in urban culture, exiled by sexuality, relegated to marginality, silenced, objectified, expunged.

Although a celebrated modernist manifesto, *A Room of One's Own* departs significantly from the traits that have "often been taken as a common base for a *definition* of Modernism": "[the] movement towards sophistication and mannerism, towards introversion, technical display, [and] internal self-scepticism".[9] Instead of assuming a polished distance from its audience, Woolf's essay deliberately reaches out—first to the young female students at Newnham and Girton who were its first audience, and now to us as readers—soliciting our engagement and response. Moreover, the essay cultivates a deliberately unsophisticated authorial position, from the opening musings on women and fiction to the concluding emphasis on the collaborative, grass-roots creation of a female literary tradition. Given the essay's grounding in practical realities, it is neither irrelevant nor insignificant that Judith Shakespeare's journey to London ends not with fame as an author, but with pregnancy and suicide; success as an artist results, the essay tells us, not from individual technical brilliance, but from the material conditions necessary for artistic creation. The story of Shakespeare's sister dramatizes Woolf's understanding that the city's meaning for women is concrete, specific, and dramatically determined by society and biology—by the inescapable fact that Judith's "poet's heart" is "caught and tangled in a woman's body." (AROO, 49–50)

The essay's recommendations for the modern woman writer have a similar gritty concreteness: the modern woman writer must articulate the experiences and emotions of the ordinary women who swell the city streets. Here too, Woolf stresses the important locus of difference in a *woman* writer's urban experience: her marginal status, which has silenced her in the past and even now makes speech a struggle for women. If London destroyed the talent of Judith Shakespeare in the sixteenth century, in the twentieth century it everywhere bodies forth the female condition as the proper subject of her art. As Woolf explains to the descendant of Judith Shakespeare, the fictitious novelist Mary Carmichael,

> All these infinitely obscure lives remain to be recorded, I said . . . and went on in thought through the streets of London feeling in imagination the pressure of dumbness, the accumulation of unrecorded life, whether from the women at the street corners with their arms akimbo, and the rings embedded in their fat swollen fingers talking with a gesticulation like the swing of Shakespeare's words; or from the violetsellers and matchsellers and old crones stationed under doorways; or from drifting girls whose faces, like waves in sun and cloud, signal . . . the flickering lights of shop windows. All that you will have to explore, I said to Mary Carmichael, holding your torch firm in your hand. (AROO, 93)

Woolf's advice to Mary Carmichael both reflects her own experience of being silenced and marginalized by the London environment, and contains her solution to that problem: the formulation of an aesthetic that enables female articulation because it celebrates "those infinitely obscure lives" embedded in the urban surroundings.

In this celebration of the vibrant variety of ordinary street life, Woolf's vision departs dramatically from the more aloof, abstract aesthetic often identified with literary modernism. As Peter Faulkner defines it, modernism includes "the devotion to an ideal of Art," "acutely rendered material . . . [organized] in an illuminating way," and stress on the writer's impersonality rather than direct emotional expression, through the use of what T. S. Eliot called the "objective correlative."[10] The difference between this concept of the artist as an objective, impersonal and distanced observer serving an abstract ideal of Art and Woolf's engaged vision of the woman artist as a female Diogenes rambling London streets in search of a concrete, and even indecorous, reality (an "honest woman?") reveals the shortcomings of the critical construct that is canonical high modernism.

Perry Meisel problematizes that critical category in his study *The Myth of the Modern*, dubbing it "[the] usual Oedipal paradox in overdrive—the will to modernity—Pound's emblematic injunction to make it new." To a feminist reader, the greatest myth of the modern might well be the claim for inclusiveness implicit in Meisel's subtitle, "British literature and criticism after 1850."

Meisel's study shares with much of modernist criticism its elegant refusal to consider the untidy margins to the field in question, yet it is precisely those margins that raise questions of central importance if we want to elucidate, rather than merely to enshrine, the critical myth that is modernism. Arguing that modernism arises "against, and as a function of, the authority that empowers it," Meisel ventures several definitions of modernism in the brief span of his introductory chapter: "[Modern] literature acts out the loss of something primary that it wishes to regain," "[m]odernism is, in all its historical manifestations, the recurrent desire to find origins or ground despite the impossibility of ever doing so for sure", and "modernism is . . . a structure of compensation, a way of adjusting to the paradox of belatedness that is its precondition."[11]

Redolent of male oedipal anxiety and competition, envy of female procreative power, and the impossible wish for a certainty of origins that such female procreative potency makes possible, these definitions reveal the shortcomings of any construction of modernism that relies on the model of masculine identity creation. Such a modernism will have less analytic utility for the works of women writers, who will have more concern about the suppression of a tradition than about its weight on newcomers, and whose stronger locus of anxiety is more likely to be issues of authorship than influence.[12]

This is not to argue that female modernists had an unproblematically unitary perspective, or that they felt no anxiety of influence, no fear that they could never be as original as their towering precursors. Rather, it is to mark as characteristic of many female modernists the split focus or doubled gaze. As Woolf expresses it—with a characteristically urban twist—in her manifesto for the modern woman writer, *A Room of One's Own*, "if one is a woman one is often surprised by a sudden splitting off of consciousness, say in walking down Whitehall, when from being the natural inheritor of that civilisation, she becomes, on the contrary, outside of it, alien and critical." (AROO, 101) Woolf exhibited that split consciousness by virtue of her own personal history as well as her position as a woman in her culture and society, sharing the iconoclastic perspective of her modernist contemporaries, yet because of her experience as a woman, making a different assessment of the modern writer's task.

Despite her origins in the British intellectual aristocracy as the daughter of Sir Leslie Stephen, and despite her membership in the generation rebelling against their high Victorian precursors, for much of her life Woolf felt an outsider from the intellectual realm that was London. Brenda R. Silver has observed how the

"dual awareness of inheritance and exclusion is vividly portrayed
by the twenty-one-year-old Woolf in a diary entry called "The
Country in London" and subtitled 'Getting ready for Salisbury,
by which I mean laying in books.' "[13] Woolf compares the sense
of marginality and disenfranchisement that she felt when in London with the sense of intellectual heritage and belonging that
was hers in the country:

> I read some history: it is suddenly all alive, branching forwards &
> backwards & connected with every kind of thing that seemed en-
> tirely remote before . . . I think I see for a moment how our minds
> are all threaded together—how any live mind today is . . . of the
> very same stuff as Plato's & Euripides . . . I feel as though I had
> grasped the central meaning of the world, & all these poets & his-
> torians & philosophers were only following out paths branching
> from that centre in which I stand. (Silver, 5–6)

In contrast, London is inimical to women: "The London atmosphere is too hot—too fretful. I read—then I lay down the book
and say—what right have I, a woman, to read all these things
that men have done? They would laugh if they saw me."[14] Such a
disembodied sense of artistic filiation, empowerment and centrality was difficult or impossible to attain in an urban environment,
Woolf believed. While the country permitted an unmediated experience with literature as a solitary reader, the city mingled the
literary realm with the social, mediating the pleasures of reading
with the pains of enforced gender roles. Women were inevitably
confronted with the actual physical fact of their gender difference
and so were excluded from the city's literary and social world(s).

This stress on marginality and the struggle for artistic self-
expression appears in Woolf's first published London essay,
"Street Music," a celebration of the street musician as urban artist. The essay presents a vision of a city-based art that is collaborative, populist, and rooted in the labor of people who are
ordinary, even obscure. Woolf does not elevate art over the quo-
tidian—as did so many male modernists—but rather elevates the
texture of ordinary street life *into* art. So, in "Street Music" she
strikes the note which was to resound through her mature works:
recognition of the countless potential artists among us who, for
want of the right material conditions (the right encouragement,
environment, or gift of expression) go unnoticed:

> Whatever the accomplishment, we must always treat with tender-
> ness the efforts of those who strive honestly to express the music
> that is in them; for the gift of conception is certainly superior to
> the gift of expression, and it is not unreasonable to suppose that

Street Music.

> the men and women who scrape for the harmonies that never
> come while the traffic goes thundering by have as great a posses-
> sion, though fated never to impart it, as the masters whose facile
> eloquence enchants thousands to listen. (SM, 145)

Woolf's first urban essay anticipates the representation of the
city in Woolf's later works in its formulation of an aesthetic that
affirms the texture of ordinary life and in its use of the urban
environment to explore literary issues, such as the possibility of
hostile criticism, the importance of an artist's education—or lack
thereof—and the issue of payment for artistic production. However, it is particularly interesting for the way it links gender politics and poetics to the urban environment.

Woolf affirms her connection to all urban outsiders by drawing
the implicit parallel between the positions of the street musician
and the woman writer. Like the woman writer, the street musician is not generally a socially welcome creature: " 'Street musicians are counted a nuisance' by the candid dwellers in most
London squares, and they have taken the trouble to emblazon
this terse bit of musical criticism upon a board which bears other
regulations for the peace and propriety of the square" (SM, 144).
Like the woman writer, the street musician is outside the bounds

of propriety; just as she is barred from the library, lawns, and chapel of Oxbridge in *A Room of One's Own*, so the street musicians are forbidden to enter the city squares wherein they must ply their trade. Like the woman writer who perseveres, the street musician has learned not to pay "the least attention to criticism." Like women writers (and women in general), the street musician is poorly paid—or not paid at all—for his or her labors. And just as the woman writer has seemed, to male writers from Dr. Johnson to D. H. Lawrence, a scandalous aberrance from the customary feminine role, so the street musician plies a trade which seems "vagrant and unorthodox" to the well-ordered mind of the legitimate householder.

Against the machismo of male modernism, advanced most vividly by Ezra Pound's definition of creativity as "driving any new idea into the great passive vulva of London," Woolf's street musicians—and by extension other modernist artists—are feminized.[15] They join "artists of all kinds" in being seen as "unmanly," because they "give expression to the thoughts and emotions . . . which it should be the endeavor of the good citizen to repress" (SM, 145).[16] Emotional and expressive, unconventional, unpaid or poorly paid, liable to hostile criticism, socially ostracised—the street musician is a powerfully charged metaphor for Virginia Woolf's early sense of her own position as a woman writer in twentieth century London.

The death of powerful precursors provides a second chance; with the death of Sir Leslie Stephen, Virginia—along with her siblings—felt the typically modernist determination to remake the social and aesthetic approaches of her Victorian precursors. Characteristically, Woolf represented that impulse in urban terms, remapping the city to accord with the new aesthetic and political position she shared with her siblings. As she recalled in *A Sketch of the Past*, "Vanessa—looking at a map of London and seeing how far apart they were—had decided that we should leave Kensington and start life afresh in Bloomsbury" (MB, 162). With the changed city space came a corresponding change in social relations and aesthetic aspirations: "We were full of experiments and reforms . . . we were going to paint; to write . . . Everything was going to be new; everything was going to be different. Everything was on trial" (MB, 163).

The split consciousness revealed by Woolf's different representations of London figures in the works of modern women writers on many levels, from ideological and psychological to formalist, and provides a different point of entry to the characteristic modernist problem of belatedness and originality. Not only does the modern woman writer reveal the familiar modernist concern with constructing a workable position in relation to the (largely male) literary tradition preceding her, but she also must deal with the additional problem we might call prematurity: the problem of coming too early, when a recognized *female* tradition does not yet exist. Virginia Woolf thus frames as the crucial problem for Shakespeare's sister the difficulty of *forging, or articulating, a tradition* from the lives around her, because and in spite of the cultural silencing of women. "All these infinitely obscure lives remain to be recorded," the narrator of *A Room of One's Own* tells Mary Carmichael.

The implications of this problem reach past politics to poetics, for not only is the *content* of the modern woman's writing different, but the *form* as well. When Mary Carmichael goes, torch in hand, into the city streets to forge a tradition out of the "accumulation of unrecorded life" she finds there, she must struggle with the problem of plots and plausibilities: the absense of appropriate forms for the new plots of modern women writers.[17] The result is a formal difference from the writing of her male colleagues which, once again, Woolf expresses in urban terms:

> She had broken up Jane Austen's sentence . . . Then she had gone further and broken the sequence—the expected order. Perhaps she had done this unconsciously, merely giving things their natural order, as a woman would, if she wrote like a woman. But the effect was somehow baffling; one could not see . . . a crisis coming round the next corner. (AROO, 95)

In her mature works, Woolf experimented more and more with the formal possibilities inherent in "giving things their natural order, as a woman would, if she wrote like a woman." She also continued to turn to London to explore the experience of marginality, through the more formalist strategy that we might call urbanism of the margins.[18] By that phrase I mean a representation of the city that strategically decenters it, reframing as central what has previously been seen as marginal, in accordance with Woolf's celebrated admonition to modern writers, "Let us not take it for granted that life exists more fully in what is commonly thought big than in what is commonly thought small." Two very different works exemplify Woolf's strategy of using a decentered perspective to represent the city: the "Six Articles on London Life" (1931–32) and *Flush: A Biography* (1933). These works are marginal both by virtue of their genres—the former are urban travelogues published in *Good Housekeeping*, the latter is the biography of a dog—and to different degrees both present a deliberately decentered, feminist perspective on their subjects.

Although the "London Scene" essays celebrate the high modernist setting, their approach diverges from the typical city of modernism. Rather than documenting the city as an "environment of personal consciousness, flickering impressions, Baudelaire's city of crowds, Dostoyevsky's encounters from the underground, Corbière's (and Eliot's) *mélange adultère de tout*," these essays figure a London informed by the same socially and materially grounded feminist consciousness that suffuses *A Room of One's Own*.[19] In their early drafts, these essays employ the strategic decentering Woolf used in *A Room of One's Own*, where she redirected her reader's attention from William Shakespeare to Judith. Here she shifts our attention from the central male subject to the marginal female subject, and reframes the whole social field. For example, in the initial draft of "The Docks of London," rather than celebrating her announced subject—the docks—as a splendid realm of imperial commerce, Woolf shifts her gaze upriver to figure London as a messy master in whose wake the feminized garbage barges incessantly labor to recreate cleanliness and order.

The split focus or doubled gaze is also characteristic of these works, which reveal identity-in-contestation as Woolf struggles between identification with insiders (men, the upper classes) and outsiders (women, the working classes). The essays also exemplify the strategies she forged to acommodate her vision to the aesthetic and ideological demands of her vehicle, whether it be the book publishing trade or as here the middlebrow women's magazine, *Good Housekeeping*. In the changed representation of the city between first and final drafts, "The Docks of London" reflects Woolf's conflicted identifications, for Woolf revises to exclude all of the explicit social criticism. In its finished version, the essay provides a self-congratulatory celebration of the consuming class, while the workers have become invisible.

An even more authoritative decentering operates, with a return to the theme of housecleaning, in "Great Men's Houses," where Woolf inverts the adulatory tour of the great man's home to focus on the labor of his wife and maid, which provided the material conditions for his greatness. The spatial imagery of the house of Thomas and Jane Welsh Carlyle explicitly connects sexual and class oppression, mistress and maid. Emphasizing the amount of time women spend in physical labor each day, the essay suggests that the forms of labor, rather than familial or class ties, really define women's place in society. Because both Jane Welsh Carlyle and the maid are responsible for the hot water, clean rooms, and regular meals that Thomas Carlyle requires to write his history, the women are both associated with the same

space in "his" home. While the great man fills the top floors, the
women cluster in the lower regions: kitchen, washroom, scullery,
basement. As with Woolf's life-long representation of London, so
here spatial organization contains within it a politics and poetics
of gender. Just as the women's domestic tasks confine them to
the lower reaches of the home, so they limit them to the lower
reaches of society.[20] And while this essay is concerned with Victorian writers, the implications for Woolf's view of modern writers are clear. As Jane Marcus has pointed out, "Only a woman
like Virginia Woolf could conceive of the metaphor of the artist as
charwoman to the world." If Joyce imagined the modern artist
paring his fingernails above his creation, Woolf's modern artist
was down on her knees with a broom and dustpan, sweeping up
nail parings right alongside the housemaids.[21]

Despite their powerful moments of social criticism, the urbanism of the margins embodied by Woolf's decentered perspective
on London in the "Six Essays on London Life" too often falls victim to Woolf's internal struggle between identification with the
regnant central subject of her masculine colleagues and with the
disenfranchised position of women and other marginal groups,
and is subsumed by the middlebrow travelogue appropriate to
Good Housekeeping. (It is precisely this sort of conflict within the
creative process that a feminist analysis of the gender politics and
poetics within modernism has enabled us systematically to identify.) But in Flush: A Biography, the work in which she lets a span-
iel stand in for the similarly marginalized position of woman in
Victorian society, Woolf's conflicted identifications are nearer resolution. She signals this in the plot by providing her canine protagonist with a metaphoric journey of liberation from London,
the city of the patriarchs, to Florence, the maternal city. The
choice of a dog as protagonist has run the gamut of critical commentary, from the dismissive judgement that Woolf was simply
being "silly" (the preponderance of critical opinion, abetted by
her own reference to the novel as "a joke"), to my own analysis
of the novel's metaphoric exploration of gender relations expressed through the parallels between the tale of the kidnapping
of Barrett Browning's dog and the Ripper murders, and finally to
Pamela Caughie's current, engaging refusal of the very dialectics
between silliness and seriousness.[22] Yet this silliness is an aspect
of Woolf's entire corpus that is worth taking seriously, for it
poses a real challenge to modernist values and decorum and so
shows how in modern women's writings, gender politics and poetics often deepen and complicate the formalist project of modernism, so that to adopt a deliberate silliness can be to take a
more politically serious position, in feminist terms, than to adopt
the most portentiously allusive narrative style.

Decentering the Canonical Vision of the Modern City.

Given the formal and thematic implications of the gender politics and poets I have been discussing, the tradition forged by
Shakespeare's sister will necessarily differ from her brother's, in
both content and form. In contrast to Meisel's sense of the "strikingly uniform structure of modernism as a whole," feminist
critics of modernism remark on the differences within it. Modern women writers negotiate spaces within modernism for different and uncanonical genres such as the diary, the autobiography,
and the letter and for their different gendered perspective(s) on
such issues as the possibility of originality and the response to
tradition.[23]

Woolf's most extended play with the questions of tradition and
originality is her mock biography *Orlando*. This novel, written in
homage to Vita Sackville-West, exemplifies the modernist woman

writer's characteristic slant on these issues. *To the Lighthouse* was the novel in which Woolf dealt with the issue of social belatedness, laying to rest forever the ghost of her parents in order to establish herself as an independent adult. In *Orlando* Woolf confronted the issue of literary originality, anxiety concerning belatedness, and the influence of her literary fathers, in order to create a place for herself in the English novelistic tradition. I have analyzed elsewhere how Woolf's defiance of the plots and plausibilities of the "Defoe narrative" functions to make Orlando "a serious work of criticism *in and of* the tradition of Leslie Stephen" as well as "Woolf's gesture of literary emancipation."[24] Here I will merely highlight one moment in that *jeu d'esprit*, to sketch out how Woolf's response to her situation as a modern woman writer, in relation to her tradition and to contemporary society, results in a feminist revision of canonical modernist concerns, including the portrait of the modern city.

Woolf's treatment of London in *Orlando* provides a telling example of the materially-grounded critique and analysis she embodied in her representation of the city. Alluding to, and subverting, T. S. Eliot's *The Waste Land*, which Hogarth Press published in 1923, Woolf embodies the split focus or doubled gaze of the female modernist; she is attentive to (male) textuality, but concerned to forge a new female tradition. Literal and literary filiations collide when Orlando's son is born, offstage, in a passage in which Woolf celebrates the social, sexual, and literary possibilities of the modern city. Here is the passage in question from *Orlando*:

> Wait! Wait! The kingfisher comes; the kingfisher comes not. Behold, meanwhile, the factory chimneys, and their smoke; behold the city clerks flashing by in their outrigger . . . Behold them all. Though Heaven has mercifully decreed that the secrets of all hearts are hidden so that we are lured on for ever to suspect something, perhaps, that does not exist; still . . . we see blaze up and salute the splendid fulfillment of natural desires for a hat, for a boat, for a rat in a ditch . . .
>
> Hail! natural desire! Hail! happiness! divine happiness! and pleasure of all sorts, flowers and wine, though one fades and the other intoxicates; and halfcrown tickets out of London on Sundays, and singing in a dark chapel hymns about death, and anything, anything, that interrupts and confounds the tapping of typewriters and filing of letters and forging of links and chains, binding the Empire together. Hail even the crude, red bows on shop girls' lips . . . kingfisher flashing from bank to bank, and all fulfillment of natural desire, whether it is what the male novelist says it is; or prayer; or denial; hail! in whatever form it comes, and may there be more forms, and stranger. (*Orlando*, 192–93)

Forced by biographical conventions to veil Orlando's *accouche-ment*, an indecorous topic unsuitable for the staid biographer's pen, Orlando's narrator substitutes a description of the city. Yet the repressed returns, for the London passage is redolent with the social and sexual license of the censored event—female pro-creation with its [male] anxiety-producing overtones of potency, centrality, originality. In a choric interlude whose images recall Eliot's *The Waste Land*—flowers and factory workers; rats on the riverbank; typists, clerks, and shop girls; day excursions to Lon-don's parks; hymn singing in dark city churches; the myriad shapes of natural desire—Woolf's urban portrait revises the ca-nonical representation of the modernist city to offer an alterna-tive response to the issues of tradition and identity. Rather than the familiar anxiety about belatedness (what Meisel called "that old Oedipal paradox in overdrive,") here we find a celebration of origin, in the social, biological, and intellectual sense. While Eli-ot's poem circles obsessively around issues of domination and control, and reflects an anxious search for individual autonomy, Woolf's passage celebrates human connectedness and glories in whatever nurtures subversive freedom.

Although in its imagery this passage clearly alludes to *The Waste Land*, the passage as a whole, like the novel/biography where it appears, departs from and so significantly subverts Eliot's vision. Encircling the whole passage is the image of the "kingfisher flashing from bank to bank," an opaque natural inversion of the Fisher King myth central to *The Waste Land*. Woolf's strategic inversion typifies the feminist revision of mod-ernism; anxiety about cultural, intellectual and even sexual bar-renness in Eliot becomes celebration of a natural rather than mythic fertility—cultural, intellectual and sexual—in Woolf. Eli-ot's poem figures all the varieties of unsatisfying sexuality—from sterility to impotence to abortion—while this passage celebrates satisfying sexuality in all its varieties, including the birth in which this episode culminates. Neither hellish wasteland nor babel-ridden purgatory of chaotic commercialism and debased over-stimulation, Woolf's London is instead a gloriously mun-dane and fertile heaven.

This brief passage from *Orlando* emblematizes Woolf's strate-gies as a writer throughout her career, in its appropriation and revision of androcentric images of the city to express her own au-thentic feminist perspective. From "The Journal of Mistress Joan Martyn" to *Orlando*, Virginia Woolf's representation of the city exemplifies the concerns and strategies of female modernism, as critics are newly defining them: attention to the problem of speech and silence and to the experience of marginality; a concern with gender politics and poetics, which complicates and deepens the formalist agenda; the strategic use of a decentered perspective; and a split focus or doubled gaze resulting from conflicted identification. As she "dramatise[d] London perpetually," Woolf revealed the eclipsed face of female modernism.

NOTES

1. Woolf's actual London experiences were a rich counterpoint to the representational relation to London I am addressing here, and have been the subject of a number of books since Dorothy Brewster's pathbreaking study, *Virginia Woolf's London* (New York: New York University Press, 1960).
2. Susan Squier, *Virginia Woolf and London: The Sexual Politics of the City* (Chapel Hill and London: The University of North Carolina Press, 1985).
3. Susan Stanford Friedman, *Psyche Reborn: The Emergence of H.D.* (Bloomington: Indiana University Press, 1981); Marianne DeKoven, *A Different Language: Gertrude Stein's Experimental Writing* (Madison: University of Wisconsin Press, 1983); Rachel Blau DuPlessis, *Writing Beyond the Ending: Narrative Strategies of Twentieth-Century Women Writers* (Bloomington: Indiana University Press, 1984); Catharine R. Stimpson, "The Mind, the Body, and Gertrude Stein." *Critical Inquiry* 3 (1977): 491–506 and "Reading Gertrude Stein," *Tulsa Studies in Women's Literature* 4 (1985): 265–271; Shari Benstock, *Women of the Left Bank: Paris, 1900–1940* (Austin: The University of Texas Press, 1986); Sandra M. Gilbert and Susan Gubar, *No Man's Land: The Place of the Woman Writer in the Twentieth Century*, Vols. I and II, (New Haven and London: Yale University Press, 1988, 1989); Bonnie Kime Scott, *The Gender of Modernism* (Bloomington: Indiana University Press, 1990); Mary Lynn Broe and Angela Ingram, *Women's Writing in Exile* (Chapel Hill: The University of North Carolina Press, 1989); Carolyn Burke, "Getting Spliced: Modernism and Sexual Difference," manuscript courtesy of the author. Another version of this essay appears in *American Quarterly*, 39:1 (Spring 1987). Elizabeth Abel's study of Virginia Woolf in relation to the work of Melanie Klein, and Sigmund Freud, *Virginia Woolf and the Fictions of Psychoanalysis*, has been published by the University of Chicago Press.
4. Carolyn Burke, *op.cit.*, p. 2.
5. Benstock, *op.cit.*, 32.
6. For an early statement of this perspective, see my *Women Writers and the City: Essays in Feminist Literary Criticism* (Knoxville: The University of Tennessee Press, 1984). Christine Sizemore's study of the image of the city in the works of modern British women writers, *A Female Vision of the City: London in the Novels of Five British Women* (Knoxville: The University of Tennessee Press, 1989) continues this work of feminist reevaluation.
7. For this phrase, I am indebted to Carolyn Burke's discussion of Gertrude Stein, which has many suggestive parallels to Virginia Woolf's understanding of the gendered—indeed, the sexual—subtext of a woman writer's relation to the urban environment, especially as she figures it in the story of Judith Shakespeare.

> [It] has not often been noticed that Stein's formulation of modernist technique—for the splice makes possible one kind of juxtaposition—contains a poetics of gender hidden within its apparently formalist concerns. Moreover, Stein's implicit parallel between verbal connectives and

the modes of human intercourse raises important questions about the participation of women writers in literary modernism and the sexual poetics of its projects.

Carolyn Burke, "Getting Spliced: Modernism and Sexual Difference," manuscript courtesy of the author. Another version of this essay appears in *American Quarterly*, 39:1 (Spring 1987).

8. Virginia Woolf, *A Room of One's Own* (New York: Harcourt, Brace & World, Inc., 1929; rpt. New York and Burlingame, Harcourt, Brace & World, Inc., 1957).

9. Malcolm Bradbury and James McFarlane, "The Name and Nature of Modernism," *Modernism: 1980–1930* (Harmondsworth, England and New York: Penguin Books, 1976, 1986), 19–55, 26.

10. Peter Faulkner, *The English Modernist Reader, 1910–1930* (Iowa City: The University of Iowa Press, 1986), 13–30.

11. Perry Meisel, *The Myth of the Modern: A Study in British Literature and Criticism after 1850* (New Haven and London: Yale University Press, 1987) pp. 1, 4, 5.

12. Gilbert and Gubar's definition of the "anxiety of authorship" in distinction to Bloom's "anxiety of influence" is obviously my referent. For an extended discussion of the difference between these two responses to literary creation, see Chapter One, "The Queen's Looking Glass: Female Creativity, Male Images of Women, and the Metaphor of Literary Paternity," Sandra M. Gilbert and Susan Gubar, *The Madwoman in the Attic: The Woman Writer and the Nineteenth-Century Literary Imagination* (New Haven and London: Yale University Press, 1979). Susan Stanford Friedman makes a similar point when she points out that the androcentrism of modernist myth-making necessarily posed serious obstacles to H.D.'s project of identity creation as a writer.

> [As] woman mythmaker, H.D. was faced with raw materials of poetic vision that did not validate her experience or perspective as authentic, but rather projected a feminine image of woman's "otherness" or deviation from the masculine human norm. To construct a new symbolic system that did not objectify her self as woman, her mythmaking necessarily included a subversive aspect that set her distinctly apart from her fellow poets. Like theirs, her transformation of old mythologies was a new synthesis of symbol. But unlike theirs, her synthesis included a revision of patriarchal foundations. For H.D., mythmaking from a woman's perspective began in a negation of male perspectives. (Friedman, *op.cit.*, 211–12)

13. Brenda R. Silver, *Virginia Woolf's Reading Notebooks* (Princeton: Princeton University Press, 1983), 5–6.

14. Virginia Woolf, "The Country in London," Hyde Park Gate Diary, 1903 courtesy of Louise A. DeSalvo and Mitchell Leaska.

15. Ezra Pound, "Postscripts to *The Natural Philosophy of Love* by Remy de Gourmont," in *Pavannes and Divagations* (New York: New Directions, 1958), p. 207." Cited in Burke, *op.cit.*, p. 10.

16. Carolyn Burke, "Getting Spliced: Modernism and Sexual Difference," unpublished paper courtesy of the author.

17. Nancy K. Miller, "Emphasis Added: Plots and Plausibilities in Women's Fiction," *PMLA*: 96 (January 1981), 36–48. See also Rachel Blau DuPlessis, *op.cit.*

18. Friedman writes of H.D.'s act of grounding political attitudes in personal experience and developing a "political syncretism, a modernism of the margins rather than the reactionary center." Friedman, "Modernism of the 'Scattered

Remnant': Race and Politics in H.D.'s Development," *H.D.*, edited by Michael King. (New York: National Poetry Foundation, 1986), cited in Shari Benstock, 30–31.

19. Malcolm Bradbury, "The Cities of Modernism," 100.

20. The strategic decentering of the London realm in the "Six Essays on London Life" is characteristic of the urban representations of modern women writers. See my essay, "The Modern City and the Construction of Female Desire," *Tulsa Studies in Women's Literature*, Summer 1989.

21. Jane Marcus, "*The Years* as Greek Drama, Domestic Novel, and *Gotterdammerung*," *Bulletin of the New York Public Library* 80 (Winter 1977): 276–301, 301.

22. Considering *Flush* in the context of feminist responses to modernism, once again I weigh in on the side of seriousness. I am now struck by its links to another important trend within female modernism only recently identified: the feminist tendency to identify across species lines. This tendency characterizes the tradition of feminist vegetarian pacifism that Carol Adams identifies, a tradition that appeared in England and America, at the time of the First World War.

   Benstock reminds us that one of the main readings of Modernism "defines it specifically as a post-World War I phenomenon, that emphasizes the role the war played in creating the psychology of despair in which the ensuing literary movement would ground itself," and she cites Susan Stanford Friedman's powerful analysis of the birth of modernism in the death of a human centered world organized around the Enlightenment vision. While "The Waste Land" powerfully articulates the sense of despair arising from such a shattered universe, another response to the decentering of man was the flowering of feminism.

   And we can also locate at the same moment another decentering, producing a new awareness of the other species that populate the earth with "man." To argue that *Flush* is an early example of such a cross-species identification, also to appear in the works of feminist vegetarians and most recently to be found in the science fiction writings of Octavia Butler, is not of course to argue that *Flush* is an example of feminist vegetarian pacifism. And indeed, it is to err on the side of overseriousness. But it is to point out that Woolf's habitual tendency to participate imaginatively in the lives of non-human creatures (from birds to dogs to marmosets) is not only an intertexual fact (*pace* Keats and his sparrow) but can also be understood in a philosophical and even political (broadly construed) context. Woolf described Flush as "a joke" in a letter written in 1933 to Lady Ottoline Morrell. (L, V: 161–62). Carol J. Adams's essay on feminist vegetarian pacifism as a tradition within literary modernism, "Feminism, the Great War, and Modern Vegetarianism," appears in *Arms and the Woman: War, Gender, and Literary Representation*, edited by Helen M. Cooper, Adrienne Auslander Munich, and Susan Merrill Squier (Chapel Hill and London: The University of North Carolina Press, 1989). Pamela Caughie, "*Flush* and the Literary Canon: On the Uses of 'Silly' Fiction." Paper presented at the Tulsa Comparative Literature Symposium, "Redefining Marginality," March 31, 1989.

23. Meisel, *op.cit.*, p. 1. For a discussion of the letter as a rediscovered form in female modernism, see Catharine R. Stimpson, "The Female Sociograph: The Theater of Virginia Woolf's Letters," *The Female Autograph*, ed. Domna C. Stanton and Jeanine Parisier Plottel (New York: New York Literary Forum, 1984), 193–203.

   Jean E. Kennard extends the feminist critique of canonical modernism when she points out that it has led critics to overlook "a counter-tradition to the dominant male modernist mode of exile and alienation."

Brittain and Holtby are representative of many women writers in the twentieth century who worked in a basically realistic mode. Several of these women—Rebecca West, Storm Jameson, Phyllis Bentley, Hilda Reid, Beatrice Kean Seymour, for example—were personal friends, many of them fellow Somervillians. Together with these women and others, Brittain and Holtby, I suggest, continued a tradition of English fiction exemplified by George Eliot.

Jean E. Kennard, *Vera Brittain & Winifred Holtby: A Working Partnership* (Hanover and London: University Press of New England, 1989), 22–23.
24. Susan M. Squier, "Tradition and Revision in Woolf's *Orlando*: Defoe and "The Jessamy Brides," *Women's Studies*:12 (1986), 167–77, p. 75.

REFERENCES

Elizabeth Abel. *Virginia Woolf and the Fictions of Psychoanalysis*. Chicago: The University of Chicago Press, 1989.

Carol J. Adams. "Feminism, the Great War, and Modern Vegetarianism," *Arms and the Woman: War, Gender, and Literary Representation*. ed. Helen M. Cooper, Adrienne Auslander Munich, and Susan Merrill Squier. Chapel Hill and London: The University of North Carolina Press, 1989.

Shari Benstock. *Women of the Left Bank: Paris, 1900–1940*. Austin: The University of Texas Press, 1986.

Malcolm Bradbury and James McFarlane, "The Name and Nature of Modernism," *Modernism:1980–1930*. Harmondsworth, England and New York: Penguin Books, 1976, 1986.

Dorothy Brewster. *Virginia Woolf's London*. New York: New York University Press, 1960.

Mary Lynn Broe and Angela Ingram. *Women's Writing in Exile*. Chapel Hill: The University of North Carolina Press, 1989.

Carolyn Burke, "Getting Spliced: Modernism and Sexual Difference," manuscript courtesy of the author. Another version of this essay appears in *American Quarterly*, 39:1 Spring 1987.

Pamela Caughie, "*Flush* and the Literary Canon: On the Uses of 'Silly' Fiction." Paper presented at the Tulsa Comparative Literature Symposium, "Redefining Marginality," March 31, 1989.

Marianne DeKoven. *A Different Language: Gertrude Stein's Experimental Writing*. Madison: University of Wisconsin Press, 1983.

Rachel Blau DuPlessis. *Writing Beyond the Ending: Narrative Strategies of Twentieth-Century Women Writers*. Bloomington: Indiana University Press, 1984.

T. S. Eliot. "The Waste Land." *The Collected Poems*. New York: Harcourt, Brace & World, 1970.

Peter Faulkner. *The English Modernist Reader, 1910–1930* Iowa City: The University of Iowa Press, 1986.

Susan Stanford Friedman, "Modernism of the 'Scattered Remnant': Race and Politics in H.D.'s Development," *H.D.*, edited by Michael King. (New York: National Poetry Foundation, 1986).

—————— . *Psyche Reborn: The Emergence of H.D.* Bloomington: Indiana University Press, 1981.

Sandra M. Gilbert and Susan Gubar. *No Man's Land: The Place of the Woman Writer in the Twentieth Century, Vols. I and II.* New Haven and London: Yale University Press, 1988, 1989.

Jean E. Kennard. *Vera Brittain & Winifred Holtby: A Working Partnership.* Hanover and London: University Press of New England, 1989.

Jane Marcus, "*The Years* as Greek Drama, Domestic Novel, and *Gotterdammerung,*" *Bulletin of the New York Public Library* 80 (Winter 1977): 276–301, 301.

Perry Meisel. *The Myth of the Modern: A Study in British Literature and Criticism after 1850.* New Haven and London: Yale University Press, 1987.

Nancy K. Miller, "Emphasis Added: Plots and Plausibilities in Women's Fiction," *PMLA*: 96 (January 1981), 36–48.

Ezra Pound, "Postscripts to *The Natural Philosophy of Love* by Remy de Gourmont," in *Pavannes and Divagations* (New York: New Directions, 1958).

Bonnie Kime Scott. *The Gender of Modernism.* Bloomington: Indiana University Press, 1990.

Brenda R. Silver. *Virginia Woolf's Reading Notebooks* Princeton: Princeton University Press, 1983.

Christine Sizemore. *A Female Vision of the City: London in the Novels of Five British Women.* Knoxville: The University of Tennessee Press, 1989.

Susan M. Squier, "The Modern City and the Construction of Female Desire," *Tulsa Studies in Women's Literature*, Summer 1989.

—————— , "Tradition and Revision in Woolf's *Orlando*: Defoe and "The Jessamy Brides," *Women's Studies*:12 (1986), 167–77, p. 75.

—————— . *Virginia Woolf and London: The Sexual Politics of the City.* Chapel Hill and London: The University of North Carolina Press, 1985.

—————— . *Women Writers and the City: Essays in Feminist Literary Criticism.* Knoxville: The University of Tennessee Press, 1984.

Catharine R. Stimpson, "Reading Gertrude Stein," *Tulsa Studies in Women's Literature* 4 (1985): 265–271

—————— , "The Female Sociograph: The Theater of Virginia Woolf's Letters," *The Female Autograph.* Eds. Domna C. Stanton and Jeanine Parisier Plottel. New York: New York Literary Forum, 1984, 193–203.

—————— , "The Mind, the Body, and Gertrude Stein." *Critical Inquiry* 3 (1977): 491–506

Virginia Woolf, "The Country in London," Hyde Park Gate Diary, 1903 courtesy of Louise A. DeSalvo and Mitchell Leaska.

—————— . "The Docks of London." *Good Housekeeping* 20:4 (December 1931): 16–17, 114, 116–17.

—————— . "Great Men's Houses." *Good Housekeeping* 21:1 (March 1932): 10–11, 102–3.

—————— , *Flush: A Biography.* New York: Harcourt Brace Jovanovich, 1961.

—————— . "The Journal of Mistress Joan Martyn." *The Complete Shorter Fiction of Virginia Woolf.* Edited by Susan Dick. New York: Harcourt Brace Jovanovich, 1985.

—————— . *The Letters of Virginia Woolf.* Edited by Nigel Nicolson and Joanne Trautmann. New York: Harcourt Brace Jovanovich. VI, 1936–41 (1980).

———. *The London Scene*. New York: Frank Hallman, 1975; London: Hogarth Press, 1982.

———. *Orlando: A Biography*. New York: Signet, 1960.

———. *A Room of One's Own*. New York: Harcourt, Brace & World, Inc., 1929; rpt. New York and Burlingame, Harcourt, Brace & World, Inc., 1957.

———. "Street Music." *National Review* 45 (1905): 144–48.

CINGRIA AND HIS CITIES

Eugène Nicole

Among the main traditions of literature of the City in twentieth century France, the tradition of the "promeneur", or the stroller, is well illustrated by Apollinaire's *Le Flâneur des deux rives*, by Fargue's *Le Piéton de Paris*, and by Larbaud's prose pieces, to quote only a few. I would like to add to this category one of the least classifiable of writers: Charles-Albert Cingria. A vagabond, contradictory and almost legendary personality, his complete works make up about ten volumes, of which I will limit myself to a selection of four titles and four towns; Paris in *Bois sec bois vert* (1948); Rome, the subject of *L'Eau de la dixième milliaire* (1932) and, *Musiques de Fribourg* and *Impressions d'un passant à Lausanne*, of 1945 and 1932 respectively.

This means, of course that I shall only be able to skim the surface of my subject and that I must renounce any detailed analysis of Cingria's narrative poetics. I will limit myself, therefore, to situating Cingria's urban imaginary, and to pinpointing some of his narrative and poetic particularities.

It might be an exaggeration to say that the city holds a privileged place in Cingria's chronicles. Not only because in Cingria every narrative or thematic frame, every referential pretext or every *topos* is constantly traversed by unexpected, often proliferating digressions, but also because, other places, other landscapes share his interest: the country roads he usually travels by bicycle, river landscapes (in particular the banks of the Loire), and every place containing reeds. Cingria has a passion for reeds, which he seeks out enthusiastically on the edges of cities as well as within them. He savors empty lots, the grass between monuments and, in a general way, everything that flourishes among stones, including street urchins and abandoned cats. This *Città in campagna* has not prevented him, however, from studying the city as the locus of the concentration and the diffusion of civilization. Cingria's towns are also the holy and learned towns of the West. To Rome and Fribourg should be added, in passing, Saint-Maurice and Saint-Gall, but also Aix-en-Provence and Byzantium. At this point we might be able to highlight the historical dimension, of the urban imaginary evident in so many texts. It reflects the melancholy of change, as Baudelaire, in a celebrated line, inscribes it in French Letters, or the cynical and passionate record of Haussman's transformations of Paris, described in Aragon's *Passage de l'Opéra*, or all the mythology of the past, which forms one of the obsessions of Butor's *La Modification*.

The history of the countryside, as illustrated by Gaston Roupnel's fine book of that title, is a relatively new idea; whereas the city is profoundly linked to its history, and to history in general, of which it is the centrifugal and driving force.

The danger here would be to dissolve the urban real into this history, to dissociate history from its present, daily reality, in the manner in which travel guides present a historical synopsis as material prefatory to visiting a city. For, clearly, with Cingria, we do not leave "the real world", and none of the texts that I am examining here belong in the category of "fiction". A Cingria town, in this sense, is neither the referential frame of a story (as, for instance, Paris in certain episodes of *Les Misérables*), nor the profound and symbolic subject of a novel (like Bleston in Butor's *L'Emploi du temps*). It is, if I might say, the direct given of the text, at times inscribed in the title (*Souvenirs d'un passant à Lausanne*; *Musiques de Fribourg*) and at other times appearing in a kind of justificatory preface in which the narrator reveals his reasons for speaking:

> He who writes these lines has something of a right to consider himself an inhabitant of Fribourg since it is in this town that his fitness to vote was first ascertained.[1]

or, in an opening statement about the town itself:

> There are towns on the map which, par excellence, incarnate mystery . . . Marseille, for example, or Saigon. And also, perhaps, Lausanne, a terribly mysterious town when you understand that you do not know to whom it belongs.[2]

In this respect, Cingria's text is also distinguishable from travel diaries, even when, as with Stendhal, they are entitled *Promenades dans Rome*. For with Cingria, walking is always ahead, if one might say, of the town. Thus, the town will never be presented as successive sectors, cut out according to the economy of a time-table, or historical subdivisions. (However, despite their titles, *Le Flâneur des deux rives* and *Le Piéton de Paris* proceed in just that way, investing urban space district by district.)

If Cingria's city distinguishes socio-cultural spaces within itself, it does so only by traversing them, by intersecting them, in the broken linearity of an itinerary. The *itinerary* is the frontier, the itinerary makes sense, founds, through caprice or design, the paradigmatic order, and, in its continuity, the "discrete quality" of the sign of urban language. This randomness, moreover,

reveals a profound truth of the City, namely that its own "cadas-
tre", the lay-out of its streets, structures the itinerary up to a
certain point and restricts its liberty, leaving it only the choice of
modality: discovery, speed, or repetition. However, although it is
thus modeled by the urban space, this progression brings with it
the subjective supremacy of the gaze. Cingria plays on this with
a charming airiness. In the following sentences, for example, he
pretends that on the itinerary of the tram he takes in Fribourg, a
linguistic frontier begins in the middle of a street, at a place
where a little shop bears the sign: "Zur Stadt Paris":

> That is, instead of speaking French as is done from the Ocean to
> the Channel to the ascending slopes of the Jura—one begins, with-
> out any warning, to speak a German dialect—which is incercep-
> tibly transformed into the Bern dialect, then Alsatian towards the
> North, then into other still Alpine dialects around Vienna, and
> further away, until you reach Carinthia and Pannonia where Slavic
> idioms and Islam predominate and the other disappear.[3]

This linguistic revery is only one example among many of what
appears in Cingria as the hyperbolic choice of detail in urban
space. Here, it is a window and a sign on a store which suppos-
edly divides the world into two cultures. Elsewhere it will be the
beauty of broken letters and illegible inscriptions on the frontispiece of Roman temples, letters truer than the Latin language reproduced in texts, because they are encountered here, says
Cingria, in their place, in their original incarnation. Elsewhere, it
can be a rabbit locked in its cage, its body shaking like a ball of
mercury, in the market square. Inscriptions of culture, of history,
or fleeting encounters with an animal waiting to be bought, everything is a sign for the stroller, and, among these different objects, of course, all hierarchy is abolished, all of the stratified
organization of the urban subject is reoriented into the imaginary
textuality of the poem, and the movement of the itinerary. Therefore, although *not* fictitious, Cingria's urban textuality is novelistic in the sense that, in the novel, every object, no matter how
insignificant, is a sign, by the simple fact of being mentioned,
and all the more so, perhaps, in that it seems insignificant. To
sharpen this comparison, one should recall Cingria's very original idea, the axiom of his poetics of place: there is no need for
plot, no need, therefore, for fiction in the traditional sense, because plot is inscribed in the real, because landscape is a plot,
because place is a plot. In this sense as well, walking, the route,
merely respond mimetically to the intrigue of place. The intrigue
is the itinerary, the itinerary *is* the narrative structure of the in-

trigue; it is the novel of the real, if by that we mean not its systematic exploration (which is precisely the *telos* of the specialised guide), but its poetic unveiling of the subjective, selective construction of an experience which, however, is always expressed as necessary and primordial. For the interest of Cingria's urban itinerary is constituted by the paradox that although it has no laws, it follows a course. A course or a thread which, moreover, can also be perceived in the web of an ideological discourse. Cingria's itinerary is resolutely inscribed against the commonplace. It consists in running counter to received ideas. Cingria is an artist of the paradox, and his urban poetics illustrate this figure all the better precisely because it is inscribed in verifiable and geographical knowledge. One might say that his is the opposite of the discourse of encyclopedic dictionaries.

Many examples could be given of this, on all levels of his texts, which obviously cannot be summarized. For the two versions of his "great" text on Rome (1932 and 1939), for example, Cingria chooses the respective titles, *L'Eau de la dixième milliaire* and *Le Comte des formes*. In both cases, he alludes to a network of aqueducts ("formae") that fed imperial Rome. One of these waters, *l'Aqua Tepula*, which reached the capitol, had its source in the field of Lucullus, near the tenth milestone of the Latin Way. It is in this country place that, in both versions, Cingria's Roman journey ends with this salutary reminder:

> I must finish here, No literature about capital cities that today captivate the literary market pays even the most furtive homage to a particular poetic pungency of water.[4]

Thus the oversight has been corrected in a particularly effective way since through the title, which throughout fifty pages maintains its intriguing character, the entire eternal city is placed under the poetic sign of water, as well as under the sign of rain—Roman rain—to which Cingria devotes several pages of his text. The text is therefore "oriented", not only because it leads us, through random walking, to the place of its title, but because it carries a certain number of peremptory theses on how to look at Rome. On this level there is no difference in Cingria between the analysis of the urban place, the meditation on its essence and the poetic illumination of the object.

Thus, Cingria's urban text constructs its labyrinth (the walker constantly exclaims: "Ah, Where am I?") at the same time it unwinds its Ariadne's thread. Sometimes this thread is unwound, so to speak, at the outset, as in *Impressions d'un passant à Lausanne* in which the reader knows very quickly that the walker is trying

to go up the Flon, a river he has followed through the countryside, and which goes underground in the city. (How can one not
see in its disappearance and reappearances the very modality of
Cingria's texts which lose their thread only the better to recover
it?) Elsewhere, in *Musiques de Fribourg*, for example, the itinerary
is less spatial than temporal. Beginning with the staircase in the
house he lives in, then passing on to considerations of bilingual-
ism, stopping at the library—which provides the occasion for a
few reflections on musicology—,then on to the market and finally to the lower town where the catastrophic collapse of the
Pont du Gotteron on May 9, 1919, at 3:55 p.m. is described in
detail, this exploration is a function of the familiarity of a long
residence and of its habits. This produces abundant analyses of
the inhabitants of Fribourg, of its press and even, paradoxically
since the entire text was written in winter, of the serious question of mixed bathing at the baths Cingria likes to visit in order to
hear "the variety of accents in children's speech".[5] Among Cingria's texts of this kind, I should mention his legendary lecture of
July 10, 1941, entitled "Twenty-one years in Paris", of which, un-
fortunately, only a few written fragments remain. We know that
it closed with these words: "Let's say I have finished, Gentlemen,
otherwise this speech would be interminable."[6]

But Cingria's urban texts are not interminable. They never ex-
ceed forty or so pages, in which they reproduce the rhythm of
walking and the impulsiveness of conversation. To properly char-
acterise them, they should be analysed in the detail of their style
and imagery, and above all, they should be abundantly quoted.
Very briefly, and without any illusions as to the inherent reduc-
tiveness of this kind of analysis, I shall try to delineate several of
their voices and *topi*.

First, there is in Cingria a rather solemn and polemical voice
that defines a certain ontology of the city, and the quality of its
appropriate expression. For example, at the beginning of *Impressions d'un passant à Lausanne* we find an epistemology of urban
discourse:

> The error when one tries to speak of a place is that one tries to do
> geography, that is, history, and one is immediately lost. For history
> lives, for example, in legs climbing a staircase. The sound of a
> voice, an accent, contain more information than books (usually
> badly written) on the past of cities. A differentiation acquired in
> this way is a wonderful notion. My friends never understand it.
> Those from Paris especially, who are very remarkable, pay no at-
> tention to habitation. They traverse a city and that's that. It's fin-
> ished. But it is *they* who are finished. A city has a multitude of

things the equivalent of which nothing, in what is thought or seen, can reproduce.[7]

In fact, this dichotomy between experience and knowing, between the impregnation of a place through osmosis and knowledge acquired from books, sums up Cingria's conception of history, that is, of the being of the city. Nowhere, certainly, is this question posed with so much urgency as in the case of Rome. "The study of Humanities, writes Cingria, be it the Oxford edition of Virgil, or spending one's life in an orchard reading Horace, do not make it possible for someone who has not been to Rome to really converse with someone who has that place in his marrow."[8] You must be able to pay homage to the new neighborhoods" which are perhaps more striking than the old".[9] You had to see "the price of wine written in charcoal on the walls".[10] Above all in Rome you must avoid being an antiquarian.

Cingria's second urban *topos* is the unusual quotation, the paradoxical list of signs expressing the specific urbanity of a place. In Rome, for example, there is "the Etruscan specification of bread which is flat, which smokes, the archetypical "galette" of the gods who mistrust each other—and which continues in the cooperatives".[11] Then again, Saint-Jean-de-Lateran, "much more imposing than the Vatican", the immensity of which, however, Cingria has already impressed upon us since he writes of its 20,000 rooms, twenty courtyards, eight monumental staircases, adding that, in Saint-Pierre-de-Rome the acoustics are no longer human—"for, if you spit on the floor, you don't hear a sound".[12] Then there is the grass. For everything is grass, here, grass and water, rather than thought. And on the church doors, the humanised, leather, loin-cloths. And obelisks. But not domesticated obelisks: the forgotten and broken ones which, before arriving in Rome, waited for centuries piled up on the banks of Alexandria, where they were used as latrines; among them we have the obelisk of Totmes IV or of Theodosa whose hieroglyphics Cingria abundantly describes, wishing, however, that Mustapha Kemal would come and take it to Angora. For after all, Cingria exclaimes, "this obelisk is Turkish".[13]

From the obelisk of Hadrian, transported to Rome in memory of Antinoüs and which also, before becoming the obelisk of the Pincio, spent many centuries lying in a vineyard, we slide quite naturally to the quality of wine in Rome, to the sunset over the Pincio, to the problem of heating in cold weather. Evening falls. "The last bit of the obelisk still vibrates. It is like meat. There are some children in a corner who, with short sticks are hitting small pieces of wood that jump and turn in the air."[14] This provides an opportunity for reminding us that the same game was played by the Ancients, and that it used to be called "baculum". It is also an opportunity for recalling the two meanings of the word history: that which is situated in history, and that which forever begins again.

Another aspect of the topos of paradoxical quotation in Cingria would be what one might call the *topos* of inclusion: a paradoxical figure par excellence since it consists in qualifying one town through another one, entirely foreign, if possible, to its geographical and cultural field. Moreover, this *topos* is well known. In its current lexicalised form, it derives from the rhetorical figure called antonomasia. Thus, one calls Amsterdam "the Venice of the North". Urban literature uses it in a much more subtle and original way. A fine example occurs in Valery Larbaud who, like Leopardi in his *Appunti*, evokes, or rather defines Bologna in these terms:

> Bologna and its one thousand twelve hundred pink, grey, and yellow towers, in the East, Emilian plain, an arrival in New York, the Middle Ages.[15]

Here definition functions in the mode of a comparison suggested by the visual similarity between mediaeval towers and skyscrapers. In Cingria, the connections are less global and above all less motivated. Certainly, at times, the text itself forces a certain metonymic superimposition between the present place and the absent one. For example, Egypt is so allusively present in *L'Eau de la dixième milliaire* that it is hardly surprising that the Roman sunset is described in terms borrowed from pharaonic mythology:

> It is no longer Horus of the horizon, nor Ra of the middle of the day, but Atoum or Toum, or Atoum-Ra who no longer lives but through himself.[16]

But Cingria's geographical and cultural imaginary does not always yield its keys, and its contexts are often less apparent. Thus the staircase in the author's house in Fribourg recalls Rimbaud, Delacroix's *Noces Juives*, and the Orient. Yet Cingria makes it clear that this Orient has nothing to do with the orientalism of bazaars, but with the eternal and classical Orient (both being the same for Cingria), which, on the level of the noble, the level "sub specie aeternitatis", no longer stands in opposition to the West. As for the telephone placed on the staircase, when it rings, "it is just the same as at Addis Ababa".[17] In the heart of Switzerland, Fribourg has a French air to it; this because of its religion. Protestant countries will always seem English—of rather poor class, Cingria informs us, and Catholic countries always seem Spanish. This is followed by a peremptory statement: "The appearances of countries and their divisions or cantons depend uniquely on religion".[18] Essentially, Cingria's city is rather like that specialized encyclopedia, the Stokvis, that the author consults at the Fribourg library;

> You are looking for the Valois or a genealogy of Lichtenstein, and happen upon the inconceivable nomenclature of Caribbean dynasties.[19]

In effect, the whole world files by with each page. The Gare de Flon at Lausanne recalls Anvers. On the left, that is at lakeside, the country becomes Polynesia. One town thus always recalls another. Now, writes Cingria, "there is nothing more amusing or more fruitful than being distracted from one thing by another."[20]

These paradoxical equivalencies, of which one could quote a thousand other examples, are doubtless both profound and humorous. It would, however, be false to see in them an expression of a kind of cosmopolitanism "à la Larbaud". In contrast to Larbaud, Cingria does not classify his towns in categories, no matter how poetic. Cingria's city remains unique and incommensurable. It has its own genius, the *genus loci* of the Ancients. Nowhere in the universe, writes Cingria, does one see anything like the streets of Lausanne.

However, if, beyond such particularism, one were to seek a level on which "The City" transcends cities, one might find it, in Cingria, profiled around a notion whose social sense proceeds from the very concept of the city. This word is precisely, "urbanity" the best expression of which Cingria finds in people's faces: "An extraordinary acuity visible in the eyes, features filled with fine madness".[21] We find the same thing in Paris after the Occupation: "No one has aged. Paris preserves. There, faces remain indefinitely textual".[22] Urbanity, again, in the following:

> There is a right to exist and to lose oneself in the crowd without having to account for anything to anybody.[23]

Unlike Baudelaire, Cingria in this sense, is not a "rôdeur". If, as Foucault says, one writes in order to lose one's face, then the city is indeed the place of this liberty of anonymity. But the writer in Cingria's work does not go from "I" to "He". Resolutely fixed on the axis of the first person, Cingria's urban text is the privileged space in which the poetic idiolect is inscribed in the sociolects of history, which he explores in the multiplicity of his voices and the illumination of his gazes.

Unlike the narrator of *l'Emploi du temps*, Cingria knows immediately that the town cannot be totalized. For him, to script the town will be to attain, in the movement of the writing, the individuality of the place, all the while knowing that one must stop somewhere. Without which, as he himself says, "it would be interminable".

NOTES

1. "Musiques de Fribourg" in *Florides helvètes et autres textes*; p. 167; L'Age d'Homme, Lausanne, 1983. All translations from the French are mine.
2. "Impressions d'un passant à Lausanne" in *Florides helvètes et autres textes*; p. 7.
3. ibid. p. 173.
4. "L'eau de la dixième milliaire", in *La Fourmi rouge et autres textes*; p. 156; L'Age d'Homme, Lausanne, 1978. Also in: "Le Comte des formes" in *Bois sec bois vert*; p. 286; Gallimard, Paris, 1948.
5. "Musiques de Fribourg" in *Florides helvètes et autres textes*; p. 191
6. *Oeuvres de C. A. Cingria*; ed. L'Age d'Homme, vol. 6, p. 189.
7. "Impressions d'un passant à Lausanne", opus cit. p. 8.
8. "L'Eau de la dixième milliaire", opus cit. p. 136.
9. ibid. p. 136.
10. ibid. p. 136.
11. ibid. p. 137.
12. ibid. p. 106.
13. ibid. p. 127.
14. ibid. p. 142.
15. Valéry Larbaud: *Oeuvres*, Bibliothèque de la Pléiade, p. 827.
16. "L'Eau de la dixième milliaire", opus cit. p. 173.
17. "Musiques de Fribourg", opus. cit. p. 173.
18. ibid. p. 175.
19. ibid. p. 178.
20. "Musiques de Fribourg", opus cit. p. 179.
21. "Impressions d'un passant à Lausanne", opus cit. p. 11
22. *Bois sec bois vert*, p. 100.
23. ibid. p. 101.

THE NEW YORK WRITER AND HIS LANDSCAPES

Alfred Kazin

Oneself I sing, a simple separate person,
Yet utter the word Democratic, the word En- Masse
> Walt Whitman: Inscription *Leaves of Grass*

There is something in all life untranslatable into language. He who
keeps his eye on that will write better than others, and think less
of his writing, and of all writing. Every thought has a certain im-
prisoning as well as uplifting quality, and, in proportion to its energy on the will, refuses to become an object of intellectual
contemplation.
> R. W. Emerson: Opening Number Of *The Dial* (1840)

the savage's romance,
accreted where we need the space for commerce—
the centre of the wholesale fur trade
. . .
it is not the plunder,
but 'accessibility to experience.'
> Marianne Moore: "New York"

One of the great war aims is to get to New York.
> Yehudi Menhuin—1943

From my windows on the Upper West Side I look out on buildings that clash so violently in age, style, size, shape, color, and
purpose that I must locate myself within this mad geometry.
A maze of upright parallelograms running into each other take
each other up and finally absorb one another into a dizzying urban mix.

When young I studied the city from the family fire escape, the
neighboring roof, from the Third, Sixth and Ninth Avenue EL
passing between open windows of ancient tenements in which
people showed their lives, like their bedding, on the window sill.
Now the heavens are as crowded as the earth. Bridges travel between buildings; police helicopters patrolling the unending highway stream will soon swoop down on every errant driver;
satellites already rusted and outworn impinge on fresh ones no
doubt already capable of hearing conversations in the bedroom.
The twentieth century is finally here. Exactly as previsioned in
the "Amazing Stories" I used to read as a boy. But what the

129

utopian fantasists of the early century did not guess was that the
nineteenth century would still be with us. Up on Amsterdam Avenue, not yet gentrified, there are old German Lutheran old-age
homes, green with decay and surrounded by the leftovers of Hispanic poverty, that remind us of the many discarded churches
that are just obstructions to the real estate lobby.

Henry James on his return to his birthplace in 1905 noted the
"increasing invisibility of New York churches." The end-of-
century scene on the upper West Side is so crammed jammed
jostled together that the crowdedness heavy on the eyes is the
fact most omnipresent and therefore hardest to take in, to describe, and certainly to love. The impact on the senses is sometimes too dim to be recoverable. I take it in only as fits and starts,
the outline of the daily friction and threatfulness of New York,
the undeclared state of war that will suddenly flash out in the
subway over a dropped newspaper and leave behind bodies broken, dead, while the spectators of the "fracas" flee the police.

Amazing how little of this mad crowdedness, the very fever of
our daily being, gets into the best writing about New York. If it
were not for the endless food stores, health stores, restaurants,
coffee shops, greengrocers—all necessary to feed and encourage
the thousands packed away just above Broadway itself, it would
be easy for a writer to think of the city as equal to his individual
consciousness. Loneliness, secrecy, introspection are the understandable response to so much mass in friction. As opposed to
the daily death headline in the New York Post—MOM KILLED
BY RAPIST AS CHILDREN WATCH—the most sensitive writing
finds it natural to describe a writer's vulnerability rather than the
weight of all these opposed races, classes, theologies and social
habits.

Photography can aim at this crowd as the writer may be afraid
to. The News photographer Weegee did a famous shot, July 28,
1940, 4 P.M. as he proudly noted, of a million at Coney Island.
There is no sand to be seen. But photography can earn its short-
lived triumph at too emphatic a price of professional indifference
and even malice. Journalistic photography must glide over what
it attempts to "reproduce." It is generally technology in action, as
is natural to an age informed by instruments, an age whose history may yet be confined to the history of instruments.

Unsere ist eine optische Zeit read the sign over the ruins of postwar Cologne. "Ours is a visual period." The irony was not inten-
tional. At the same time in New York, abstract expressionism
made the city "the capital of modern art." This international favorite was rooted by many in the rediscovery of their native land,
New York, painters of immigrant stock, who had been radicals
and children of the depression, but now throbbed in expansive

postwar New York to the violent colorfulness of New York streets and sky. In its sense of newfound power, "Action painting" was inspirational. It was typical New York aggressiveness. The idea is "to fuck up the canvas," said the critic Harold Rosenberg. He explained that "Action painting, like the new atomic physics, has the power to release trapped energy, to set great forces at work at liberty for good and evil." The new painting was wonderful in the subversive colors and rhythms that breathed the variety and excitement of New York, a town where native sons notoriously gape in wonder and feel like recent arrivals. It was even more wonderful in its cachet of expensiveness. Long before environmental art sought to loop hillsides together, the new painting became favorite images on executive walls and the nonpareil investment and example of ostentatious consumption for the newly rich, who identified with painters because *they* were newly rich.

By contrast, the poetry of the same period turns out to be very pale indeed. And had become very easy to write, for as Freud didn't have to say, internal consciousness, unlike the external world, is always on tap.

Oneself I sing, a simple separate person / Yet utter the word Democratic, the word En- Masse. Only Whitman among New York writers a century ago sought the crowd as a correlative to his "ongoing soul," caught the note of his key term *ensemble.* Whitman even called *Leaves Of Grass* a city, just as Auden called Eros the founder of cities. "I can hardly tell you why," Whitman wrote after the Civil War to his friend William O'Connor, "but feel very positively that if anything can justify my revolutionary attempts & utterances, it is such *ensemble*—like a great city to modern civilization & a whole combined cluttering paradoxical unity, a man, a woman." Whitman's lovable archaic myth was that New York was a true community made by the future as well as the present. It was not just a legal tie. In the most expressive poem I know about New York as an ideal, *Crossing Brooklyn Ferry,* Whitman portrayed himself as one of a crowd. And the crowd on the ferry between Fulton Street in Brooklyn and Fulton Street in Manhattan was as alive and irresistible, because it gave scope to the poet in its midst, as the tidal movements of the East River. Of course Whitman could feel separated from the life around him:

I too felt the curious abrupt questionings stir within me . . . I too had been struck from the float forever held in solution. He had faith in his future reader, as much as in the crowd around him.

> *Closer yet I approach you,*
> *What thought you have of me now, I had as much of you—*
> *I laid in my stores in advance.*
> *I considered long and seriously of you before you were born.*

He put in *Crossing Brooklyn Ferry* "the glories strung like beads on my smallest sights and hearings, on the walk in the street and the passage over the river,"—the crowd entering the gates of the ferry, the shipping of Manhattan and the heights of Brooklyn, the Winter seagulls floating with motionless wings but in slow-wheeling circles and their gradual edging toward the south, the shadowy group of steam-tug, barges, hay-boat, belated lighter, the foundry chimneys burning high and glaringly into the night, their flicker of black contrasted with wild red and yellow light over the tops of houses, and down into the clefts of streets.

At the end of *Crossing Brooklyn Ferry* these city surfaces reveal themselves as the dumb, beautiful "ministers"—the "appearances"—"you have waited, you always wait." We fathom you not—"he cries at the very end—"we love you—there is perfection in you also," because "Great or small, you furnish your parts toward the soul." The most ordinary day to day fixtures of the landscape can be absorbed into the deepest urges of our being. Such a connection to be grasped out of the tidal heart of being in New York! As Yeats said, belief makes the mind abundant. Whitman's genius was to cast an erotic haze over his confidence in radical democracy. Besides, he had nowhere to go but up, this child of Brooklyn's streets who from street pals learned the bravado that enabled his poems to make conjunction not only with the most ordinary materials but with the immortality of the earth itself.

Seventy years later Hart Crane in Whitman's Brooklyn set out in the Poem to *The Bridge* a more wistful effort at connection with New York's fullness:

> *O harp and altar, of the fury fused,*
> *(How could mere toil align thy choiring strings!)*
> *Terrific threshold of the prophet's pledge,*
> *Prayer of pariah, and the lover's cry,—*

His aim: in fifteen sections to envelop American history stemming westward from Brooklyn Bridge, the actual setting the dream-long day from dawn in "Harbor Day" to midnight in "Atlantis." Through the dream, the single day takes in vast stretches of time and space: from a subway ride in the morning to a railroad journey to the Mississippi, then going beyond DeSoto to the primeval world of the Indians, then forward to the West of the pioneers.

Like so many American poets before and after him, Crane conceived an epic poem about American history as personal myth rather than ongoing narrative. It was not the poets but the "romancers"—Melville in *Moby-Dick* and Mark Twain in *Huckleberry Finn*—who captured in consecutive terms the strain and hardihood of the national experience. What Crane really expressed in his effort to turn Brooklyn Bridge into all American history was the material confidence of the 1920s. Lindbergh, the Empire State and Chrysler Buildings, the Florida boom, the first cross-country highway system. The Empire State Building was climbing a story a day to the height of 102 floors. Stifling in an advertising agency, Crane admitted, "Maybe I'm just a little jealous of Lindy." To Waldo Frank in 1926 he also admitted—"Intellectually judged, the whole theme and project seems more and more absurd, these forms, materials, dynamics are simply non-existent in the world . . . The bridge today has no significance beyond an economical approach to shorter hours, quicker lunches, behaviorism and toothpicks."

A month later, having composed the Poem, "I feel an absolute music in the air again, and some tremendous rondure floating somewhere." The Poem provides so powerful an entrance to *The Bridge* that the forced eloquence of the rest, with random shots of American history yoked together hit and miss by Crane's amazingly chromatic straining of language, is an inevitable letdown. But the Poem on New York proper is wonderful. Crane by a fortunate accident had come to live at 110 Columbia Heights. There Washington Roebling, son of the bridge's master builder, John Augustus Roebling, had directed the actual completion of his father's bridge from the wheel chair to which he was consigned by the paralysis he suffered at the bottom of the East River overlooking work on the foundations of the Brooklyn tower. The concluding section of *The Bridge*, "Atlantis," opens powerfully

> Through the bound cable strands, the arching path
> Upward, veering with light, the flight of strings,—
> Taut miles of shuttling moonlight syncopate
> The whispered rush, telepathy of wires.
> Up the index of night, granite and steel—
> Transparent meshes—fleckless the gleaming staves—
> Sibylline voices flicker, waveringly stream
> As though a god were issue of the strings . . .
>
> And through that cordage, threading with its call
> One arc synoptic of all tides below—

Crane said of this "I have attempted to induce the same feelings of elation, etc.—like being carried forward and upward simultaneously—both in imagery, rhythm and repetition, that one experiences in walking across my beloved Brooklyn Bridge."

What is personal and even intimate in the opening and closing sections of *The Bridge* seems more lasting than all the rest.
*Under thy shadow by the piers I waited;/ Only in darkness is thy shadow
clear.* Crane was of course a stranger in New York, another writer
from the heartland in the supreme power center. Vladimir Maya-
kovsky from Moscow was also fascinated by the Brooklyn Bridge
in the 20's

> Hey, Coolidge boy,
> make a shout of joy!
> When a thing is good
>   then it's good.
> Blush from compliments
>   like our flag's calico,
> even though you're
>   the most superb united states
>   of
> America.

And so was Federico Garcia Lorca from Granada, who as a sometime student at Columbia wrote "Unsleeping City: Brooklyn
Bridge Nocturne," identified the bridge not with some historical
material epic, as Crane wanted to do, but with the loneliness
Crane actually evoked. Lorca did not cry, as Crane seems to,
"Only connect!" He openly excoriated the city he identified with
sleeplessness—

> Life is no dream! Beware and beware and beware!
> We tumble downstairs to eat of the damp of the earth
> or we climb to the snowy divide with the choir of dead dahlias.
> But neither dream nor forgetfulness, is:
> brute flesh is. Kisses that gather our mouths
> in a mesh of raw veins.
> Whomsoever his woe brings to grief, it will grieve without quarter.
> Whom death brings to dread will carry that death on his
>   shoulders.

The 1920's marked the triumph of American entrepreneurship
conceived as rugged individualism—nowhere more blatantly
than in the city most famous for Wall Street. Hegel's favorite student, as he called himself, John Augustus Roebling the utopian
communist and amateur metaphysician from Muhlhausen had
fled to this country from the Prussian police and had actually
kept a kind of commune in Saxonburg Pennsylvania where he
first tested the wire rope he invented that made Brooklyn Bridge
possible. Everyone who recognizes its uniqueness still marvels
over the central promenade—the latest bridges of course have no
promenade at all. But Roebling an Hegelian in Germany, in
America a transcendentalist said, "It is a want of my intellectual

nature to bring in harmony all that surrounds me. Every new harmony I discover is to me another messenger of peace, another pledge of my redemption." In his "The Condition of the United States Reviewed By The Higher Law," he urged us to consider the country not as a business partnership but a family—"a parental estate." This amazing engineer actually believed: "Whoever discovers harmonies of nature, without being able to reconcile them, will discover that the idea of disharmony originated in his own mind, and was only reflected in that which surrounds him. Whatever you wish to perceive you can see . . . Bring your own interior nature in union with the outer world, and harmony will be established."

"This elevated promenade," Roebling wrote in his prospectus, "will allow people of leisure and old and young to stroll over the bridge on fine days. I need not state that in a crowded commercial city such a promenade will be of incalculable value." Roebling the everlasting visionary had designed the great stone towers after the Gothic Cathedral in Muhlhausen. He never could separate the greatest engineering feat of his day from the ancient myth of connectedness and protection embodied in bridges. The individual walking Brooklyn Bridge was now to be included and developed in some mighty work of harmony. The theme was not E. M. Forster's wistful cry "Only connect!" but connection made social. This in the tumultuous brutal city of New York by synoptic experience of the greatest harbor, the already imperial city, always in sight of the immigrant's passage and the power in freedom that became the immigrant's dream.

The drive to own and exploit every fraction of New York's limited space was so marked early in the nineteenth century that the intellectual leaders of the city—the once romantic poet and now editor of the New York Post, William Cullen Bryant, was a leader in this—were able to conceive of a central park to keep the masses from crowding each other to death. What still astonishes and exhilarates me about the plan offered by Frederick Law Olmsted before he became superintendent is the vision of a public place that would somehow elevate and expand what this extraordinarily practical visionary called the soul.

Olmsted detested the terrible regularity of New York streets, the gridiron plan, then suffering what Edith Wharton, a native daughter, said of the brownstones that once covered New York—"cursed with universal chocolate-colored coating of the most hideous stone ever quarried." Olmsted wanted a rural unkemptness for his park, picturesque roads, and in the vast planting to replace the old swamp wasteland, wild plants, random tufts, a thick growth of low brambles, ferns, aster, gentians, irregularly spaced trees. And of course the boulders of rock. "Fine old trees may be left standing," he wrote "and to save them, the wheelway carried a little to the right or left, or slightly raised or lowered. Such conditions . . . far from blemishes . . . add to other charms of picturesqueness, and they are a concession to nature, tending to an effect not of incongruity and incompleteness, but of consistent and happy landscape competition. Olmsted in collaboration with the professional landscape architect Calvin Vaux and Jacob Wrey Mould designed every structure, miniature bridge, terrace, arch, stairway, fountain, bench, every piece of masonry work, fence, gate, lamp post and mosaic design, never overlooking the innumerable details of every description that needed to be drawn for fabrication.

Olmsted described the park to be as "throughout a single work of art, and as such subject to the primary law of every work of art, namely, that it shall be framed upon a single, noble motive, to which the design of all its parts, in some more or less subtle way, shall be confluent and helpful . . What artist so noble as he who, with far-reaching conceptions of beauty and designing-power, sketches the outlines, writes the colors, and directs the shadows of a picture so great that Nature shall be employed upon it for generations before the work he has arranged for her shall realize his interiors?"

> I shall venture to assume to myself the title of artist. . . . The main object and justification is simply to produce a certain influence in the minds of the people . . . The character of this influence is a poetic one and it is to be produced by means of scenes, through observation of which the mind may be more or less lifted out of moods and habits into which it is, under the ordinary conditions of life in the city, likely to fall. . . .

Of course Whitman was right to complain that the plan was suited to New York's elite. Fifteen miles of perfect roads and bridle paths mainly attracted the "carriage-riding classes," "the full oceanic tide of New York's wealth and 'gentility.' " But he admitted that the park "represented at least a trial marriage of art and enlightened enterprise, nature and the life of the city." Even Harvard's super-refined Charles Eliot Norton said that of all American artists Olmsted stood "first in the production of great works which answer the need and give expression to the life of our immense and miscellaneous democracy."

Olmsted did see the representative New Yorker as someone walking through the Ramble, as he christened and planned it, taking in the air in a Wordsworthian access of sublimity. Little could he anticipate the sexual mayhem now more common in the Ramble. New York the "promised city," to the world—Yehudi Menhuhin was to say in 1943 that one of the principal war aims was to get to New York—was to become in literature what one native son, Herman Melville, described as the city of darkness, of orphanage, of crushing anonymity. Still another native son, Henry James, was on his return to New York at the beginning of the twentieth century to lament the crush of democracy itself. James could be amusing about the pressure on Central Park; he compared it to an innkeeper compelled to take in everybody. But what he most admired, as a thrill to his majestic sensibility, was the power that the twentieth century city now exhibited. The masses, especially as reflected in the immigrants thronging his old streets in lower New York, he called the agency of future ravage.

James like no other writer of the day on New York—not Dreiser in *Sister Carrie*, Wharton in *The House of Mirth*, Stephen Crane in *Maggie*, Jacob Riis in *How the Other Half Lives* or Howells in *A Hazard Of New Fortunes*—caught in his impressions of a native's return in *The American Scene*, the **physical** thrill of modern New York, the boundless energy and impatience expressed in the harbor, the new skyscrapers and bridges.

Henry Adams in the *Education*—"As he came up the bay again, November 5, 1904, he found the approach more striking than ever—wonderful—and like nothing he had ever much cared to see. The outline of the city became frantic in its effort to explain something that defied meaning. Power seemed to have outgrown its servitude and to have asserted its freedom. The cylinder had exploded, and thrown great masses of stone and steam against the sky. The city had the air and movement of hysteria, and the citizens were crying, in every accent of anger and alarm, that the new forces must at any cost be brought under control. Prosperity never before imagined, power never yet wielded by man, speed never reached by anything but a meteor, had made the world irritable, nervous, querulous, unreasonable and afraid." HJ—the native son—could not feel *that* alien. "The subject was everywhere—that was the beauty, that was the advantage; it was thrilling, really, to find oneself in the presence of a theme to which everything directly contributed, leaving no touch of experience irrelevant." Before leaving the country thirty years before James had thought of **Europe** as the great imperial idea, contrasting it with the "thin empty lovely American beauty."

Now in the presence of the powerhouse he wrote that "The aspect the power wears then is indescribable; it is the power of the most extravagant of cities, rejoicing, as with the voice of the morning, in its might, its fortune, its unsurpassable conditions, and imparting to every object and element, to the motion and expression of every floating, hurrying, panting thing, to the throb of ferries and tugs, to the plash of waves and the play of winds and the glint of lights and the shrill of whistles and the quality and authority of breeze-borne cries—all, practically, a diffused, wasted clamour of detonations."

Of Brooklyn Bridge James saw only the force, and this he (perhaps subconsciously) identified with the mass surge he regretted.

> The universal *applied* passion struck me as shining unprecedently out of composition; in the bigness and bravery and insolence, especially, of everything that rushed and shrieked; in the air as of a great intricate frenzied dance, half merry, half desperate, or at least half defiant, performed on the huge watery floor. This appearance of the bold lacing-together, across the waters, of the scattered members of the monstrous organism—lacking as by the ceaseless play of an enormous system of steam shuttles or electric bobbs (I scarce knew what to call them), commensurate in form with their infinite work—does perhaps more than anything else to give the pitch of the vision of energy. One has the sense that the monster grows and grows, flinging abroad its loose limbs even as some unmannered young giant at his "larks," and that the binding stitches must for ever fly further and faster and draw harder; the future complexity of the web, all under the sky and over the sea, becoming thus that of some colossal set of clockworks, some steel-souled machine-room of brandished arms and hammering fists and opening and closing jaws. The immeasurable bridges are but as the horizontal sheaths of pistons working at high pressure, day and night, and subject, one apprehends with perhaps inconsistent gloom, to a certain, to fantastic, to merciless multiplication.

James's impressionistic genius dominates the harbor and the bridge. This is truly, as he said of the ideal critic, "perception at the pitch of passion." But what has he done with his own, his native city? He has turned it into an art object. In that extraordinary book of his late genius, *An American Scene*, James's consideration of the life in the streets is that democracy is on a rampage, that the intrusiveness of people—some actually eating in these streets—is unbearable. The "land of consideration," as he called the society he thought he found in England, seems totally unintelligible in New York. And when James in his abundant memoirs of earliest youth, *A Small Boy And Others*, lingers fondly on New York sights and sounds before the Civil War, one sees genius at work in his assimilation to and devouring subjectivity of what was still Walt Whitman's city. Compare Whitman in **Song Of Myself**—"The blab of the pave, tires of carts, sluff of boot-

soles, talk of the promenaders," Whitman tries to do justice to
New York's mass life, with James remembering himself as always
alone, and so getting everything on lower Broadway, as he says,
to rub his contemplative nose. "For there was the very pattern
and measure of all he was to demand: just to be somewhere—
almost anywhere would do—and somehow receive an impression or an accession, feel a relation or a vibration."

Did the old James of 1905 revisiting New York overlook anything of consequence in the modern city? Nothing whatever; this
is already our New York, and none of us in our more harried
moments at the rush hour can safely rebuff James's picture of
"the consummate monotonous commonness of the pushing male
crowd, moving in its dense mass—with the confusion carried to
chaos for any intelligence, any perception; a welter of objects and
sounds in which relief, detachment, dignity, meaning, perished
utterly and lost all rights." The city has indeed become so pressing and unsafe that the crudity James merely sniffed at has been
translated into a constant fear of the city—even on the part of
those most stimulated by its possibilities.

James's magnificently estranged assessment of modern New
York turns the city into an esthetic object. He could never have
noticed what another sometime New Yorker, Tom Paine, did in
early Greenwich Village—"The contrast of affluence and wretch-
edness is like dead and living bodies chained together." The city
becomes an esthetic object when you become totally fascinated
by the energy and multifariousness of the surface, when the urban mix comes to seem beautiful *because* it is such an exciting as-
sault on your senses. English intellectuals are especially good at
this. Cyril Connolly after the war could not get over Greenwich
Village bookstores open at midnight. New York became the "supreme metropolis." "If Paris is the setting for a romance, New
York is the perfect city in which to get over one, to get over anything. Here the lost *douceur de vivre* is forgotten and intoxication
of living takes its place . . . " John Russell calls New York "one of
the supreme subjects of the century."

In *The Art Of The City* (Oxford, 1984) a brilliant English critic,
Peter Conrad, has written a book all about New York as art object
in which the last word is the most telling. The people, he concludes, are *irrelevant*. A world city—and New York has become
for the last half of the twentieth century the very capital of the
century—is by the very nature of its fascination a city for visitors.
Life in the Bronx, Queens and most of Brooklyn seems to them
as uneventful as Keokuk.

When London was a world city, Dickens had no trouble describing the routine life of the metropolis; nor did Balzac in a
comparable time for Paris. But even the novelists of New York in

our day are swamped by excessive power and self importance of
the center, with its hypnotizing domination by magazines, book
publishing, television, information, entertainment. The "glitzy"
city, with its concomitant violence, is a landscape for journalists,
for fleeting views, for unemployed actors reciting specialty
dishes to yuppy computer programmers in restaurants. It is a
godsend to the expert manipulators of illusions, layout, and
newsflash. Never, as in the media, were there so many conventional minds in power, and never did so much sophistication so
clearly replace intelligence. Never was there so much blatant con-
formism, corporate ambition and the crudest self-interest made
so spectacular by images. The impersonation of art is a major industry now. Never were there so many painters, such mobs at
the art museum, so much conspicuous and driveling fantasy
manufactured and sold in the name of post modernist sensation-
alism, so much music and information and entertainment in the
unsleeping city twenty four hours a day, so much empty emula-
tion of fashion in the name of creativity.

But this human landscape lends itself to literature by strangers
celebrating their alienation and even aloneness. W. H. Auden, a
New Yorker in New York for decades after 1939, made New York
the arch symbol of rootlessness in the current world and even
celebrated rootlessness as necessary to the age of anxiety. To at
least one of the many admirers who were startled by the appearance in St. Marks Place of the cleverest English poet since Dry-
den as a sort of East Village slob somehow famous for his lack of
underwear and giving lectures in carpet slippers, it was clear
that New York certainly turned the poet on but otherwise was
not worthy of respect. A key note in the poetry of the New
Yorker is the contrast between the city as the communal life of
mankind, civilization, and New York the ideal playground of the
one-night stand. "Eros, founder of cities," indeed is one of his
great lines. Eros is clearly no American deity. Auden in *New Year
Letter* recalls: *An English area comes to mind, / I see the nature of my
kind / As a locality I love.*

Auden defended himself to English friends, shocked that he
stayed away when war broke out in 1939, by insisting that the
notion that a man belongs to a place no longer means anything.
The Machine Age, he told them, has destroyed all sense of community, replacing the village with the factory. Everyone is now
isolated and alone. The American, Auden said with his usual authority, worships industry, not God—the "fully alienated land, /
An earth made common by the means / of hunger, money and
machines." "Aloneness is man's real condition. In America one's
rights come not from being a member of a community but from

"being of use." The planet itself he wittily described as a heavy, old, lumbering woman "with no ambition in her heart—

> Eccentric, wrinkled and ice-capped,
> Swarming with parasites and wrapped
> In a peculiar atmosphere,
> Earth wabbles down her career
> With no ambition in her heart

About America, he wrote in his introduction to James's *The American Scene*, an extraordinarily impassioned rejection of much that James lingered over with old love and new regret: "The truth is, Nature never intended human beings to live here, and her hostility, which confined the Indian to a nomad life and forbids the white man to relax his vigilance and his will, for one instant, must be an important factor in determining the American character." And in one of his most beautiful poems, "In Praise Of Limestone," he celebrates, as the mark of the European character, the friable landscape: "We the inconstant ones, are consistently homesick for, because it dissolves in water, makes a secret system of caves and conduits, furnishes a private pool for its fish and carving, its own little ravine whose cliffs entertain / The butterfly and the lizard; / examine this region / Of short distances and definite places."

How very different from an English poet's New York, who remembers his old friends at home and his band of brothers; "accustomed to a stone that responds / They have never had to veil their faces in awe / Of a crater whose blazing fury could not be fixed; Adjusted to the local needs of valleys / Where everything can be touched or reached by walking. . . ."

That landscape of limestone is contrasted at the end with "immoderate soils where the beauty was not so external / But "these modifications of matter into / Innocent athletes and gesticulating fountains, / Made solely for pleasure, make a further point: / The blessed will not care what angle they are regarded from, / Having nothing to hide." And at the very end: "when I try to imagine a faultless love / Or the life to come, what I hear is a murmur / Of underground streams, what I see is a limestone landscape."

So alienation turns New York into a metaphysical statement. Strangeness apparently is all. Saul Bellow in *The Victim* (1948), one of the few significant novels touching on The Holocaust, opens with an extraordinary shot of New York. His protagonist Asa Leventhal, a man of no particular gifts, easily disheartened and confused by his summer loneliness, takes the ferry to Staten Island—

The towers on the shore rose up in huge blocks, scorched, smoky, gray . . . The notion brushed Leventhal's mind that the light over them and over the water was akin to the yellow revealed in the slit of the eye of a wild animal, say a lion, something inhuman that didn't care about anything human and yet was implanted in every human being too, one speck of it, and formed a part of him that responded to the heat and the glare . . . even to freezing, salty things, harsh things, all things difficult to stand.

As for myself—writing all this very early in the morning, my time for writing anything, summoning myself at daybreak—I see not the brilliant New York night created for guests at the Plaza Hotel—but another daybreak landscape half a century ago. In 1932 or so working class immigrant families rise together because at five Papa goes to work—sometimes to paint subway tracks and stations, sometimes even Brooklyn Bridge. Mama, a home dress-maker used to no America but her kitchen workshop, is too work-driven even for breakfast and drinks her tea at the old Singer sewing machine.

Even now, the hard pressures of the old life can turn my night into penance, something to get through before my work begins. But the morning is rebirth. Now, thank God for the morning, looking east to Central Park, I wait for the first light to hit the hard green metal partitions that divide terrace from terrace (where no one sits) above the clamorous street, along the vast housing complexes of gentrified Columbus Avenue. When the light finally hits those partitions and makes them glitter like er-satz emeralds, all of that green rejoices me. It is so loud, strident, New York. I can now get up in good conscience. A little Bach with my coffee and I am off—and why should I not write about my landscape as well?

But mine does not always include what in my Brooklyn child-hood we called New York—their city, not ours. Or as the taxi driver outside the St. George in Brooklyn Heights said many years ago when I asked him if he couldn't make better time to the airport going through Manhattan—"*What* Manhattan?" I can hardly believe some things in my own landscape of memory. Watching a demonstration of the unemployed in Union Square, I once saw police on all the neighboring roofs holding machine guns. It is easier now to remember my mother leading a pack of women to put an evicted family's furniture back into the house. It is also more joyful to remember the old open trolley cars to Coney Island where the conductor collected his fares swinging from pole to pole along the outside platform. You knew you were approaching the water—finally—by the grass you saw between the tracks and the German beer gardens that announced the way to Steeplechase.

I also see myself as a small boy bringing my father's Passover lunch to him as with a gang of painters he sits on one of the ascending cables of Brooklyn Bridge painting away on each side of him like an Eskimo propelling a kayak.

What a distance the bridge travelled as it flung itself across the river. Everything seemed far as well as powerful. New York the far flung, New York the city of distances, in which—other times, other customs—I read myself sick on the endless subway journey to and from college. The distance now seems longer than ever, time replacing space. The sense of being just a transient here, even in my native landscape, is difficult to bear. Of all the great city writers, James M. Joyce, who never saw it, knew best how to identify the grief of mortality with New York:

> One born every second somewhere. Other dying every second. Since I fed the birds five minutes. Three hundred kicked the bucket. Other three hundred born, washing the blood off, all are washed in the blood of the lamb, bawling maaaaaaa.

> Cityfull passing away, other cityfull coming, passing away too; other coming on, passing on. Houses, lines of houses, streets, miles of pavements piled up bricks, stones. Changing hands. This owner, that. Landlord never dies they say. Other steps into his shoes when he gets his notice to quit. They buy the place up with gold and still they have all the gold. Swindle in it somewhere. Piled up in cities, worn away age after age. Pyramids in sand. Built on bread and onions. Slaves Chinese wall. Babylon. Big stones left. Round towers. Rest rubble, sprawling suburbs, jerrybuilt, Kerwan's mushroom houses, built of breeze. Shelter for the night.

> No one is anything.

But as Marianne Moore said of the city to which she was not born, the thing about New York—and not just in the fur district!—is "not the plunder but the accessibility to experience." And that accessibility is so rife and ripe, comes in such cascades, such thunderclap of too much proximity to other people's faces, other people's knives and forks and conversations as they sit alongside you at the next table, that one wants to register so much impact, get it down on paper. Where, in the living voice, in the exchange between mind and mind, writer and reader, it may just be that community exists.

Snark/Art Resources, S19476. E. Levick, Immigrants arriving to U.S.A. Washington, Library of Congress.

5

NEW YORK TO PARIS

Andromaque—I am thinking of you, but not just you; nostalgia goes past myth and legend, and is with us still. Breaking up or down, strolling or weeping, no one's narration is the same. Is that the same swan we are looking at, or has it just become some sign or other? Those windows we used to see through so transparently, how did they get reframed? Where is Paris now?

THE BREAK-UP OF THE CITY AND THE BREAK-DOWN OF NARRATIVE: BAUDELAIRE'S "LE CYGNE" AND JAMES MERRILL'S "URBAN CONVALESCENCE"

Arnold Weinstein

The two poems that form the basis of this discussion are written in separate languages, appear a hundred years apart, and would appear to describe two separate cities: Paris and New York. It seems worthwhile, then, to state at the outset, what common ground I find in these works, and which of their features will be salient in this analysis. Both poems are significantly provoked by the poet's encounter with "urban renewal," the new Paris that Haussmann was constructing in mid-19th century, and the city block that is being torn up in modern New York. For each poet, this encounter has something of the traumatic in it, a trauma whose force depends on our believing, even if subliminally, that buildings outlast people. Surely much of our fascination with buildings of the past lies in the fact that they are the Past. Stone would seem to have a lifetime that dwarfs human duration, and the great cities that have been decimated in the past—the fires of London, the destruction of Pompei and Herculanean, the ravaging of Dresden and Hiroshima—evoke a sense of apocalypse. Yet, the modern city is undeniably in a state of perpetual transformation: whole blocks are razed, and much of any city today is constantly under scaffolding. One might describe this feature of modern cities as a kind of permanent passing gear, a cycle of development that makes our biological time seem almost static. As a result, few city dwellers can keep up with the image of their city, and we are now, even more than Baudelaire was 130 years ago, in an age where the youngest of us is a storehouse of memories, a graveyard of structures and bricks and stone that are long gone. "As usual in New York," Merrill says, "everything is torn down before you have time to care for it." The spectacle of change and dismantling leads both poets to a meditation on the Past that is at once personal and urban, and in both cases there is considerable emphasis on the generative powers of language as it rebuilds and "restores" what is gone. The central themes of loss, discontinuity and alienation loom large in each poem, and each text displays, in its very structure, the decentered, origin-severed condition of the city-dweller, a condition termed exile in Baudelaire and homelessness in Merrill. Finally, each poem has a peculiar spatial dimension, as the poet probes into the whereabouts of the Past, and by considering these two poems together, we can learn something about the memorializing role of poetry and the special tasks of narrative as a time-laden construct.

First, however, we need to consider each poem, briefly, and, for this, we need to see the texts themselves.

Charles Baudelaire   LE CYGNE

A Victor Hugo

Andromaque, je pense à vous! Ce petit fleuve,
Pauvre et triste miroir où jadis resplendit
L'Immense majesté de vos douleurs de veuve,
Ce Simoïs menteur qui par vos pleurs grandit,

A fécondé soudain ma mémoire fertile,
Comme je traversais le nouveau Carrousel.
Le vieux Paris n'est plus (la forme d'une ville
Change plus vite, hélas! que le coeur d'un mortel);

Je ne vois qu'en esprit tout ce camp de baraques,
Ces tas de chapiteaux ébauchés et fûts,
Les herbes, les gros blocs verdis par l'eau des flaques,
Et, brillant aux carreaux, le bric-à-brac confus.

Là, s 'étalait jadis une ménagerie;

Là je vis, un matin, à l'heure où sous les cieux
Froids et clairs le Travail s'éveille, où la voirie
Pousse un sombre ouragan dans l'air silencieux,

Un cygne qui s'était évadé de sa cage,
Et, de ses pieds palmés frottant le pavé sec,
Sur le sol raboteux traînait son blanc plumage.
Près d'un ruisseau sans eau la bête ouvrant le bec

Baignait nerveusement ses ailes dans la poudre,
Et disait, le coeur plein de son beau lac natal:
"Eau, quand donc pleuvras-tu? quand tonneras-tu, foudre?"
Je vois ce malheureux, mythe étrange et fatal,

Vers le ciel quelquefois, comme l'homme d'Ovide,
Vers le ciel ironique et cruellement bleu,
Sur son cou convulsif tendant sa tête avide,
Comme s'il adressait des reproches à Dieu!

Paris change! mais rien dans ma mélancolie
N'a bougé! palais neufs, échafaudages, blocs,
Vieux faubourgs, tout pour moi devient allégorie,
Et mes chers souvenirs sont plus lourds que des rocs.

Aussi devant ce Louvre une image m'opprime:
Je pense à mon grand cygne, avec ses gestes fous,
Comme les exilés, ridicule et sublime,
Et rongé d'un désir sans trève! et puis à vous,

Andromaque, des bras d'un grand époux tombée,
Vil bétail, sous la main du superbe Pyrrhus,
Auprès d'un tombeau vide en extase courbée;
Veuve d'Hector, hélas! et femme d'Hélénus!

Je pense à la négresse, maigrie et phthisique,
Piétinant dans la boue, et cherchant, l'oeil hagard,
Les cocotiers absents de la superbe Afrique
Derrière la muraille immense du brouillard;

A quiconque a perdu ce qui ne se retrouve
Jamais, jamais! à ceux qui s'abreuvent de pleurs
Et tettent la Douleur comme une bonne louve!
Aux maigres orphelins séchant comme des fleurs!

Ainsi dans la forêt où mon esprit s'exile
Un vieux Souvenir sonne à plein souffle du cor!
Je pense aux matelots oubliés dans une île,
Aux captifs, aux vaincus! . . . à bien d'autres encor!

James Merrill   AN URBAN CONVALESCENCE

Out for a walk, after a week in bed.
I find them tearing up part of my block
And, chilled through, dazed and lonely, join the dozen

In meek attitudes, watching a huge crane
Fumble luxuriously in the filth of years.
Her jaws dribble rubble. An old man
Laughs and curses in her brain,
Bringing to mind the close of *The White Goddess*.

As usual in New York, everything is torn down
Before you have had time to care for it.
Head bowed, at the shrine of noise, let me try to recall
What building stood here. Was there a building at all?
I have lived on this same street for a decade.

Wait. Yes. Vaguely a presence rises
Some five floors high, of shabby stone
—Or am I confusing it with another one
In another part of town, or of the world?—
And over its lintel into focus vaguely
Misted with blood (my eyes are shut)
A single garland sways, stone fruit, stone leaves,
Which years of grit had etched until it thrust
Roots down, even into the poor soil of my seeing.
When did the garland become part of me?
I asked myself, amused almost,
Then shiver once from head to toe.

Transfixed by a particular cheap engraving of garlands
Bought for a few francs long ago,
All calligraphic tendril and cross-hatched rondure.
Ten years ago, and crumpled up to stanch
Boughs dripping, whose white gestures filled a cab,
And thought of neither then nor since.
Also, to clasp them, the small, red-nailed hand
Of no one I can place. Wait. No. Her name, her features
Lie toppled underneath that year's fashions.
The words she must have spoken, setting her face
To fluttering like a veil, I cannot hear now,
Let alone understand.

So that I am already on the stair,
As it were, of where I lived,
When the whole structure shudders at my tread
And soundlessly collapses, filling
The air with motes of stone.
Onto the still erect building next door
Are pressed levels and hues—
Pocked rose, streaked greens, brown whites.
Who drained the pousse-café?
Wires and pipes, snapped off at the roots, quiver.

Well, that is what life does. I stare
A moment longer, so, and presently
The massive volume of the world

Closes again.

Upon that book I swear
To abide by what it teaches:
Gospels of ugliness and waste.
Of towering voids, of soiled gusts.
Of a shrieking to be faced
Full into, eyes astream with cold—

With cold?

All night then. With self-knowledge.

Indoors at last, the pages of *Time* are apt
To open, and the illustrated mayor of New York,
Given a glimpse of how and where I work,
To note yet one more house that can be scrapped.

Unwillingly I picture
My walls weathering in the general view.
It is not even as though the new
Buildings did very much for architecture.

Suppose they did. The sickness of our time requires
That these as well be blasted in their prime.
You would think the simple fact of having lasted
Threatened our cities like mysterious fires.

There are certain phrases which to use in a poem
Is like rubbing silver with quicksilver. Bright
But facile, the glamour deadens overnight.
For instance, how 'the sickness of our time'

Enhances, then debases, what I feel.
At my desk I swallow in a glass of water
No longer cordial, scarely wet, a pill
They had told me not to take until much later.

With the result that back into my imagination
The city glides, like cities seen from the air,
Mere smoke and sparkle to the passenger
Having in mind another destination

Which now is not that honey-slow descent
Of the Champs-Elysées, her hand in his,
But the dull need to make some kind of house
Out of the life lived, out of the love spent.

Baudelaire's swan-poem is a central document for any discussion of poetry and polis but it so well known that I shall only discuss those features of it central to my argument. All critics have noted the ubiquitous exile motif that runs through the poem: Victor Hugo, Andromache, Ovid, the swan, the "négresse, amaigrie et phthisique," the meager orphans and the shipwrecked sailors. This list of exiles carries very considerable pathos with it, and Baudelaire ranges freely over both history and motive: the politics of exile do not change all that much from the Trojan War to Napoléon III, and poets as well as warriors and widows can be cast out from their homeland; the consumptive Black woman tramping the Parisian mud is radically severed from proud Africa, just as the pitiable swan is stranded on the dry urban cobblestone, separated from the "beau lac natal" that now exists only in his heart. One can observe, I think, that these figures are strangely communalized in Baudelaire's poem, much as they are in the famous evocation of artists in "Les Phares" and that they represent a bizarre series or set of analogical images, each obviously a face of the other, none developed fully at the expense of the others. One may say that the poem moves simultaneously along all these circuits at once, and indeed it is this "decentered" feature of the piece that flaunts its modernity. But, we cannot fail to see that these simultaneous circuits are all broken circuits, that each of these figures is tragically displaced, removed from its origin and past, dispossessed of its homeland. Each one of subjects has been cut off, arrested in its developmental curve, set adrift, much like a derelict, in the psychic and urban landscape of the poem. This is broken narrative. Those vital connections that articulate a life-in-time-and-space have all been severed. That, Baudelaire seems to be telling us, is the character of life in the city.

As has been widely recognized, the poem moves increasingly toward the multiple, the unspecified, the open-ended, as the poet sets about making his analogies, spewing forth his repertory of exiles, and this activity, in itself, establishes, as it often does in Baudelaire, a strange new family, an eery kind of kinship, one which powerfully links the *poet* to the creatures of his memory. The vital spawning power of thought and memory are akin to the energy and generative power of semiosis itself, and the *calembour* of the title figures largely in many of the poem's interpretations. The poem as a whole can be seen as a tribute to the imagining powers of the poet, the demiurgic source of these strange images, the creator of analogy and the forger of connection.

"Andromache, je pense à vous," the 19th century Parisian poet says, and his whole poem is, in some sense, adumbrated in that line. *Thinking* restores Andromache and indeed the entire Trojan War to 19th century Paris: indeed, where else is the classical past located, if not in the minds and memories of those who come after? So, too, can the exiled poets be brought home by memory: Ovid and Victor Hugo remember their homelands, and we remember Ovid and Victor Hugo. "Le beau lac natal" and "les cocotiers absents de la superbe Afrique" live, bitter-sweetly, in memory, absent from the city of stone and pavement, yet present and reachable through recall. Memory completes the circuits that life has broken, and exile comes to be seen as the condition of all living people, not just the down-trodden and the exploited, but all who yearn for the Past, whether it be their own, or their city's or their culture's. More than the grand avenues that Haussmann was building, thought is the privileged channel of communication and traffic, the access route that cannot be closed or barricaded. Usually conceived as fleeting and mobile and even capricious, thought becomes, for Baudelaire, the garantor of fidelity and permanence in a fickle world of stone.

"Le vieux Paris n'est plus"; but, then, where is it? "La forme d'une ville change plus vite, hélas, que le coeur d'un mortel." The city of the past is a product of mind, not of matter. Thus we have the magnificent reversal in the second part of the poem:

> Paris change! mais rien dans ma mélancolie
> N'a bougé! palais neufs, échafaudages, blocs,
> Vieux faubourgs, tout pour moi devient allégorie,
> Et mes chers souvenirs sont plus lourds que des rocs.

Here we see a world of pure spirit where the claims of fidelity and permanence have their own ghostly authority, where the moving, material city becomes transparent and fixed with meaning. The heavy world of stone, wonderfully rendered by the guttural, harsh tonalities of "bougé, palais neufs, échafaudages, blocs, / Vieux faubourgs," has been made porous, luminous with pattern and fable, allégorie. And conversely, of course, the inner world of memory has become so tangible and authoritative, so present, as to be "plus lourds que des rocs." The poet, through his language, evokes a city that time cannot alter, that lives on beyond and behind the alterations and renewals of the planners; in like manner memory becomes the civic virtue par excellence, the means of hallowing the city's fullness and restoring one's own estate.

We are now in a position to examine briefly Merrill's counterpart to Baudelaire's poem, "An Urban Convalescence." The 19th century Romantic icons—swans, shipwrecked sailors—are gone, and in their place is an ironic, post-Prufrock idiom of fatigue and self-reflexiveness. Merrill's speaker, like Baudelaire's, will be called on to create a rival city of his own, to erect an edifice of spirit that can fill in the "towering voids" left by the planners. But the ante has been upped, technologically, and the weakened, convalescing city-stroller seems no match for the dinosaur-like

crane whose "jaws dribble rubble." Once again, however, the
precious alchemy reappears, the transformation of matter into
spirit, and we see that the city of mortar and steel is strangely
organic, that it has roots which still live, even after it has been
savagely deconstructed. Thus, Merrill, like Baudelaire, celebrates
the restorative power of thought and memory, and he offers us a
wonderful close-up of how it all works. The disappeared building
gives rise to a remembered one, of which only a single, etched
garland over the lintel remains; and with this floral icon, Merrill
follows the associative meanderings of the mind: stone fruit,
stone leaves, the poor soil of my seeing, and from there the
transatlantic flight to Paris to a cheap engraving of garlands, now
made of paper, wrapping paper to be exact, crumpled up to
stanch boughs dripping, and the reader follows, sleuthlike, the
lovely process of birth itself, as the New York stone completes its
seachange leading us to that absent bouquet of which Mallarmé
wrote, to white gestures, even to a small red-nailed hand; and
that is it, no further. The final touches—the words she spoke, her
name and features—won't quite come, but the voyage has been
quite epic enough as it is, and the speaker fully realizes that this
far-flung tale of metaphoric garlands is his own *vita nuova*, the
transcription in art that truly *restores*.

At this midway point the Merrill poem does something noteworthy. It takes a hard look at that devasted cityscape, and it acknowledges something akin to the futility of poetry. The raped
building is exposed, once more: "Wires and pipes, snapped off at
the roots, quiver." And the tone becomes streetwise: "Well, that
is what life does." The world of matter "closes again," and the
poet pledges to face the ugly facts:

> Gospels of ugliness and waste,
> of towering voids, of soiled gusts,
> Of a shrieking to be faced
> Full into, eyes astream with cold—

The sneaky little rhyme that slips into these tough lines,
"Waste" and "faced," signals the remarkable tonal shift that now
takes place. Much as Baudelaire had suffused his material scene
with spirit, turned his *vieux faubourgs* into *allégorie*, so too does
Merrill demonstrate how that gritty urban world can become art.
Merrill rhymes it and wraps it and mirrors it and traps it. Echo
and rhyme are everywhere:

> . . . with cold—
>
> With cold?

It is not even as though the new
Buildings did very much for architecture.

Suppose they did.

"The sickness of our time" returns, 7 lines later, in quotation marks this time, accused of being rhetorical. Merrill seems to be testing his materials in front of our eyes, seeing what will last, striving for a toughened language much the way we "reinforce" steel to make it stronger. One senses here a powerful emphasis on language itself, language as a kind of structure, an armature that can contain and last, toughened language as protection against the vandalism and exposure that is everywhere imaged in the poem, even the poet's own apartment which is but "one more house to be scrapped." This verbal city is to rival with the one threatened by cranes and mayors, and it is to house the living memories of its inhabitants, offering a shape for lives over time, a way of recording the "life lived" and the "love spent."

Seen together, Baudelaire and Merrill make an eloquent joint case for poetry as a memorializing art, and they sense the vital connection between the historicity of the city and the temporality of individual lives. For them, urban renewal ineluctably betokens psychic loss, and they boldly present the task of restoration in terms of spirit, memory and language.

It is now perhaps time to use the twin examples of Baudelaire and Merrill as a fixed base for an imaginative, theoretical scaffolding of my own, and to generalize my remarks about the plight of narrative within the city. John Berger closes one of his essays with the remark that the greatest threat of the modern city, "with its empty space and time", is that of "impersonal ahistoricity!"[1] It is all too easy to reduce the cityscape to a timeless present, and both poems depict the well-nigh Proustian trauma of time breaking in, of being forced to alter our habitual grids. We cannot see time; we can only see images. Susan Sontag has eloquently critiqued photography along these lines, namely that it can never give us more than truncated images, and this deprives us of real understanding. "In contrast," she writes, "to the amorous relation, which is based on how something looks, understanding is based on how it functions. And functioning takes place in time, and must be explained in time. Only that which narrates can make us understand."[2] Andromache, the swan, the Black woman in Paris and the shipwrecked sailors are, with a vengeance, truncated images, but Baudelaire does us and them the service of narrating, of both highlighting their disjunction and stressing his connection to them. Cities offer their inhabitants the astounding opportunity to interface their past with

its, to let each mirror and inform the other. City life challenges us
to incessant narrative, to chronicle the past of our environment
while rediscovering our own. The great obstacle to such a
scheme, of course, is to see only retinally rather than imaginatively, to see the truncated image and miss the narrative circle
(even when it is a broken circle), to live at the surface and to
eschew the depths. In Butor's great city novel, *L'Emploi du temps*,
he offers a remarkable evocation of the compromises and sell-
outs that mark the city's inhabitants; in referring to the cowardly
bargains they have made, he speaks of

> le pain d'une tranquillité précaire, péniblement acquise à grands
> renoncements, enfoncements et abandons, à grands ensevelisse-
> ments, obscurcissements et trahisons, à grandes humiliations
> bues, exigences tues, à grands secrets perdus, à grands oublis.[3]

Narrative, in this archaeological text, is a kind of imaginative
dig. The meagerness of city life testifies to a moral failure that is
really a failure of imagination, a failure to grasp the rich resources at hand, the thick overlays and substrata of history and
culture that layer the city and echo its voice.

"The city lives," Emerson said, "by remembering." In Mumford's monumental *City in History*, he refines and amplifies this
view of the city as a place of storage and transmission:

> Through its concentration of physical and cultural power, the city
> heightened the tempo of human intercourse and translated its
> products into forms that could be stored and reproduced. Through
> its monuments, written records, and orderly habits of association,
> the city enlarged the scope of all human activities, extending them
> backwards and forwards in time. By means of its storage facilities
> (buildings, vaults, archives, monuments, tablets, books), the city
> became capable of transmitting a complex culture from generation
> to generation, for it marshalled together not only the physical
> means but the human agents needed to pass on and enlarge the
> heritage. That remains the greatest of the city's gifts. As compared
> with the complex human order of the city, our present ingenious
> electronic mechanisms for storing and transmitting information are
> crude and limited.[4]

To understand and appreciate Mumford's sharp contrast between human and mechanical means of storage and transmission, we have only to recall Godard's film *Alphaville*. There
Godard's grade B cult hero, Lemmy Caution, takes on the evil
controller of the futurist Alphaville, namely a giant computer Alpha 60. Lemmy Caution and Alpha 60 each perform their own
kind of transmission and storage. The Giant Computer, shown

over and over with its endless circuitry, stores all known information on earth, processes it logically, and then governs the city dwellers with its dictates of order and control. The Computer has grown rich and powerful in its programming, as the citizens of Alphaville have been despoiled of their language and poetry, their darkness and impulses. Each day they lose a few more words; they don't understand *conscience;* for *amour,* they have only *volupté;* they've lost *rouge-gorge* and *lumière d'automne;* they've lost *tendresse.* And of course, the city knows only a timeless present; over and over we hear that no one has ever lived in the past or the future.

Now Lemmy Caution also stores and transmits. He records all that he sees with his little Brownie camera. He is the living past: Hero of intertextuality, he opens his mouth, and out come Eluard, Pascal, Baudelaire and Borges. He teaches the heroine Natasha the word *conscience*—consciousness and conscience, human awareness and human values. He refuses to live in the present and he makes Natasha remember that she too has an origin, that she is not from or of Alphaville. With its campy detective story frame, *Alphaville* is doubtless a degraded, even an embarrassing form of narrative. But in its grotesque contrast between the procedures of Lemmy Caution and those of Alpha 60, it serves as a fitting way to begin drawing this argument to a close. The city lives by remembering, as Emerson says, and Godard shows that the opposite is also true: the city dies by forgetting. Alphaville is a Necropolis, a city of the living dead where electronic storage and transmission have entirely replaced human memory and narrative. This scenario shows us, writ large, what Baudelaire's poem implies, writ small. Baudelaire's text exploits a bold paradox: using a decentered strategy of simultaneity and analogy, Baudelaire flaunts the breakdown of narrative, the severance of origins and ends, and he proceeds in non-logocentric fashion, everywhere at once; in keeping with this refusal of narrative, he stresses the generative potential of the mind, the endless power of the sign so much so that one feels a bizarre competitiveness in the poem, an uneasy feeling that this lateral, analogical, metaphorizing activity is, itself, narrative's greatest enemy. The lost City is permanently lost, and the poet can only bear witness, elegiacally, to the alienations of war, politics and the economic order. What homeland there is, is consigned to memory and poetry. Yet he is haunted by narrative, by that vertical arrangement of life that works from origin to end and lives through memory; each of his egalitarian images is a figure of exile, of rupture from a past and a homeland; each suffers the tragedy of broken narrative.

It would be tempting to close on this note of paradox, but I would rather conclude with an image of harmony and reconciliation. I shall draw my last reference from one of the most beautiful city-texts I know, Calvino's *Invisible Cities*. As Marco Polo describes the fabulous cities he has seen to Kublai Khan, we are awed by the generative powers of language; it is clear that Marco is hardly dependent on a priori givens or fixed data, but that he has discovered the life-principle itself in fiction-making, in endless invention, in pure semiosis. Language is enlisted here in the heady enterprise of making a world, making a rival world that might allow the Khan to "discern, through the walls and towers destined to crumble, the tracery of a pattern so subtle it could escape the termites' gnawing." Marco's idealist constructions seem as free and unlimited as the human mind itself is, and it therefore comes as a surprise when the Khan asks him:

> "Did you ever happen to see a city resembling this one?" Kublai asked Marco Polo, extending his beringed hand from beneath the silken canopy of the imperial barge, to point to the bridges arching over the canals, the princely palaces whose marble doorsteps were immersed in the water, the bustle of light craft zig-zagging, driven by long oars, the boats unloading baskets of vegetables at the market square, the balconies, platforms, domes, campaniles, island gardens glowing green in the lagoon's grayness.
>
> "No, sire," Marco answered, "I should never have imagined a city like this could exist."

Now, of course, we know, and it seems that the Khan also knows what city this is, but Marco speaks on, through the entire night, until dawn, describing all the inexhaustible cities he has seen. Finally, he concludes:

> "Sire, now I have told you about all the cities I know,"
>
> "There is still one of which you never speak."
>
> Marco Polo bowed his head.
>
> "Venice," the Khan said.
>
> Marco smiled. "What else do you believe I have been talking to you about?"
>
> The emperor did not turn a hair. "And yet I have never heard you mention that name."
>
> And Polo said: "Every time I describe a city I am saying something about Venice."[5]

Here, for a very poignant moment, the high-flying Polo comes home, moves from circumference to center, from fable to history, from the ozone layers of fantasy and invention to 13th century Venice. I believe that we can see here that fuller, more harmonious deployment of narrative for which Merrill is striving at the end of his poem, that verbal, partly fictive home that would give shape and duration to the "life lived" and the "love spent." Polo and Venice and narrative are performing the work of transmission and storage, and they are performing it well. At its richest, narrative reaches both backwards and forwards, is bound to the past but invents a future. Marco Polo's response does not slight the power of the imagination to invent a world, but it humbly acknowledges that the imagination is housed in a body that was born in a place at a particular moment in time, and that all its freedoms will nonetheless be conditioned by those facts of life. By wedding imagination and history, narrative adds immeasurably to the data of our lives, both restoring what time has removed and projecting alternate models to what is. There is surely no more privileged site for such work and play than the City, the visible one of here-and-now, and the countless invisible ones as well.

NOTES

1. John Berger, *About Looking*, (New York: Pantheon, 1980), p. 102.
2. Susan Sontag, *On Photography*, (New York: Delta, 1973), p. 23.
3. Michel Butor, *L'Emploi du Temps* (Paris: Minuit, 1963), pp. 122–123.
4. Lewis Mumford, *The City in History* (New York: Harbinger, 1961), P. 569.
5. Italo Calvino, *Invisiblie Cities* (New York: Harcourt, Brace Jovanovich, 1974), pp. 85–86.

FROM MEMORY LANE TO MEMORY BOULEVARD:
PARIS CHANGE!

Sima Godfrey

La physionomie de Paris est en beaucoup d'endroits changée de fond en comble. . . . Un morceau du passé tombe avec chacune de ces pierres, où se lisait écrite sous une rouille du temps l'histoire de nos aïeux; l'alignement coupe en deux plus d'un souvenir qu'on eût aimé à garder. . . . De chères mémoires se perdent au milieu de ce remue-ménage universel; mais qu'y faire?
Théophile Gautier, reviewing *Paris démoli* by
Edouard Fournier in *Le Moniteur universel*,
21 January 1854.[1]

This paper advances a reading of Baudelaire's Parisian poetry that identifies the action of *flânerie* with the poetic vagaries of memory. In taking as my point of departure Baudelaire's famous dictum of 1846—"art is a mnemotechnics of the beautiful" ("The Salon of 1846")—I have selected for analysis the most famous of the "Tableaux parisiens", "Le Cygne" ["The Swan"]. The singular attention that this poem has commanded in recent criticism is striking to be sure. It implies, however,—unfairly, I think—the exceptional status of the poem within 19th-century French poetry and more particularly within Baudelaire's *oeuvre*.[2] Let me state from the start, therefore, that for the meanderings of memory I consider this poem exemplary rather than exceptional.

Legend holds that mnemotechnics, or the art of memory, was invented by a lyric poet, Simonides, who succeeded in naming the mangled victims of a catastrophe by recalling the seats they had occupied at a banquet-table just before the roof collapsed. Noting that it was through his memory of the places at which the guests had been sitting that he had been able to identify the bodies, he realized the principal rule for the development of memory. Cicero summarizes the invention as follows:

He inferred that persons desiring to train this faculty [of memory] must select places [*loci*] and form mental images [*imagines*] of the things they wish to remember and store those images in the places, so that the order of the places will preserve the order of the things, and the images of the things will denote the things themselves, and we shall employ the places and images respectively as a wax writing-tablet and the letters written on it.

(*De Oratore*, II, lxxxvi, 351–4)

More recently in our own century, the Soviet psychologist Alexander Luria provided the modern gloss to Simonides' feat in a memorable case study dating back to the 1930s, *The Mind of a Mnemonist*. The subject of his study, S., possessed a dazzling memory; years after encountering long lists of information, he could recite them back with total recall in any order at all. Luria summarized S.'s mnemonic technique as follows:

> When S. read through a long series of words, each word would elicit a graphic image. And since the series was fairly long, he had to find some way of distributing these images in a mental row or sequence. Most often (and this habit persisted throughout his life), he would "distribute" them along some roadway or street he visualized in his mind. Sometimes this was a street in his home town, which would also include the yard attached to the house he had lived in as a child and which he recalled vividly. On the other hand, he might also select a street in Moscow. Frequently, he would take a mental walk along that street—Gorky Street in Moscow—beginning at Mayakovsky Square, and slowly make his way down, "distributing" his images at houses, gates, and store windows. At times, without realizing it, he would suddenly find himself back in his home town . . . , where he would wind up his trip in the house he had lived in as a child. . . .
>
> This technique of converting a series of words into a series of graphic images explains why S. could so easily reproduce a series from start to finish or in reverse order . . . To do this, he would simply begin his walk, either from the beginning or from the end of the street, find the image of the object I had named, and "take a look at" whatever happened to be situated on either side of it.[3]

Luria's frame of reference for presenting the mind of his mnemonist was largely determined by scientific categories of analysis, in particular, those dealing with questions of perception.[4] Had he consulted classical rhetorical rather than psychological sources, however, he would have recognized in S.'s mnemotechnics—translating words into *imagines* and then attaching them in his mind to fixed *loci*—a "mise-en-pratique" of the very principles outlined by Cicero in his advice to orators centuries earlier.

The *locus classicus* for the discussion of memory that informed Cicero's disquisition on oratory, as well as that of Quintilian and all subsequent commentators, is the anonymous Roman treatise of about 85 B.C., the *Rhetorica ad Herennium*. The following is an excerpt from the third chapter, on Memory, as translated by Harry Caplan in the Loeb Classical Library edition.

> The artificial memory includes backgrounds [places] and images. [constat . . . ex locis et imaginibus] By [locos] I mean such scenes

as are naturally or artificially set off on a small scale so that we can
grasp or embrace them easily by natural memory—for example, a
house, an intercolumnar space, a recess, an arch or the like. . . .
The [loci] are very much like wax tablets or papyrus, the images
like the letters, the arrangement and disposition of the images like
a script, and the delivery is like reading. . . . We shall need to
study with special care the [loci] we have adopted so that they may
cling lastingly in our memory, for the images, like letters, are ef-
faced when we make no use of them, but the [loci] like wax tablets
should abide. (III, xvi, 29–31; pp. 209–11)

When Baudelaire thus states in 1846 that *art is a mnemotechnics
of the beautiful*, the allusion to the art of memory is both literal
and specific; by the standard rhetorical tradition which he—like
all educated Frenchmen of his generation—had studied in the
penultimate year of his lycée curriculum, he refers to a poetic
stenography of memory as encoded in select *loci* that support a
variety of superimposed images.[5] Accordingly, we may read
Baudelaire's self-conscious *flânerie* through the streets of Paris
somewhat like S.'s famous "mental walks": as a nostalgic "stroll
down memory-lane" to revisit the privileged *loci* of his imagined,
or memorized, past. By extension, in "Le Cygne", composed in
1859, the profound sense of alienation that the poet experiences
emerges from a direct confrontation with the fact of vanished
houses, shattered *loci* and lost footholds. The architectural transformations of Paris that are witnessed in part one of that poem
imply along with them a crisis of memory[6]: for what happens
when the fixed and lasting *loci* of memory are themselves dis-
turbed? When the streets along which one habitually takes one's
real *and* mental walks are suddenly bulldozed? When the "wax-
tablets", that should "abide," are broken? To borrow the language of modern psychology, what happens when the orienting
schemata of a cognitive map are displaced?[7]

Cognitive maps are often discussed as mental pictures of the
environment that the mind's eye can examine at leisure, while
the mind's owner is, for instance, comfortably reclined in an arm-
chair. Cognitive psychologists have remarked (following the
Greeks) that the durability of a cognitive map is determined by
the relative stability of the *loci* selected to orient it. Ulric Neisser
notes that "most errors that occur in the use of cognitive maps
are probably due not so much to general "forgetting" as to a kind
of confusion or interference. . . . Route finding and recall are
therefore most susceptible to error in situations that have frequently changed (like the locations of cats) and least in situations
that are relatively stable (like the locations of buildings)."[8] Baudelaire's *Tableaux parisiens* and more particularly, "Le Cygne," repli-

cate and provide striking insights into the physical and psychological disorientation that ensues when relatively stable points of reference, such as the buildings which one uses to find one's way suddenly vanish like cats.

The poet's cognitive map, laid out as it is in the streets of a Paris that is both real and remembered, is based on the familiar landmarks—buildings and monuments, streets and districts— that characterize the perception of city structure as defined by Kevin Lynch in *The Image of the City*. Lynch's specific concern is not with the nature of memory *per se,* but with the moral and aesthetic responsibilities that the urban planner owes to the city dweller's image of his environment, for the focal points of that image condition the dweller's sense of both physical and emotional well-being.

> In the process of way-finding, the strategic link is the environmental image, the generalized mental picture of the exterior physical world that is held by an individual. *The image is the product both of immediate sensation and of the memory of past experience,* and it is used to interpret information and to guide action. The need to recognize and pattern our surroundings is so crucial, and has such long roots in the past, that this image has wide practical and emotional importance to the individual. . . . An ordered environment . . . may serve as a broad frame of reference, an organizer of activity, or belief, or knowledge. (my emphasis)[9]

Environmental images are the result of an interactive process between the observer and his environment that brings together past and present in a familiar place. Accordingly, the perception of change in that environment will affect not only the individual's image of his surroundings, but moreover his image of self.

With this interactive "image of the city" in mind, we return to "Le Cygne": to follow the confusing directions and spatial disorientations of Baudelaire's "tableau" is to read the poet's desperate attempt to reconstruct in art the focal points of reference that will guide him back through memory to the lost images and "beauty" of a childhood whose *locus* is and was Paris.

In trying to pursue the poet's nostalgic *flânerie* across Paris and backwards into time, the critical reader needs also to reconstruct the fictions of the fixed *loci* and transient images that dictate his aleatory path. For this purpose, we turn to Baudelaire's private correspondence. The following is an excerpt from a letter written by Baudelaire to his mother on 6 May 1861, several months after the appearance of the second edition of the *Fleurs du Mal.*[10] In an extraordinarily candid moment, he recalls the privileged time in his childhood, when his mother was near and he basked in her love.

There was a time in my childhood when I loved you passionately;
listen and read on without fear. I have never spoken to you about
it in such detail. I remember a carriage ride; you were coming out
of the convalescent home to which you had been sent and in order
to prove to me that you had been thinking of your son, you
showed me some ink drawings that you made for me. Don't you
find my memory scary? Later, I recall the Place Saint-André-des-
Arts and Neuilly. Long walks together and endless tenderness!
I remember the quays of the Seine, so sad at night. Oh! those were
the good times of maternal kindness. Forgive me for calling them
good times; they were no doubt bad times for you. But I was alive
in you at all times then; and you were mine all alone. You were
both my idol and my friend. You may be surprised that I can still
speak so passionately about a time so long ago. I myself am surprised by it.[11]

The precise geography of Baudelaire's recollections allow us to
date this specific childhood memory of passionate love to the
twenty-month period that separated the death of the poet's father, François Baudelaire (10 February 1827) and the official engagement of the boy's mother to Jacques Aupick (8 October 1828),
the period during which his mother belonged, he says, to no
other man, and was his, "uniquement à moi." Sometime in the
fall of 1827, Madame veuve Baudelaire and her son moved from
the Rue Hautefeuille to the Rue and then the Place Saint-André-
des-Arts and in the early summer of 1828 they moved again to
François Baudelaire's property in Neuilly, the pastoral home that
the poet evokes so tenderly in *Fleurs du Mal 99*.

> Je n'ai pas oublié, voisine de la ville,
> Notre blanche maison, petite mais tranquille; . . .
>
> I have not forgotten the house we lived in then,
> it was just outside of town, a little white house . . .

Baudelaire's nostalgic memory of his "première jeunesse" wanders similarly across the map of "le vieux Paris [qui] n'est plus"
to define its own restless *flânerie* from the Rue Hautefeuille on
the left bank of Paris to the Rue de Seine in Neuilly. In a letter
dated 23 December 1865, he again telegraphs the happy recollections of childhood to two old addresses.

> In short, my dear mother, I am deathly bored; my one great dis-
> traction comes from thinking of you. My thoughts continually go
> out to you. I see you in your bedroom or your drawing room,
> working, moving about, doing things, fretting and fuming and
> reprimanding me from afar. And then I recall [je revois] my entire

childhood spent next to you and the Rue Hautefeuille and the Rue
Saint-André-des-Arts; but from time to time I awake from my day-
dreams . . . [12]

By October 1828, that is, the time when Colonel Aupick was
already a definite presence in their lives, the family had moved
once again to 17 Rue du Bac and this is where the map of Baudelaire's happy childhood ends.

Baudelaire acknowledges with some embarrassment that the
"good times" of maternal love must have been trying ones indeed for his mother. For a good part of her year of mourning the
young widow was confined to a "maison de santé" as a result,
one has assumed, of her weakened health. In her absence, it was
the family servant, Mariette, who looked after the young Baudelaire in Neuilly, and the poetic homage he would later pay to her
clearly addresses this time of tenderness when the faithful servant substituted for a since unfaithful mother.

> La servante au grand coeur dont vous étiez jalouse,
> Et qui dort son sommeil sous une humble pelouse,
> Nous devrions pourtant lui porter quelques fleurs. . . .
>
> You used to be jealous of our old nurse
> Who sleeps, warm heart and all, beneath the sod.
> We ought to bring her flowers, even so. . . .
>
> (*Fleurs du Mal* 100)

On 11 January 1858, several months after the infamous censor-
ship trial of the *Fleurs du Mal* (from which he emerged largely
unscathed), Baudelaire wrote to his mother, who had once more
had occasion to move as a result of her husband's death. Jacques
Aupick had died in April of the preceding year and the widow
left Paris soon after to take up residence in Honfleur. There she
impatiently awaited a visit from her son. Widowed yet again, she
had to confront "bad times" that were ironically rather "good"
once more for the poet—his volume of poems had won not only
the notorious attention of the Ministry of the Interior but also the
respect of France's leading poet at the time, Victor Hugo. His article on "The Essence of Laughter" had been reprinted in *Le
Présent* on 1 September 1857 and his two essays on caricature had
appeared in the same journal the following month; and on October 18th his article on *Madame Bovary* was published in Gautier's
journal *L'Artiste*. Madame Aupick's reaction to her son's success
was, however, less than cordial. The letters of this time poi-
gnantly illustrate Baudelaire's demoralization in the face of maternal reproach. Until her death Madame Aupick took offense at
the manifest impiety of her son that had provoked public scandal.

In 1858, therefore, Baudelaire wrote to her both to explain his delay in coming to Honfleur and to prove his poetic discretion and filial love.

> I see that you did not notice that there are two poems in the *Fleurs du Mal* that concern you, or at least allude to intimate details of our former life, to that period of widowhood that left me with such singular and sad memories—the first: *Je n'ai pas oublié voisine de la ville* . . . (Neuilly), and the second, which follows it: *La servante au grand coeur dont vous étiez jalouse* . . . (Mariette): I kept these pieces untitled and without any precise indications because I can't bear to prostitute family intimacies.[13]

Baudelaire draws attention to two "tableaux" whose settings recall the period of his mother's first widowhood; they stand in ironic contrast to her renewed state of widowhood that was less qualified by the son's sympathy. The two pieces may have been composed as early as 1843, but in 1861 Baudelaire included them in the section of the *Fleurs du Mal*—composed mostly of later poems—entitled "Tableaux parisiens." That section of the collection, most noted for the modernism of its aesthetic sensibility, is organized largely about the wanderings of a lyric persona through the streets of Paris: streets that are magically overlaid with memories to form an allegorical palimpsest of past history that is at once cultural, mythical and personal. The place of these two early poems in that stroll down streets of memory thus serves to figure the "longues promenades" and "tendresses maternelles" that Baudelaire would specifically evoke in the famous letter of 1861. That letter similarly charts a regression into the past down streets of Paris which lead back to the happy homes of Saint-André-des Arts and Neuilly, homes that were inhabited for a brief but golden moment by a young widow and her beloved son.

> Et le soleil, le soir ruisselant et superbe
> Qui, derrière la vitre où se brisait sa gerbe,
> Semblait, grand oeil ouvert dans le ciel curieux,
> Contempler nos dîners longs et silencieux,
> Répandant largement ses beaux reflets de cierge
> Sur la nappé frugale et les rideaux de serge.

> Nor those seemingly endless evenings when the sun
> (whose rays ignited every windowpane)
> seemed, like a wide eye in the wondering sky,
> to contemplate our long silent meals,
> kindling more richly than any candlelight
> the cheap curtains and the much laundered cloth.
> (*Fleurs du Mal* 99, "Je n'ai pas oublié, voisine de la ville")

Baudelaire highlights the images that he draws in the "Tableaux parisiens" against the backdrop of a broad, nostalgic, mythologized past that is no more and may never have been. In the most famous of these, "Le Cygne," fragments of "prehistory"— the prehistory of Paris and the prehistory of the poet—are resuscitated from the débris of the modern city. (That débris possesses nonetheless its own historical referent in the public world, since at the time of composition of this poem, the topographical map of Paris was being redefined in a very real sense by Napoleon III and his agent, Baron Haussman.) The poet wanders wistfully through the allegorized rubble of Paris, an exile among exiles; like the noble swan, humiliated in the dust of the city, an ironic fallen "beau de l'air" is condemned to long for the shimmering "beau lac natal" of oceanic memory. An orphaned poet, condemned to life, he reassembles the desiccated traces of a past that has been condemned to death; and this sketchy tableau provides the pretext for his ironic "swan-song" of Paris.

> Paris change! mais rien dans ma mélancolie
> N'a bougé! palais neufs, échafaudages, blocs,
> Vieux faubourgs, tout pour moi devient allégorie,
> Et mes chers souvenirs sont plus lourds que des rocs.

> Paris changes . . . But in sadness like mine
> nothing stirs—new buildings, old
> neighborhoods turn to allegory,
> and memories weigh more than stone.
>
> ("Le Cygne")

His poem of exile, dedicated to a contemporary hero in exile, Victor Hugo, opens with a dramatic address to a female "phantom" exhumed from the archives of memory and antiquity: *Andromaque, je pense à vous!* An ancient little stream inundates the poet's *"fertile memory"* leading him back to a source in the present and to the startling "newness" of a *locus* transformed, the Place du Carrousel. It also leads the reader, exiled in a fragmented world of heteroclite references and confusing signs—

> Le Cygne
>
> A Victor Hugo
>
> Andromaque, je pense à vous!—

onto the terrain of allegory and myth, where imagination decomposes all creation and creates a "new world" of its own, following private rules whose sources stem "from the depths of the soul." ("Salon of 1859")

In one of the planned prefaces for the *Fleurs du Mal*, Baudelaire explicitly states the Latin allusion to Andromache: "Virgile (tout le morceau d'Andromaque)." The reference to the *Aeneid* is doubly significant in a poem that begins with an invocation to the exiled widow, Andromache, and summons, shadow-like at its end, Romulus and Remus and the birth of Rome. The myth of a city and an empire whose future extended historically beyond the scope of Virgil's poetic vision and collapsed in a decline and fall as fierce as Troy's. That empire's distant glory underscores, nonetheless, with savage irony, the debased, bourgeois parody of an empire that Napoleon III had produced with such amateur zeal in the France of the 1850's. By analogy, Virgil's epic vision of the founding of a city is ironically inverted in Baudelaire's poem to accomodate the disintegration of a city into heaps of shattered memories. The she-wolf who nursed the hope for the future here feeds only a hungry regret for the past.

> A quiconque a perdu ce qui ne se trouve
> Jamais, jamais! à ceux qui s'abreuvent de pleurs
> Et tettent la Douleur comme une bonne louve! . . .

> [I think] of those who lose what never can be found
> again—never! swallowing their tears
> and nursing at the she-wolf Sorrow's dugs; . . .

But in a poem that explicitly echoes the parallel tragedy of ancients and moderns, the reference to Andromache recalls too the image of a neo-classical heroine, one who speaks out from the literary echo-chambers of memory in French. This is the Andromaque of Racine:

> Ma flamme par Hector fut jadis allumée;
> Avec lui dans la tombe elle s'est enfermée.
> Mais il me reste un fils. Vous saurez un jour,
> Madame, pour un fils jusqu'où va notre amour; . . .
> (Andromaque, III iv, 865–868)

> My ardent love was kindled once by Hector, long ago;
> That flame belongs to him, locked in the tomb.
> But I still have a son. One day you too will know,
> Madame, how far our love will extend for a son; . . .

For the educated French reader of the nineteenth century, the figure of Andromache rises up out of myth to recruit the memory not only of Virgil's noble widow, condemned to exile and to a marriage of betrayal—

> Andromaque, des bras d'un grand époux tombée,
> Vil bétail, sous la main du superbe Pyrrhus,
> Auprès d'un tombeau vide en extase courbée;
> Veuve d'Hector, hélas! et femme d'Hélénus!

> [I think] of you, Andromache, dragged off
> to be the booty of Achilles' son,
> Hector's widow now the wife of Helenus,
> crouching blindly over an empty grave!

—but moreover Racine's tragic heroine, the widow fiercely faithful to the memory of a dead husband and to the love of a young son. The woman who would die to protect the life of her child and the undying honor of his father. She is above all the devoted widow and mother and her majesty derives from an unwavering commitment to both those roles.

Strolling poetically through the streets of Paris, Baudelaire thus encodes the private myths of a personal history of desire and defeat within a larger myth of disinheritance and exile that is generated by jolting visions of a changing city. The *flâneur's* personal *plan de Paris* becomes a cognitive map for reading or misreading the poet's reconstructed fictions of childhood.[14] And the "dearest" memory of childhood weighs down upon his imagination—the cherished picture of a widow and her son wandering across Paris—to feed into the allegory of modern life that he builds upon the blasted foundations of the past.

In Baudelaire's poetry of the late 1850's and 1860's the streets of modern Paris are haunted by the arresting apparition of widows. It is onto these noble figures of alienation and loss, singled out from the amorphous crowd, that the poet repeatedly projects his own "avid speculations" and profound desires (as in the prose poem, "Les Veuves" ["Widows"]). Like Andromache, who underwrites the enormous majesty of widowhood and mourning, these women, condemned to loneliness, repeatedly call forth an image of nobility that cancels out the material degradations to which they have been submitted by loss. Thus it is that in the most famous of Baudelaire's Parisian sonnets, "A une passante," ["In Passing"] the woman in the crowd who suddenly compels the poet's eye and desire is a widow too.

> Longue, mince, en grand deuil, douleur majestueuse,
> Une femme passa, d'une main fastueuse
> Soulevant, balançant le feston et l'ourlet; . . .

> Tall, slender, in mourning—noble grief—
> a woman passed, and with a jewelled hand
> gathered up her black embroidered hem; . . .

Walter Benjamin has provided masterful analyses of these tableaux of public widowhood as existential allegories of modern life.[15] They contain, however, just as surely, the private myth of a family romance that the poet filters through the imaginary prisms of desire and regret. For the *flâneur*'s casual stroll through the streets of Paris is not so aimless as it might seem. Like the Russian mnemonist trying hard to remember, "at times, without realizing how it happened," Baudelaire suddenly finds himself "back in his home town"—*le vieux Paris [qui] n'est plus*—"where he would wind up his trip in the house he had lived in as a child." His poetic wanderings, like his nostalgic dreams, have an object at their end: that original and not-so-obscure object of desire who inhabits the house of his childhood and towers over the poet's imagination, the image of an idealized widowed-mother who commands desire and charges memory from discreet addresses all around Paris. These addresses—moreover the houses they refer to—represent the privileged *loci* that inspire a restless poet hungry for *souvenirs* in the streets of the city.

As memory lane is violently transformed into memory boulevard, however, the buildings along the way that house the dearest fictions of a poet's past risk being condemned. And the collapse of the house of memory brings with it, for Baudelaire, the most anxious threat of all: the loss of his own origins and of the original object of love. Like ancient Simonides before him, the poet of modernity, nostalgic mnemotechnician of the beautiful, discovers in the end that the only guarantee against time, death, and collapsing roofs is a record of *places in the art*.

In the face of urban wreckage and shaky buildings, it is to another *locus classicus* that Baudelaire will therefore confide his veiled memories and imagined desires: to that Horatian monument of poetry, more solid and lasting than bronze. A nineteenth-century monument, the *Fleurs du Mal* thus trace an exceptional blueprint for memory that defines, in the words of Barbey d'Aurévilly, a *secret architecture*, ordered by the willful design of a master draughtsman. "Les artistes qui voient les lignes sous le luxe et l'efflorescence de la couleur percevront très bien qu'il y a ici *une architecture secrète*, un plan calculé par le poète méditatif et volontaire. . . . [Les Fleurs du Mal] perdraient donc beaucoup à n'être point lues *dans l'ordre* où le poète, qui sait si bien ce qu'il fait, les a rangées." (*Le Pays*, July 1857.) To paraphrase the classical paraphrase of his friend and mentor, Théophile Gautier, Baudelaire's *oeuvre* recalls a most ancient theme: when palaces and homes crumble, "les vers *souvenirs* demeurent, plus forts que des airains."[16]

NOTES

1. Gautier's review was reprinted as the preface to the expanded third edition of Fournier's book (Paris, 1883). After its initial success in 1854, *Paris démoli* went

into a second edition in 1855. In the scant year separating the first and second editions, however, the face of Paris had changed so dramatically that Fournier added a new introductory chapter in 1855, "Voyage à travers de nouvelles ruines." Despite some wistful feelings for vanished charms, Fournier expresses above all his faith in the healthy progress and renewal of Paris. The opening sentence of this chapter stands as an ironic epigraph to Baudelaire's "Le Cygne": "Depuis un an que ce livre a paru, les ruines se sont tous les jours accumulées davantage dans l'ancien Paris, et tous les jours la ville nouvelle a continué d'en sortir plus à l'aise et plus superbe."

In the chapters that follow, *Paris démoli* revisits facades and neighbourhoods of Paris that have changed or disappeared since the 16th century; the book reads alternately like a touristic "flânerie" through ancient Paris and like a historical novel, with ancedotal references to the homes of great literary figures of the Parisian past—Boileau, Racine, Molière, Scarron, etc. Although Fournier offers no critique of the radical redefinition of Paris in the 1850's, the timing and the success of the book clearly reflect public sensitivity to the theme of "Paris demolished," an inescapable theme for Parisians during this period of major urban redevelopment. Gautier's response to *Paris démoli*, for all his praise of Fournier's erudition, is full of poignant regret for the architectural memories that the wreckers have destroyed. In his review, Gautier wanders through Paris, with Fournier as his guide, pausing to remember what once stood in the place of the new scaffolds. In theme as in spirit, Gautier's preface to Fournier's *Paris démoli* serves as a fitting preface to Baudelaire's *Tableaux parisiens*.

2. On the critical vogue for "Le Cygne" in recent years, see Ross Chambers, "Du Temps des 'Chats' au temps du 'Cygne'," *Oeuvres et critiques*, 9, no. 2 (1984):11–26.

3. A. R. Luria, *The Mind of a Mnemonist*, trans. Lynn Solotaroff (New York: Basic Books, 1968):31–33. On the subject of mnemonics, see also Ulric Neisser, ed., *Memory Observed; Remembering in Natural Contexts*, San Francisco: W. H. Freeman, 1982.

4. For the purposes of comparison with Baudelaire, it is striking that in the analysis of S.'s mnemonic technique, Luria emphasizes the importance of *synaesthesia* in S.'s system of recall. Words, sounds, numbers would all 'materialize' in S.'s mind as visual images, creating a personal system of proto-Baudelairian "correspondances" or Rimbaldian "voyelles."

> "Each speech sound immediately summoned up for S. a striking visual image, for it had its own distinct form, color, and taste. Vowels appeared to him as simple figures, consonants as splashes, some of them solid configurations, others more scattered—but all of them retained some distinct form. As he described it:

> A [a] is something white and long; и [ɛ] moves off somewhere ahead so that you just can't sketch it, whereas й [j'i] is pointed in form. Ю [j'u] is also pointed and sharper than e [j'ɛ], whereas я [j'a] is big, so big that you can actually roll right over it. . . . I also experience a sense of taste from each sound. And when I see lines, some configuration that has been drawn, these produce sounds. . . . (25–26)

By analogy with S., Baudelaire's "correspondances," may thus be considered a further extension of his specific *mnemotechnics* of the beautiful.

5. During the years that correspond to Baudelaire's lycée studies in Lyon and at the Collège Louis-le-Grand in Paris, works by Cicero figured prominently in the curriculum from the year in Quatrième (1833–4) onward; special attention was paid to Cicero's rhetoric and oratory in the class of Rhétorique (1837–38).

Baudelaire's interest and excellence in Latin during these years is, of course, well known. Moreover, it is significant that the one teacher at Louis-le-Grand to have left a positive, lasting impression on Baudelaire was his teacher in rhetoric, a classicist with a taste for modern literature, M. Jacob Wilhelm Rinn. Writing to his step-father on 17 July 1838, the young Baudelaire notes: "très souvent je vais causer avec M. Rinn, mon professeur, des ouvrages que je lis, d'idées littéraires, d'auteurs latins, de ce qu'on fait aujourd'hui, de ce qu'il faut faire dans la vie, etc. . . . M. Rinn pour moi est un oracle." Baudelaire would have no doubt known the Simonides legend and Cicero's commentary on it from his own reading of Cicero or from Rinn's lectures and general readings for the rhetoric year. (Furthermore, in 1831–2, Rinn had published an edition of Cicero.) For more details on J. W. Rinn, see David Pellow, *Charles Baudelaire: The Formative Years*, Ph.D. Dissertation, Vanderbilt University, 1971:107–118.

6. For a detailed account of these architectural transformations as they relate to sequences in "Le Cygne," see Richard D. Burton, *The Context of Baudelaire's "Le Cygne,"* Durham: University of Durham Press, 1980.

7. The term "cognitive map" was originally coined by E. C. Tolman in "Cognitive Maps in Rats and Men," *Psychological Review* 55 (1948):189–208. More recently, Ulric Neisser has expanded the discussion of cognitive maps in *Cognition and Reality, Principles and Implications of Cognitive Psychology*, San Francisco: W. H. Freeman, 1976.

8. Neisser, *Cognition and Reality*, 136.

9. Kevin Lynch, *The Image of the City* (Cambridge, Mass.: M.I.T. Press, 1960):4.

10. This expanded edition was the first to present the section entitled "Tableaux parisiens" which contains "Le Cygne."

11. Charles Baudelaire, *Correspondance*, ed. Claude Pichois, 2 vols. (Paris: Gallimard, 1973), 2:153. Unless otherwise indicated, all translations are my own. English quotations from *Les Fleurs du Mal* are from Richard Howard's translation (Boston: Godine, 1983).

12. *Correspondance*, 2:553–54.

13. *Correspondance*, 1:445.

14. Luria's analysis of S.'s "mind" in telling on this point.

> Thinking in terms of images was fraught with . . . dangers. Inasmuch as S.'s images were particularly vivid and stable, and recurred thousands of times, they soon became the dominant element in his awareness, uncontrollably coming to the surface whenever he touched upon something that was linked to them even in the most general way. *These were images of his childhood:* of the little house he had lived in in Rezhista; of the yard at Chaim Petukh's, where he could see the horses standing in the shed, where everything smelled of oats and manure. This explains why, once he had begun to read or had started one of his mental walks connected with recall, he would suddenly discover that although he had started out at Mayakovsky Square [in Moscow] he invariable ended up at Chaim Petukh's house or in one of the public squares in Rezhista. . . .
>
> Given such a tendency, cognitive functions can hardly proceed normally. The very thought which occasions an image is soon replaced by another—to which the image itself has led; a point is thus reached at which images begin to guide one's thinking . . . (emphasis added, 115–116)

Ironically, the process which the psychologist here describes as a cognitive problem (images replacing "thought") serves as a starting point for psychoanalysis and may also serve as a definition of modern *poesis*.

15. Walter Benjamin, *Charles Baudelaire, a Lyric Poet in the Age of High Capitalism*, trans. Harry Zohn (London: New Left Books, 1973).
16. Cf. Théophile Gautier's Parnassian manifesto, "L'Art," in *Emaux et Camées:*

> Les dieux eux-mêmes meurent,
> Mais les vers souverains
> Demeurent
> Plus forts que les airains.

PARIS, BAUDELAIRE AND BENJAMIN: THE POETICS OF URBAN VIOLENCE

Josephine Diamond

The title originally given to this book: "City, Text and Thought," leaves the relation between the urban, the aesthetic and the theoretical tantalizingly open. The apparently neutral "and" is a problematic conjunction, particularly in the context of modern French literature where the city is no longer simply the geographical centre of cultural production but, from realism to surrealism, occupies a privileged rhetorical place within the text itself. Indeed, Baudelaire's paradigmatic articulation of modernism is inseparable from his representation of modern Paris, brilliantly reformulated by the equally paradigmatic theoretical text: Walter Benjamin's *Baudelaire: A Lyric Poet in The Era of High Capitalism.*[1]

The rhetorical mode that expresses Baudelaire's configuration of Paris is, according to Benjamin, allegory. The thrust of Benjamin's work, of course, is to question the priority given to symbol over allegory in Romantic aesthetics as a trope which constitutes unity, identity and totalisation. Whereas the symbol projects a natural plenitude, allegory is emblematic, fragmented, arbitrary. In Baudelaire it represents history, through the débris and detritus that mark his urban landscape—one thinks, as an extreme example, of the female carcass gathering flies in the streets of "La Charogne"—as discontinuous, without progress or telos. In contrast to the auratic objects of the symbolic order that provoke transcendent epiphanies or transform anteriority into interiority, the objects of the city landscape are fetishised commodities that offer the pleasure of a passing seduction and leave the trace of non-meaning. The poet thus assumes in Baudelaire's works the ironic persona of the ragpicker, that by-product of mass production, or of the flâneur the prince of leisure in apparent opposition to the bustling and anonymous urban crowd. The on-looker, looking over the luxurious objects exposed in the new arcades, the flâneur, in Benjamin's words, is the soul of merchandise; as is, more literally, one of his favorite figures on the city streets, the prostitute.

If Benjamin describes Baudelaire's representation of Paris as fragmented and commodified, without historical continuity, he nevertheless highlights moments of acute perception, sudden shocks that create a new constellation of images and disrupt the empty repetitions of commodified history. One recalls, for example, the exchanged and ever passing glance of eyes in "Une Passante" that transforms and relocates the traditional neo-platonic topos, or "Le Cygne" in which the fragmentation of Paris, emblematised by the allegorized and stranded swan, evokes a series of associations, beginning with the exiled Andromaque, a historical flash-point in the light of which urban modernization emerges as bric-à-brac, the ruins of the past.

Theodor Adorno, in his *Aesthetics and Politics*, criticizes Benjamin's study of Baudelaire for relating the pragmatic contents of Baudelaire's work directly to adjacent features in the social and economic history of his time: "I regard it as methodologically unfortunate to give conspicuous individual features from the realm of the superstructure a "materialistic" turn by relating them immediately and perhaps even causally to corresponding features of the infrastructure. Materialist determination of cultural traits is only possible if it is mediated through the *total social process*."[2] Terry Eagleton, in his *Walter Benjamin or Towards A Revolutionary Criticism*, tends to agree with Adorno, quoting the following passage from Benjamin's study of Baudelaire as an example of his audacious mixture of metaphor and fact: "In the performance of the clown, there is an obvious reference to economy. With his abrupt movements he imitates both the machines which push the material and the economic boom which pushes the merchandise."[3] Yet Eagleton acknowledges that the problem of defining a relation between base and superstructure, while avoiding expressive, homologous or mechanical connotations, is generally unresolved in Marxist theory. Benjamin's juxtapositions remain in a state of provocative but productive interdeterminacy, his style constantly hovering between the symbolic and the allegorical.

Focusing on moments of discontinuity, fragmentation or constellating shock, Benjamin does not articulate the interrelation between the different modes of *Les Fleurs du Mal* or between the *Tableaux parisiens* and the prose poems of *Le Spleen de Paris*. However, his own readings prefigure post-modernist readings which differentiate between symbol and allegory in terms of the generic difference between the lyrics and the prose poems. I am thinking in particular of Barbara Johnson's *Défigurations du langage poétique*,[4] and Leo Bersani's *Baudelaire and Freud*,[5] which confront the significance of the greater realism of the prose poems, the more immediate imagery of the city landscape, its commodification and urban violence. Johnson reads the prose poems as defigurations of what she calls the incestuous and narcissistic sensuousness of the lyrics which corresponds to a definition of poetry as autonomous, ideal and transcendent. The prose poems, on the other hand, expose poetry as a circuit of exchange isomor-

phic with the economic code. She is very specific about this relation, stating that the system of equivalences between signifiers
and signified functions on the same principle of adequation as
that which links work to salary or product to price. Indeed, given
its excess of meaning, poetry as exposed by the prose poems corresponds to the capitalist notion of surplus value. Thus Johnson
conflates the aesthetic and economic codes, making it possible
for a metaphoric substitution of one for the other. We shall see
the logical consequence of this conflation in Jeffrey Mehlman's
reading of Baudelaire in his article "Baudelaire with Freud/The-
ory and Pain."[6]

It is theoretically jolting to turn to Leo Bersani's *Baudelaire and
Freud* which absolutely reverses the defigurative priority Johnson
gives to the prose poems. Bersani associates the lyrical poems
with mobile significance and continuous substitutions of desire
and the prose poems with a flat allegorical mode—quite different from Benjamin's use of allegory—which he equates with La-
can's Imaginary and with nineteenth century realism in general.
"Realism curiously accommodates allegory. It is as if the self-
effacement required by an aesthetic of objectivity were in fact enacted as an attempt to reappropriate a self 'lost' in the world."[7]
However, despite their diametrically opposed readings, both
Johnson and Bersani reduce the socioeconomic code to metaphor or fantasmatic illusion. Such readings become particularly
problematical when applied to the more typical of the prose
poems where violence, often sadomasochistic, is the dominant
textual event.

The prose poem I would like to look at in some detail is *Assommons les pauvres* which represents urban violence in a dramatic
and exemplary way and has elicited especially provocative and
productive readings by Leo Bersani and Jeffrey Mehlman. Both of
these concentrate on the crucial scene where the narrator meets
a beggar asking for charity, hears a demonic voice whispering
in his ear that one man is equal to another only if he proves it
and that freedom is a matter of conquest, and proceeds to test
this theory by beating up the old beggar. When the beggar finally
rises up and turns on him, he celebrates the success of his praxis,
gives the beggar his money and recommends that he disseminate
the lesson. In his "Baudelaire with Freud" Mehlman reads this
poem as typical of a process whereby a prince/dandy/narrator
disrupts the master/slave dualism but also prevents any dialectical *aufhebung*. Thus the violent scene exemplifies metaphorical
displacement and mobility of reference. This interpretation
hinges on Baudelaire's ambiguous use of the word "douleur,"
qualifying the theory he wishes the beggar to disseminate, in the

phrase "que j'ai eu la douleur d'essayer sur votre dos." Not only does "douleur" displace the "plaisir" conventional to the phrase but, to quote Mehlman, "it is curiously afloat between subject and object . . . as though the exchange of beatings were generative of a new reality, a douleur which is neither the dandy's nor the beggar's but the presence/absence of the one in the other, less the exchange of douleurs than the douleur of a certain kind of exchange."[8] Thus the violence of metaphoricity exceeds and decenters individual consciousness. Mehlman interprets Baudelaire as working on a textual level which "is analogous to our own, concerned with repetition in difference." The scene of urban violence thus emerges as a paradigm for deconstructive theory.

However, Mehlman's reading of this poem is absolutely contradicted by that of Bersani. In his *Baudelaire and Freud*, Bersani interprets the sadistic narrator who appropriates the beggar, makes him identical to himself and vicariously propagates his image throughout the world, as the immobilizer of desire. Thus, *Assommons les pauvres* exemplifies Baudelaire's refusal of metaphoric mobility in the name of the immobilizing narcissistic image. In order to get out of the impasse produced by the crucial sadomasochistic scene, we can only return to the opening of the poem where the narrator recalls its initiating circumstances. It begins with the recollection of an act of reading. For two weeks, the narrator recalls, he had locked himself in his room reading all kinds of books on how to be happy and rich in twenty four hours. Both Mehlman and Bersani, who pay little attention to the first part of the poem, incorporate these texts under the rubric of idealism which the narrator proceeds to disrupt or mirror through his act of violence. To take a cue from Benjamin who is always alert to the transformations of literature by its means of reproduction, what is highlighted here is not the idealism but the consumability of the texts. Through the speculative drive of the literary entrepreneurs feeding on the dissatisfaction of the poor and unhappy, a form of literature is manufactured which can be swallowed, consumed and easily digested. However, far from transforming the lives of its readers, this literary junk food produces the desire for further consumption and stupefaction. Thus, the narrator staggers out of his room in quest of the nearest tavern where, dizzy and stupefied, he is accosted by the beggar. The expression on the beggar's face ironically contests the entrepreneurial promise of utopia. Whereas the reduction of ideas to matter for consumption is in the aim of furthering consumption *per se*, the beggar in his resentful humiliation dreams of revolution. If spirit could move matter, writes the narrator, if magnetism could ripen grapes, the expression of that beggar would overturn

thrones. Ideas of wealth and joy are revealed to be ideological
propaganda that both mask and acerbate prevailing social conditions or else, as in the beggar's eyes, they are impotent and rag-
ing fantasies. It is here that the text turns. The impasse between
the ennui of consumption and the hatred of impotent desire, between the narrator and the beggar, is broken by the demonic
voice urging the narrator to violent action.

The narrator likens this voice to that of the demon of Socrates,
with one essential difference. It is not the great inhibitor but the
great affirmer, prefiguring Nietzsche's reversal of the negativity
of the metaphysical tradition. It is the voice of excess, of daring,
of madness, the voice that often in Baudelaire (as in the first of
the *Spleen* poems, where a cry of anguish breaks the stifling ennui emblematised in the oppressive lid of the city sky and the
bars of the rain) disrupts the idealist/materialist impasse by ironic
dramatization. It is the voice of the metteur en scene initiating
some outrageous production. However, given the caricatural, parodic and ironic mode of the sado-masochistic scene, it is difficult
to take it, as does Mehlman, as a metaphor of violent metaphoricity. What is being caricatured by Baudelaire is the instant transformation promised by the literary self-help manuals. Equality
through conquest emerges as another slogan and it is deconstructed by the pathetic but farcical scene of urban violence.
Within the interplay of sudden blows the beggar's body is turned
into a deranged machine, a piece of steak to be battered; because
of the rapidity and ease of the narrator's movements, it seems at
the same time insubstantial, like a mobile figure in a comic strip.
Similarly, it is disturbing to take the narrator as paradigmatic of
the post modernist deconstructor when he reveals himself as the
archetypal dandy, lamenting a broken nail as he knocks out the
beggar's teeth, and as the archetypal bully and coward keeping a
wary eye open for the policeman on the block. The bold pre-
Nietszchean program reduced to a slogan and disfigured into fascism is delineated through him. Baudelaire does not use this
scene as an exemplum but as the ironic caricature of an exemplum. The narrator welcomes the chiasmic reversal when the old
carcass turns on him with a look that seems "de bon augure"
and beats him up in turn with a blatantly ironic encomium to
philosophy: "O miracle, O jouissance du philosophie qui vérifie
l'excellence de sa théorie." Not only does the hyperbolic rhetoric
of this exclamation undermine the seriousness of the narrator's
exemplary experiment, but he equally puts the outcome into
doubt by implying that he ends it, like a sophist, not because
of its success but because he wants to avoid further beating.
Similarly, to suppose that the beggar, money in hand, will

keep his theoretical promise is, to say the least, to beg the question. Rather than an exemplum of metaphoricity or the mirror of narcissistic self-projection, the scene enacts the violence that is implicit but repressed in social or Christian philanthropy. It is a challenge to social philanthropists as becomes especially clear if we put back the last line of the poem, omitted by the original publisher as being too *ad-hominem*, that is: "Qu'en dis-tu Proudhon?"

If, on one level, the scene exposes the violence that is stupefied by consumerism or that remains only as an expression in the humiliated beggar's eyes, on another level, its hyperbole, its use of the rhetoric of excess, takes that violence into another dimension. One might recall that what Baudelaire found wanting in Proudhon, as he wrote to Victor Hugo in 1858, was the excess inseparable from gallantry, chivalry, mysticism and heroism. The scene of urban violence is a *mise en scène* of the violence of ideology and the violence ideology would repress but it is also a hysterical farce, a comic caricature in which Baudelaire creates the linguistic parallel of the pantomime where mutilated and battered bodies are resurrected in moments of fantastic reversal. One recalls the pantomime Baudelaire describes in *L'Essence du rire* in which a very English Pierrot is involved in a farcical plot which culminates when his head rolls off at the foot of the guillotine but which he retrieves before he walks off the stage. The effect produced by this mime is what Baudelaire himself calls vertiginous hyperbole. The chiasmus, the change of places between the beggar and the narrator is part of this more general rhetorical figure of excess, the disruption of an aporctic impasse, by a figural madness. Thus the stupidity produced by consumerism, the impotent rage produced by poverty are exploded. Such transitions from what Baudelaire calls here the vertigo of stupor to excessive and manic or hysterical activity are commonplaces in his work, particularly in the *Tableaux parisiens* and the *Spleen de Paris*. Indeed, an excess of stupor is often the prelude to its opposite. To refer, once again, to *L'Essence du rire*, the ennui of everydayness is broken when the actors spit in their hands and rub them together as if to perform some great feat; indeed, in the pantomime a tumultuous destiny and great disasters await them but also the lightness of fantastic play and paradox.

Like Nietzsche and Freud, Baudelaire has generated extraordinary post-modernist readings, but *Assommons les pauvres* suggests that to dissolve all the elements of the text into a code of metaphoricity suppresses the difference between the fragmentation, fetishism and sadomasochistic violence of a specifically modern mode of economic, predominantly urban production, and the heterogeneity and mobility of metaphoric discourse. The figures used by Baudelaire, caricature, parody and hyperbole, all maintain a tension between a critique and a transformation.

Post-modernist readings of Baudelaire celebrate fragmentation and the scene of language as a mobile play of difference. It is not surprising that Benjamin's work on Baudelaire, with its exposure of historical discontinuity and the absence of totalization, with its emphasis on the arbitrary and the fragmentary, should now be especially illuminating. However, Benjamin always situates the reader, always situates his representation of Baudelaire within a specific frame of socio-economic transformation, and he resists the absorption of the city into the metaphoric totalization that often characterizes the work of his post-modernist descendants.

Within the different poetic modes of *Les Fleurs du Mal* Baudelaire sets up a play of contrasts between desire and its commodification. *Assommons les pauvres,* and the prose poems in general, submit the fragmented and violent images of the urban text to a caustic and ironic critique while at the same time initiating a carnivalesque transformation. Operating on both the levels of ideological exposure and aesthetic play, it is a far cry from the estheticizing of violence, that Benjamin himself identifies with the specifically modern and urban phenomenon of fascism.

NOTES

1. Walter Benjamin, *Charles Baudelaire: A Lyric Poet in the Era of High Capitalism,* translated by Harry Zohn (London: NLB, 1973).
2. Theodor Adorno, *Aesthetics and Politics,* (London: NLB, 1977), p. 129.
3. Eagleton, p. 53.
4. Barbara Johnson, *Défigurations du langage poétique,* (Paris: Flammarion, 1979).
5. Leo Bersani, *Baudelaire and Freud,* (Berkeley: University of California Press, 1977).
6. Jeffrey Mehlman, "Baudelaire with Freud/Theory and Pain," *Diacritics,* Spring 1974, pp. 7–13.
7. Bersani, p. 111.
8. Mehlman, p. 8.

FRAMING THE CITY: TWO PARISIAN WINDOWS

Christopher Prendergast

'Paris est Paris, voyez-vous' remarks the chief of police at the moment of unmasking the master criminal, Vautrin, in Balzac's *Le Père Goriot*.[1] It is significant that the remark is made by a policeman in a work that is in some ways an embryonic version of what will become the detective novel. The latter is, of course, not only a distinctively urban form; it also proposes a specific form of knowledge of the urban itself, predicated on the belief that an increasingly heterogeneous and intractable urban reality can be successfully monitored and mastered. Yet, although presented as an exemplary figure of knowledge, an expert in mapping and tracking the Parisian labyrinth, Balzac's policeman here in fact combines both power and impotence; at once full and empty, his tautology connotes knowledge but contains no information. The logical form of much writing about Paris (and cities generally) is like this; for those who truly understand the city, 'Paris' (or 'London' or 'New York', etc) is what goes without saying, either too obvious or too complex for anything other than the knowing or weary self-evidence of tautological statement.

What then does the city represent, and how to represent the city, to see it as form and 'identity' (in the double sense of giving identity to the city and finding identity in the city)? These were in fact pressing questions for many of the artists and writers of the nineteenth century, once the closed logic of the stereotype and the naturalising ideologies it served were challenged and dismantled. Since the stereotypes nevertheless remained active, and continue to do so, they are also questions for us, both in our own experience of the city and as we look back trying, with the requisite effort of historical imagination, to grasp the world of the nineteenth-century city. But to pose the questions thus risks resurrecting Balzac's fantasy of omnipotence and control, assuming privileged access to what lies 'behind' tautology and stereotype, to what, in the 'Avant-propos' to the *Comédie humaine* is called the 'sens caché' of the modern world. We might therefore wish to take the opposite view, that the city lies beyond intelligibility and workable forms of representation; that, like Newman's city (cited here by Gerhard Joseph), the city is that for which we 'have no map'. But this too is problematic: the proposition that the city defies understanding is also a stereotype; it will be strongly naturalised in urban writing and painting in late nineteenth-century

France, and is arguably linked to ideological interests wishing the understandable (orders of power and systems of control) to remain non-understood. Alternatively, we can adopt a resolutely pluralistic approach—that of multiplying critical perspectives within a multiplicity of given perspectives, a juxtaposition, and often a clash, of representations. One image for this way of investigating images of the urban could be Henry James's figure for the relation between fiction and the world: the image of the window. Since we are dealing with a field of representations, taken from an archive so large as to be potentially unmanageable, it would seem that the only way to conduct an enterprise of this sort is by way of a more or less improvised eclecticism—that is, in the spirit of an analogy between the diverse imaginings of the city and James's house of fiction with its many windows. James's pluralistic figure moreover suggests both a model and a further metaphor (or rather a mixture of the literal and the figurative), whereby one moves about the house and its variegated views in the form of a series of urban walks. This is the model based on that characteristic denizen of the literature of nineteenth-century Paris, the *flâneur*, and the corresponding notion of the city as a special kind of visual and social space, peculiarly open to the random gaze and the unforeseen encounter.

The present volume accordingly supplies us with many points of view and takes us to many places, both geographical and theoretical. But if, in its rehearsal of both subject matter and sources, the book is appropriately construed as an open-ended series of windows on and trajectories through forms of urban experience, nevertheless a strategy of free-wheeling methodological eclecticism also carries serious intellectual risks. The attractions of the eclectic and the aleatory are considerable (particularly to fans of the postmodern city), but they can also serve to mask important difficulties of interpretation embedded in the material under consideration itself. The convenience of approaching the latter on the analogy of a stroll through the varied rooms of the house of the city is simply too convenient, and may well end by recapitulating one of the major ideological moves of the modern urban imagination—occlusion of the question who is *master* of the house in favor of the idea of the city as a 'free field'[2] of stimulus and adventure for the relaxed and skillful connoisseur.

For, as a centrally active theme in nineteenth-century literature, the category of *flânerie* is problematical as well as enabling, especially in the complex moves and tensions of Baudelaire's writings. This of course is the great lesson of Benjamin, and Benjamin's *Charles Baudelaire: A Lyric Poet in the Era of High Capitalism* figures as a prominent and recurring reference in the pages of this book. The Paris Benjamin was concerned with is the Paris he describes as the 'capital of the nineteenth century'. By capital of the nineteenth century he meant that in the developing forms of life exemplified by Paris we see some of the distinctive features of 'modernity' in general and their complex, unsettling effects on both society and the psyche. Benjamin's strategy was that of the micrology, the close-up focus on a specific phenomenon, the nineteenth-century arcades, but with a view to uncovering a more general social and cultural logic. The arcade is posed as the site and perfect emblem of the emergence of the culture of the 'commodity', a culture of movement and dislocation in which the eye and the mind are increasingly solicited by an unprecedented range of stimuli. It is the world adumbrated by Balzac in the image of a ceaseless 'turning', what in *Illusions perdues* Lucien de Rubempré, newly arrived in the capital, experiences as 'la rapidité du tournoiement parisien',[3] a mobile, swirling landscape dominated by chance encounter, fast transaction, frenetic circulation of money, goods and bodies. Speed, as Benjamin reminds us, is the fundamental condition of the new commodity culture. And this will not only have profound effects on ways of life, undermining notions of 'tradition' and 'community', or, as Benjamin's German puts it, removing from the immediacy of *Erlebnis* the sanctioning framework of *Erfahrung*.[4] It will also implicate the fate of art, both practically through its growing incorporation into the market, and formally in the development of an art more and more committed to the registration of the sudden *aperçu*, mobile point of view and fugitive sensation. Although one must of course resist the reductive schemes of causal explanation associated with a naive base/superstructure account of culture and society, Benjamin's claim seems entirely persuasive: that the sense of the city as an increasingly uncertain and unpredictable perceptual field is a crucial determinant in the emergence of an art geared to an entirely new set of rhythms, an art based on the principles of surprise and 'shock', disruption and displacement of any assumption of a coherent 'center' to experience—whether in the 'snap-shot' technique of later nineteenth-century verse poetry, the jerky, nervous registers of the prose poem, the fluctuating and disintegrative rhythms of the novel after Flaubert.

Benjamin himself, in his work on Baudelaire, the surrealists and in his own autobiographical essays, prowled ambivalently around these developments, as a kind of *rôdeur* sniffing out what was evasive and problematical in the stance of the *flâneur*. But one thing he remained permanently alert to, as part of the seductive myth-making of a certain version of 'modernism', is what Alfred Kazin in his contribution points out (precisely in connection

with Henry James on the subject of New York): that the logical
terminus of literary (and a fortiori scholarly) *flânerie* is the construction of the city as esthetic object ('The city becomes an esthetic object when you become totally fascinated by the energy
and the multifariousness of the surface . . . '). The notion of the
city as providing a happy space for mobile reverie simply edits
out fundamental constituents and determinations of the object
under investigation. The point has moreover acquired a certain
urgency in the light of the new revisionist politics of urban histo-
riography, as represented, for example, by Donald Olsen's recent, and widely praised book, *The City as a Work of Art*. Olsen
explicitly excludes from his purview what he calls urban history
as 'social pathology'.[5] The terms of the excluded are themselves
interesting—they reproduce a stock nineteenth-century figure, in
the reduction of manmade forms of urban misery to the medica-
lised vocabulary of illness and disease. But, more important, no
sooner is the reduction effected than it is despatched to the waste
paper basket of history. Reduced and then removed, what might
otherwise obstruct the 'vista' of the estheticist historian is conveniently forgotten so as to allow the field to be exclusively occupied by a cultural and ideological fiction: the city as a work of art.
Not surprisingly, Paris, on this view, becomes, along with imperial London and Vienna, 'a privilege to inhabit', and 'the embodiment of nineteenth-century urban civilization, a realized ideal'.[6]
But *whose* privilege, an ideal realized for whom? Clearly so for
the property speculator, the genteel resident and the well-to-do
tourist (whose perspective, quite literally at the level of quoted
sources, is consistently adopted by Olsen, in marked contrast to
his contempt for major literary testimony; Dickens's London is
dismissed as 'false image' and 'perverse vision'[7]); but scarcely so
for the ragpicker, the beggar and the slum dweller. Commenting
on Haussmann's provision of public parks, Olsen quotes with evident approval the astonishing remark of a contemporary observer: 'Paris has been developing into Arcadia . . . '.[8] We know
what happens in a great deal of nineteenth-century literature and
painting to the attempted importation of pastoral imagery into
representations of the city, its ironic cancellation in the novels of
Balzac and Zola, the poetry of Baudelaire and Laforgue, the
paintings of Manet and Seurat. Certainly, the notion that the
park functioned as a space for the bucolic fraternizing of all Parisians, suspending the frictions and divisions of social hierarchy
and class conflict, could be dismissed as simply laughable, were
it not that it is also symptomatic of the terms and tone of the
revisionist approach in general. It gives one very good reason
why Olsen's endorsement of the imagery of rural arcadia is ap-

propriately met and challenged by the implications of Benjamin's urban arcades. The arcade moreover, as an early form of the shopping center, returns us to the image with which I began, the image of the window. One way of unstitching the kinds of fiction bound up with the estheticist reading of urban history and culture might then be by problematising that particular image, or rather by considering the ways in which some major nineteenth-century writers themselves both deployed and problematised it.

As the wild, hallucinatory itinerary through nocturnal Paris of Lautréamont's poem-novel, *Les Chants de Maldoror*, reaches its climax, we are, bizarrely, invited for a moment to window-shop: 'Les magasins de la rue Vivienne étalent leurs richesses aux yeux émerveillés. Eclairés par de nombreux becs de gaz, les coffrets d'acajou et les montres en or répandent à travers les vitrines les gerbes de lumière éblouissante'.[9] We are not however dazzled for long. Abruptly, the lights go out, not just the shop lights, but all the lights of the city, in dramatic and ironic negation of a recurring nineteenth-century theme—Paris as 'spectacle'. The idea of Paris as an endless adventure and feast for the eyes, a vast and inexhaustibly interesting catalogue of *choses vues* (in the title of Hugo's collection of note-books), is basic to the more optimistic side of the nineteenth-century urban imagination. Spectacle, in this context, meant several things, but it was rarely far from the fascination with the commodity. Indeed the presence of light itself, both natural and artificial (at first the gas lamps, later electric light) came to be seen as one of the most precious commodities in the increasingly commodified culture of the city. The provision of ever more lighting in public places was one of Haussmann's more cherished ambitions in the project of transforming a dark and dangerous *vieux Paris* into a fully spectacularised and efficiently policed center of Imperial civilization. In the 1830s gaslight was a novelty; by the 1850s 3000 new gas lamps had been installed on the streets, along with the practice of all-night lighting.[10] On its public surface Paris seemed altered beyond recognition, supplying at once the promise of excitement and the reassurance of security, as the place where it was safe to look at, and for, what you wanted. More lights meant more tourists and less crime; it also meant better value for money (the prostitutes could—in theory—be seen with greater clarity). In more allegorical mode, the public provision of light represented a triumph over social and cultural 'darkness'; light meant *lumières* in more than one sense; the project of the illuminated city became cognate with the idea of the enlightened city.[11] The urban

experiment with light generated a whole minor literature, from
the learned monograph and inspector's report to that specialised
version of the memoir and the guide-book, the observations and
musings of the nocturnal *flâneur*. It also entered decisively into
the inspiration of many of the major forms of nineteenth-century
art and literature. At the end of the century, the Symbolist poet
Gustave Kahn will describe the lights of the Parisian street as
producing a veritable symphony of polychromatic colour: 'La rue
actuelle, la Polychromie de la rue par les couleurs de façades, les
affiches et les lumières'.[12] This account, of course, rehearses the
terms of Impressionism, the conjunction of the urban theme and
the techniques of *plein-air* around the Impressionist painters' interest in the play of light. The famous street scenes of Monet,
Pissarro and Renoir emphasise airiness and luminosity, the
blending of natural and artificial light, often in contexts celebrating urban sociability and festivity (as, for example, in Pissarro's
Boulevard Montmartre. La Nuit, where the street lights are represented as twinkling star lights). This search for the lyric tone,
however, was not the only response. Manet's great painting, the
Rue Mosnier. Les Paveurs, is great because of the way the lyric harmony of its representation of light is checked, and challenged, by
its representation of urban labour in the foreground of the picture; whatever the light means to the 'paveurs', it is not as an
object of aesthetic pleasure or as focus of pastoral fantasy. Similarly the brilliant electric light shed on the scene of *Un Bar aux
Folies-Bergère*, with its glittering reflections in the mirror behind
the counter, is refused all connotation of innocent conviviality by
virtue of the complete absence of light in the neutral, distancing
gaze of the serving girl's eyes.[13] Manet's pictorial ironies and dis-
sonances also have their poetic equivalent in Baudelaire, for example, in his macabre, ironic version of that traditional poetic
topos, dawn over the city. In 'Crépuscule du matin', we are a
long way from the purifying and unifying light that comes with
daybreak over Wordsworth's London in 'Westminster Bridge'.
The natural light that appears over Baudelaire's Paris is from the
start poisoned by its passage through the artificial light of the gas
lamps, the light of Evil rendered in the dramatically violent image of the bleeding eye ('Où, comme un oeil sanglant qui palpite
et qui bouge / La lampe sur le jour fait une tache rouge'.[14])

Light (and its absence) clearly meant different things to different people. It depended of course on where exactly you went,
and, more importantly, where exactly you lived. Many of the urban poor saw very little of it, especially the natural sort. As the
contemporary reports of Villermé and others make clear, the cellars and ground floor dwellings in the narrow streets inhabited

by the destitute of the city rarely, if ever, saw the light of day, and in the descriptive literature regularly produced the analogy of an 'underground' population resembling a race of primeval cave dwellers.[15] It is not surprising that the painters of modern life do not, to my knowledge, seek to represent the typical interiors of the urban poor. They furnish little or no possibility for the effect of sunlight pouring through the window into enclosed domestic space that is the hallmark of the seventeenth-century Dutch painters (famously, Vermeers's "patch of yellow") rediscovered in the later nineteenth century. Without light, painting has nowhere to go, especially when the commitment is to the methods of *plein-air*. Literature, on the other hand, will take us there, notably in the descriptions of the urban slum in the novels of Hugo, Sue and, later, Zola. The physical absence of light will moreover generate a counter-symbolism of protest. In Hugo the theme of light will be the focus of an intertwining of republican ideology and Christian eschatology serving a vision of social and spiritual 're-demption'. Light, both literal and figurative, will also play a part in the utopian imagining of the alternative city as the site of progress and justice—from, say, Fourier's dream of the future *cité ouvrière* to the prophetic visions of urban harmony in Zola's late novel, *Paris*.

But, in terms of urban actuality, the essential preoccupation remained with light in its artificial rather than its natural or symbolic forms. The lights of the city are linked to the lure of the city, the beckoning signs of what is deceptively promised by the new and fast growing leisure and pleasure culture. Paris as illuminated 'spectacle' is Paris offered for consumption, and nowhere, of course, did gas and electric lighting more directly contribute to the function of the city as dream-machine than in the glitter it conferred on the commodity. This took the form of both private and public display. The ostentatiously lighted interiors of Balzac's Birotteau and Crevel signify, awkwardly and crudely, the acquisition of wealth, as will later the invention of electroplating, designed to give a fake aura of luxury to the household utensils of the bourgeoisie.[16] These were attempts at 'spectacle' on a small scale, enclosed and privatised. Its more dramatic manifestations occurred in public space—in the construction of those super-windows on the commodity, the huge glass edifices of the Exposition Universelle, or in the exploitation of the large shop window in the new department store during the Second Empire. Boucicaut, the inventor of the *Bon Marché*, quickly grasped the commercial advantages of saturating merchandise with all manner of lighting, subtle or strong. The introduction of sheet glass and electric lighting for the ground floor displays not only enticed potential purchasers (mainly women) into the store; it made window-shopping along the boulevards a standard form of Parisian *flânerie*. The lighting systems of the boulevards and the department stores instituted a whole new relation between the gaze and the commodity, the spectacularising and fetichising relation bound up with what Rachel Bowlby has called 'just looking'.[17]

The new systems appear to have entranced nearly everyone, including critics from the Left. An index of their power over the urban imagination is given by the response of none other than that fiercest of critics of contemporary capitalism, Jules Vallès. Here is Vallès's Aladdin's cave version of the city lights:

> Pas une ville au monde n'offre le spectacle de ces boulevards parisiens, surtout à certaines heures. Le soir, quand le gaz s'allume, quand théâtres, cafés-concerts, grands bazars, estaminets dorés ou pauvres, allument leurs enseignes et leurs candelabres, quand les fenêtres des grands cercles flambent, quand sur le pavé les trainées d'électricité font comme des rivières d'argent, qui parlera des *a giorno* de Venise et des illuminations de l'Orient![18]

And specifically on the windows of the department store:

> Toute l'actualité frissonne le long de ces tonnelles de verre, bariolées de réclames joyeuses.[19]

An important term in this description is the word *bariolées*. It is difficult to translate, but broadly connotes a multiple and mobile play of colour. It is a key term in the perceptual vocabulary of the later nineteenth-century literary equivalents of Impressionism, from Rimbaud to Zola, and a complex nodal word in the representational economy of the nineteenth-century urban imagination. In Rimbaud's prose poetry (for example, 'Nocturne vulgaire') it is linked to the experience of perceptual unhinging bound up with the programme of systematic 'dérèglement' of the illusion of the integrated ego. In Zola, on the other hand, a characteristic, though by no means exclusive, context for the term is commercial, notably in the novel of the department store, *Au Bonheur des Dames*, where it designates the swirl of perception and desire around the 'colorful' article for sale. Similarly, the exciting *bariolage* of Vallès's window displays marks one of the disturbing points at which commerce and art cross in the modern city, and provides one of the contexts for Lautréamont's spectacular annihilation of spectacle when the lights go out in *Les Chants de Maldoror*. Lautréamont's window darkens and disappears, and with it the arresting power of the commodities it displays. But let us now consider, in more detail, what happens to spectacle with, or through, two other literary windows, in Baudelaire's prose poem, 'Les Yeux des Pauvres' and Zola's novel, *La Curée*.

Baudelaire is fascinated by the urban window, almost as much as he is by the human eye (indeed in one of the verse poems, the former becomes a figure for the latter ('Tes yeux, illuminés comme des boutiques'[20]). The window, whether of the private dwelling or the shop, is a key staging-post in the itinerary of the Baudelairean *flâneur*. One of the earliest entries in the notebooks which record Baudelaire's self-imposed exile from 1864 in the detested Brussels laments the absence of a supreme Parisian pleasure—'La flânerie devant les boutiques, cette jouissance'.[21] The window, like the eye, is an invitation to a journey, a voyage of the imagination. In 'Les Fenêtres'[22] the act of looking through a candlelit window from the street generates a veritable proliferation of some of the major terms of Baudelaire's poetic lexicon: 'Il n'est pas d'objet plus profond, plus mystérieux, plus fécond, plus ténébreux, plus éblouissant qu'une fenêtre éclairée d'une chandelle'. The window is fertile ('fécond') in that it opens a space for the productivity of the imagination, supplies a passage from vision into reverie and a release from self into otherness.

Yet the assumed fertility of the encounter between poet's gaze and window proves to be potentially deceptive, and is hedged about in the text by various uncertainties. Through another window, seen from a distance in the rooftops of Paris, the poet glimpses a woman, poor and aging ('une femme mûre, ridée déjà, pauvre'), The poet constructs a whole life behind the window, the sad 'story' of the woman: 'Avec son visage, avec son vêtement, avec son geste, avec presque rien j'ai refait l'histoire de cette femme, ou plutôt sa légende, et quelquefois je me la raconte à moi-même en pleurant'. But in its concluding moment the poem turns against and equivocates its own expansive imaginative claims. The 'story' appears ultimately as self-referring rather than other-referring, and the glass pane less a window than a mirror reflecting back not the 'truth' of the other, but an enabling fiction for the self: 'Peut-être me direz-vous: "Es-tu sûr que cette légende soit la vraie?". Que m'importe ce que peutêtre la réalité placée hors de moi, si elle m'a aidé à vivre, à sentir que je suis et ce que je suis?' Baudelaire here says that the collapsing of other into self, of story into fiction ('légende') does not matter ('Que m'importe') But of course it matters; knowledge of the (ethical) distinction between self and other is as important as knowing the distinction (cognitive) between what, in 'La Corde' is called 'illusion' and 'le fait tel qu'il existe en dehors de nous'.[23] The concluding declaration of the poem thus seems more a piece of rhetorical bravado masking an anxiety and a failure—the failure to pass through the window, to connect the inward imperatives of the imagination with the outward forms of the real.

'Les Fenêtres' tells us, then, of the ambivalent and unstable relation between self and other in Baudelaire's city poetry, and in particular of those critical moments of resistance and breakdown experienced by the Baudelairean psyche in its efforts to project out into the alien flux of contemporary urban life. The gaze through the window is but one inflection of this complex psychic and social drama. It is, however, a privileged one, in that it directly implicates the figure of the poet himself and the very act of writing poetry about, or against, the city. The window may invite a fertile transaction between the poet and the city, but more often it serves to open up a gap between subject and object, to bring about clivage rather than communication. This is the scene of Baudelaire's great prose poem, 'Les Yeux des Pauvres'.[24] The setting of 'Les Yeux des Pauvres' is a cafe on one of Haussmann's new boulevards still in process of construction ('un café neuf qui formait le coin d'un boulevard neuf, encore tout plein de gravois et montrant déjà ses splendeurs inachevées'). Through the window the two protagonists of the poem—the poet and his beloved—are drawn to the dazzling lights and decorations of the cafe's interior:

> Le café étincelait. Le gaz lui-même y déployait toute l'ardeur d'un début, et éclairait de toutes ses forces les murs aveuglants de blancheur, les nappes éblouissantes des miroirs, les ors des baguettes et des corniches, les pages aux joues rebondies trainés par les chiens en laisse, les dames riant au faucon perché sur leur poing, les nymphes et les déesses portant sur leur tête des fruits, des pâtés et du gibier, les Hébés et les Ganymèdes présentant à bras tendu la petite amphore à bavaroises ou l'obélisque bicolore des glaces panachées; toute l'histoire et toute la mythologie mises au service de la goinfrerie.

In its accumulation of the fake, the vulgar and the incoherent, this proliferating description is reminiscent of Flaubert's account of the grotesque structure of Emma Bovary's wedding cake. Like Flaubert's cake, this too is pure confection, a spectacle proposed literally for consumption ('goinfrerie'), both physical and emotional. What is seen through the window is the dream-machine in action, presenting the terms on which the city entices into a fantasy of comfort, luxury and gratification. More specifically here, the café offers an equivalent of the decor of the edenesque love affair, the recovery through urban artifices of a paradisiac image of lovers' happiness; the café scene prolongs a previously formed illusion of communion and harmony ('Nous nous étions bien promis que toutes nos pensées nous seraient communes à l'un et à l'autre, et que nos deux âmes désormais n'en feraient plus qu'une . . . ').

Abruptly, however, the illusion snaps, in a characteristic instance of the Baudelairean tactic of poetic 'shock'. The text works structurally as a kind of extended zeugma, the incongruous yoking of clashing worlds: on the one hand, the self-absorbed world of the lovers, on the other hand, an intruding public world. Suddenly, the lovers become aware of the presence on the pavement of a poor family, a father and his two children, all in rags ('tous en guenilles'), looking in mute amazement through the café window:

> Droit devant nous, sur la chaussée, était planté un brave homme d'une quarantaine d'années, au visage fatigué, à la barbe grisonnante, tenant d'une main un petit garçon et portant sur l'autre bras un petit être trop faible pour marcher. Il remplissait l'office de bonne et faisait prendre à ses enfants l'air du soir. Tous en guenilles. Ces trois visages étaient extraordinairement sérieux, et ces six yeux contemplaient fixement le café nouveau avec une admiration égale, mais nuancée diversement par l'âge.

This, in another idiom, is again Paris as 'spectacle', but no longer from the point of view of the consumer or the happy *flâneur*. What the eyes of the poor see, and what they say, is that the poor are excluded, that spectacle and the pleasures it promises are a matter of class. They do not say this insistently: Baudelaire's text does not, either here or elsewhere in the prose poems, deal in a polemically contrived image of 'class', but in the brute reality of class, simply there, obdurate, intractable, as that which will not go away. The poor do not protest, they disrupt by virtue of their sheer presence. In particular, their stupefied gaze distracts, and destroys, the mutually communicating gaze of the lovers. Understanding becomes conflict, harmony is converted into dissonance. Confronted with the poor, the poet feels uncomfortable, guilty, moved to humanitarian sentiment ('attendri par cette famille d'yeux . . . un peu honteux de nos verres et de nos carafes, plus grands que notre soif'). He looks into his partner's eyes for signs that his own stirring of conscience is shared, but is immediately repulsed: 'Ces gens-là me sont insupportables avec leurs yeux ouverts comme des portes cochères! Ne pourriez-vous pas prier le maître du café de les éloigner d'ici?'.

The twin motifs of the window and the gaze have by now acquired quite different connotations. For the lovers the window initially frames a scene of urban pastoral[25]; for the poor it is a barrier. From the clash of those two sets of meanings, the relations of looking and seeing *issue* in a splintering of the images the poetic subject wishes to find and have confirmed. For the lover, the eyes of his mistress refuse reciprocity. For the woman, the eyes of the poor usurp what is not properly theirs; in the revealing comparison of the eyes with the 'portes cochères', they belong where servants and tradesmen belong, at the margin and behind the scenes, in the area of both the un-seen and the non-seeing. The poem ends with one of Baudelaire's typically deceptive maxims, secure in the inherited authority of its form, but ambiguous as to its exact target: 'Tant il est difficile de s'entendre, mon cher ange, et tant la pensée est incommunicable même entre gens qui s'aiment'. This is not just another piece of Baudelairean misogyny, the scarcely veiled violence of aggressive feeling directed towards the feminine (what at the beginning of the poem is called 'l'imperméabilité féminine'). It is, of course, a poem about the life and death of desire, the transformation of love into hate. But its psychological concerns are inseparable from its social concerns. The woman's callousness has a precise ironic function in relation to the poem's wider theme of social division. It undoes one of the great fictions of Second Empire Paris: that the culture of the boulevard has been fully democratised, and that the city of pleasure is available to all. In her heartless way, the woman says it how it is, that the poor have no place where the lovers are; and, if the man comes to hate her, it is because her words expose the bad faith involved in trying to combine incompatibles—physical and emotional well-being with a good conscience.

There is here, then, a politics of urban pleasure and pain, traced out in the fractured intimacy of a personal exchange. While it is doubtless excessively reductive to see in the reactions of the man and the woman a representation of political positions (the man standing for the 'liberal left' and the woman for 'the right, the Party of Order'[26]), it is quite wrong to say that this poem evades and defuses the politics of class by displacing attention away from the situation of the poor on to a lovers' private quarrel.[27] The point is precisely their conjunction. In his city poetry, Baudelaire is the great artist of the intermeshing of the public and the private, those moments at which the most delicate kinds of personal feeling—generally the sexual—are deeply affected and mediated by the social history of the city as a whole. The window of 'Les Yeux des Pauvres' is a site of exactly that kind of mediation.

The other window on nineteenth-century Paris I want to look at, or through, is from a passage in that remarkable novel of appropriations and expropriations (from real estate to bodies), Zola's *La Curée*.[28] Like Baudelaire's, Zola's window involves a café scene, a pair of lovers and a problematic construction of 'spectacle': it is the window of the private dining room in the café Riche, through which the semi-incestuous lovers, Renée and Maxime, look out on to the boulevard below. What initially they see, or rather what initially is presented through their point of view is, in the terms of Zola's more elaborate and detailed prose, a version of Vallès's account of the city lights as evoking a kind of magical fairyland (later in the passage, the play of light and colour is described as 'tohu-bohu féerique'): the exotic comparison of the newspaper kiosks with the Venetian lanterns, and its further qualification by the important adjective 'bariolées'; the blaze of the gas lamps on the café tables; the perceptual trick whereby the night lights of the shop fronts create the illusion of daylight. But if Zola's own discourse here recapitulates the myth of the illuminated city, it also distances and ambiguates the myth by relativising the perspective on the boulevard to a specific point of view—initially, that of the two lovers, and, in the subsequent development of the passage, the trajectory of Renée's gaze. What we are invited to notice is essentially what she notices ('Renée remarqua' . . . 'la jeune femme les suivait du regard' . . . 'Renée crut' . . . 'Elle entendait'; . . . 'Elle s'arrêta aux annonces d'un kiosque' . . .). Renée's way of looking at the boulevard is interested, mobile, it flickers from one object to the next, but at the same time it is blanked out, detached from the flow of life it witnesses.

This marks an important difference from Baudelaire's method. In Baudelaire's poem, looking in and at the city is revealed as a dangerous business: the eye has to be on its guard, constantly wary, screening out unwelcome information, and yet permanently vulnerable to sudden interventions in a visual field it cannot ultimately control. One way of putting this might be to talk of a tension in Baudelaire between the gaze and the glance.[29] The gaze, fixating and fetishising, seeks to hold the objects of the urban environment in a safe relation to the subject's desires, to confer meaning and 'depth' on the appropriated visual material. The glance entails a quite different kind of attention to the life of the city; it picks up on what the gaze excludes, restores the primacy of the ever-changing surface over the illusion of depth, permits the random irruption of the real into the otherwise censored space of vision. The enactment of this tension is moreover naturally suited to the medium of the prose poem: its economy and speed make for abrupt and ironic switches of thematic direction, forms of ellipsis through which the unexpected suddenly comes into focus (in 'Les Yeux des Pauvres', the poor are brought into view without narrative warning, in the elliptical movement between the end of one paragraph and the beginning of the next).

Zola's text also has its strategies for the ironic undoing of the settled gaze, the perspective of mastery on the city. But, because it is a novel, these work more by processes of accumulation and delay than by unanticipated local reversals of perception. Renée's encounter with the boulevard does not run the same risks as those experienced by Baudelaire's lovers. The latter are on the pavement, sitting on the café terrace, uncomfortably close to the action of the street. Renée is inside, and moreover high up; from the refuge of the private dining room (refuge not only of illicit lovers, but also of the rich), the window supplies access to 'spectacle', but also protects and innures against what might be demanding or threatening in the spectacle. What Renée sees is at once a lot and a little. Her eyes take in the whole of the boulevard from one end to the other ('allant d'un bout du boulevard à l'autre'); she notices the kiosks, the shop windows, the cafe tables, the drinkers, the pedestrians, the omnibus, the ticket collector, the hatter's advertisement. But, if she is passively receptive to diverse bits of information, it is information neutralised in the relative indifference of her gaze. Intensely present to the eye, the bright and mobile forms of the city finally produce a 'blur' in the consciousness of the observer, merge into the condition of the indistinct and the undifferentiated: the further reaches of the avenue appear as 'tumultueux et confus'; the crowd of pedestrians becomes an anonymous swirl, a black swarm ('un grouillement noir'), a crowd without identity-distinctions ('étrangement mêlé, et toujours le même'); and then, in the gathering of people at the omnibus station, a collection of mechanical dolls ('l'éternelle procession de petites poupées mécaniques'). Renée's gaze, a sequence of largely disconnected observations, has no way of making sense of the artifacts and forms of life it meets; as information, it does not pass into reflection, translate into knowledge. If this is Paris as 'spectacle', it is also Paris effectively derealized, seen as in a dream, resistant to sense. In the sequence, there is no point of purchase from which the eye might construct a meaningful whole. All the gaze can do is to focus momentarily on contingent particulars, and then move on, as in the shift of attention from the omnibus station to the hatter's advertisement ('qu'elle ne comprit pas').

Renée's gaze, we might want to say, announces or prefigures the alienated perspective of 'modernity', the existentially estranged viewpoint on the city characteristic of a great deal of twentieth-century literature. On the other hand—and this is surely the point of Zola's text—the conditions of Renée's estrangement are socially specific, the privilege of wealth and class, alienation *tout confort*. What the view from the Café Riche tells us is that being released from the demands of sense-making is a luxury. And, although the blur in Renée's perceptions necessarily implicates the prose which dramatises her point of view, it does not entirely obliterate its potential critical force. Zola distinguishes himself from Renée precisely by sustaining distinctions and oppositions which her way of looking tends to collapse. He recovers sense from blur by way of essentially three contrasts. In the first place, the brightness of the lights may suggest a fairyland, but it also serves to throw into relief the exhausted pallor on the faces of the people who actually live and work in the city ('et c'était surtout au centre de cet ardent foyer qu'ils voyaient les faces blêmes et les rires pâles des passants'). The contrast turns again on questions of class and money. This is further accentuated by a more specific contrast at the level of sex: in the teeming crowd, what Renée particularly notices are the women, especially the prostitutes plying their trade and taking a drink. (In other circumstances they would not be seen at all; one of the interesting features of the social history of the Parisian window is that, whereas it was crucial to the soliciting force of one sort of commodity (in the shops), it was proposed to ban it for the display of the sexual sort; according to the recommended regulations for the policing of prostitution, 'the windows of a brothel under police supervision must remain closed'.[30]) But, although the sight of the women 'interests' Renée ('elles intéressaient'), it does not really engage her. The window thus intersects another division: between inside and outside, the elegant woman in the dining room and the women who belong to the street, *les filles*, wearing 'showy dresses' and 'making loud remarks'; or the woman sitting alone, in her dress garnished with white *guipure*, sipping a glass of beer 'd'un air d'attente lourde et résignée', reminiscent of the crushed and vacant look on the face of Degas's absinthe drinker or those of the waitresses, shop-girls and prostitutes in Manet's bar pictures. Thirdly, there is the extraordinary closing moment of the passage when, as the omnibus passes the café, inside and outside briefly meet through the window, in a strange reversal of the terms of 'spectacle': the men on the omnibus raise their tired faces, 'et les regardaient, elle et Maxime, du regard curieux des affamés mettant l'oeil à la serrure'—the look of the famished briefly turned on the well-fed, the voyeurism of the poor, the window as social keyhole.

Zola's way with the window on the world of the city replays in microcosm a central ambiguity in nineteenth-century representations of the city, especially those of the later nineteenth-century. Through Renée's point of view there is staged a loss of the perspective of meaning; Renée's gaze is not one that can hold the diverse aspects of the urban scene in clear and coherent focus. This implies a particular version of the city: that it is too fluid and amorphous to be reduced to the sets of oppositions and distinctions from which meaning is produced; there are so many differences (particulars, contingencies, 'individuals') that Difference no longer counts for much; the heterogeneous proliferates, but at the same time is absorbed into the homogeneous, the 'black swarm' of the faceless crowd (arguably like the dots and blobs to which the urban population is reduced in Monet's views over the Boulevard des Capucines). On the other hand, the text also places Renée's view, shows that removal of the perspective of sense and the principle of differentiation is accomplished at a price. If the construction of an intelligible, discriminating image confers an 'identity' on the city by shutting out the anomalies which threaten the coherence of that image, then not making sense also involves a shutting out; the view of the city as unintelligible, as having *no* distinct identity, conveniently overlooks what Zola's text does not here forget: that, behind the abstract faces in the deceptively uniform crowd ('strangely mixed and always alike'), there are important distinctions, and that to represent the city as a perceptual blur is to lose sight of real social structures of difference and division, presumably only too clear to those who, as rich and poor, elegant and vulgar, hungry and replete, inhabited different points within them.[31] Along with Baudelaire's prose poem, it not only reminds us of some of the things crucially involved in 'knowing any real city' (the phrase with which this collection of essays is inaugurated). Together these two texts also frame, or are framed by, the category of the 'knowable' as such, thus returning us to another point of departure of the collection: Mary Ann Caws's opening references to the seminal work of Raymond Williams, and in particular his crucial emphasis—against the grain of certain currently fashionable orthodoxies—on thinking the city as indeed knowable, or rather as knowledge always to be struggled for (both intellectually and politically) in that complex relation of 'the random and the systematic, the visible and the obscured which is the true significance of the city [. . .] as a dominant social form'.[32]

NOTES

1. Honoré de Balzac, *Le Père Goriot*, Classiques Garnier, Paris, 1963, p. 212.

2. T. J. Clark, *The Painting of Modern Life. Paris in the Art of Manet and his Followers*, London, 1985, p. 68.
3. Balzac, *Illusions perdues*, Classiques Garnier, Paris, 1961, p. 171.
4. Walter Benjamin, 'On Some Motifs in Baudelaire', *Illuminations*, New York, 1969, p. 163.
5. Donald Olsen, *The City as a Work of Art*, New Haven and London, 1986.
6. ibid. pp. 5, 44.
7. ibid. p. 23.
8. ibid. p. 232.
9. Lautréamont, *Les Chants de Maldoror*, Livre de poche, Paris, 1963, p. 320.
10. David Pinkney, *Napoleon III and the Re-Building of Paris*, Princeton, 1958, p. 72.
11. On the crossing of the themes of light and enlightenment in connection with the history of the modern city, cf. Raymond Williams, *The Country and the City*, London, 1985, ch. 19.
12. Gustave Kahn, *Esthétique de la rue*, Paris, 1901, p. 205.
13. For a full discussion of the *Bar* picture, cf. T. J. Clark, op. cit. pp. 205–258.
14. Charles Baudelaire, *Les Fleurs du Mal*, Pléiade, Paris, 1961, p. 99. All further references to Baudelaire's writings are to this edition.
15. cf. W. H. Sewell, *Work and Revolution in France. The Language of Labor from the Old Regime to 1848*, Cambridge, 1980.
16. S. Kracauer, *Offenbach and the Paris of his Time*, London, 1937, p. 58.
17. Rachel Bowlby, *Just Looking: Consumer culture in Dreiser, Gissing and Zola*, New York, 1985.
18. Jules Vallès, *Le Tableau de Paris*, Oeuvres complètes, Vol. 13, 1971, p. 54.
19. ibid. p. 55.
20. Baudelaire, *Les Fleurs du Mal*, p. 26.
21. Baudelaire, *Sur la Belgique*, p. 1325.
22. Baudelaire, *Le Spleen de Paris*, p. 288.
23. ibid. p. 278.
24. ibid. pp. 268–269.
25. For a discussion of Baudelaire in terms of the concept of 'pastoral', cf. Marshall Berman, *All That Is Solid Melts Into Air*, New York, 1982, pp. 134 ff.
26. This is the only point on which I would disagree with Berman's impressive account of this poem, op. cit. p. 154.
27. Richard Terdiman, *Discourse/counter-discourse*, Ithaca and London, 1985, p. 317. For similar views, cf. also Jonathan Monroe, *A Poverty of Objects. The Prose Poem and the Politics of Genre*, Ithica and London, 1987.
28. Emile Zola, *La Curée*, Pléiade Vol. 1, Paris, 1960, pp. 449–451.
29. cf. Michael Riffaterre's distinction between the 'code-regard' and the 'code-coup d'oeil', *Essais de stylistique structurale*, Paris, 1971, p. 362.
30. Alain Corbin, 'Commercial Sexuality in Nineteenth-Century France: A System of Images and Regulations', *Representations*, 20, 1986.
31. cf. T. J. Clark, op. cit. p. 49: 'It is one thing to argue that the city lacks intelligible *form*, and has no coherence to speak of; it is quite another to say that it lacks *order*, that it is uncontrolled or classless.' Raymond Williams makes the same point about nineteenth-century London: '[the] miscellaneity and randomness embodies a system: a negative system of indifference; a positive system of differentiation, in law, power and financial control [. . .] For what London had to show [. . .] was a contradiction, a paradox: the coexistence of variation and apparent randomness with what in the end had to be seen as a determining system: the visible individual facts but beyond them, often hidden, the common condition and destiny', op. cit. p. 154.
32. Raymond Williams, ibid. p. 154.

Snark/Art Resource, S19480. Turn of the century photo: Distribution of free coffee on the Bowery, New York.

6

CLAIMS ON THE CITY

The pastoral is no longer any solution, if it ever was. Those words that were carved on those ancient trees, those places of the memory and for the heart, all those classical names so loved and now so lost—for them we can now make so few past claims. The chimney sweep is in the center of the image, and the beggar is at every crossroads and every corner, and in the middle of every street. Even if we have learned to misread the sign, we cannot claim not to see.

CITY, SWAIN AND SUBTEXT IN BLAKE'S *SONGS*

Frederick Garber

Blake begins the *Songs of Innocence* with three plates that play with plenitude, a fullness of condition that defines not only the state in which his figures live but also the way that state is described. The first of the plates, the frontispiece, catches a moment of encounter which is not explained until the third plate, where the child on the cloud asks the piper to pipe a song about a Lamb. That is, the piper will play and sing about a being who bears a likeness to the creatures on the frontispiece, those who live in that broad swath of yellow which is tensed into definition only as it nears the picture plane. But the piper has more than one reason to pipe and sing about those images. The play of swath and figure which fills in most of the lower half of the image shapes out a density of possession, richness of goods so thick that its components can hardly be distinguished. Their major characteristic is not their individual selves but their place in a bourgeoning mass. Together they make this shady grove a place of the utmost plenitude. The mass gives weight and gravity to the image, the fatness of the flock grounding the space within the scene as much as it grounds a present prosperity.

That grounding and the attendant fullness continue on the second plate, the title page. The apple tree that hovers over the human group stabilizes and controls the business on the plate, centering the fullness of fruit and design that takes over the space, locking that centering deep into the plate and the earth. It uses as an organizing instrument the branch which bends out from the trunk and cuts across the middle of the plate to hold both halves in place with its urgent, sinuous line. Plenitude and system have learned to work together, their product the sort of certainty that comes from having a great deal and having it firmly in place. The green growths near the top that seem both vegetable and flame emerge directly out of the language that is itself part of the lushness. The language, in its turn, holds within its contours other elements in the density of the scene, the letters becoming repositories for figures who comment variously on its contents. The celestial child of the frontispiece reappears in the "O," his arms till akimbo. He finds a new place for himself on this second plate while his youthfulness is repeated, this time in natural form, in the children reading below. On this and other plates figures frequently turn up as echoes of themselves or their likenesses, and those echoes find other echoes, just as the celestial child finds his in his natural counterparts. No place will go bare and empty in this landscape that seems to thrive on incessant multiplication.

In fact, our ways of seeing these scenes are themselves aggressively multiple. What is offered as pastoral in the first plate becomes a form of Eden in the second, complete with the fruitful tree. In the third a series of images repeat the scenes on the earlier plates—for example, the image at the top left echoes the woman and children reading, while the one below it combines the stance of both child and piper. That series continues with allied images, such as a figure sowing seed and another with a printing press, himself sowing language. On this plate which is mostly language the poem itself picks up, in a different mode of discourse, the business of the frontispiece, the mute urging of the child on the cloud now finding the words to inspire the piper. But here, again, one thing is never enough: the piper goes from piping to singing to writing, all of his modes of discourse combining with the visual mode that contains them in an attempt to encompass the Lamb. Our understanding of the Lamb seems to require all of these modes since he is himself so clearly plenitude. (The need for so many modes tells as much about the Lamb as about our problems in possessing him.) But even this meeting of modes is not entirely new, not without relation to the plates which preceded it. Hints of the meeting had already appeared on the title page, the "I" of "Innocence" supporting a piper with a broad hat, while the diagonal bar of the "N" supports a scribe who writes it all down. There are no interstices in this world, no opportunities left undone, no modes untried, nothing that is by itself and without relation. These plates take their being from a textuality of plenitude and presence. Obsessed with repetition they use all sorts of doublings to enforce the ideas of fullness and repletion. The play of echo and anticipation ensures that each of the images is somehow present in the others, each adding to the density of the others while it finds more homes for its own.

We are, in effect, being given instructions for reading and seeing, directions on how to take the plates which follow. Pastoral is identified in these plates with plenitude as well as the piping and singing that have gone along with the mode since Theocritus and Virgil. But it is also identified with a seeking for totalization, a quest for a wholeness of order, and that quest may well turn out to be endemic to the mode. What we see in the instance of poems like Marlowe's "Passionate Shepherd," everyone's model of neo-pastoral, is a determined effort to bring these elements together and create a vessel which is, at once, totally self-contained and full up to its limits. Neo-pastoral of the sort produced by the Renaissance and its successors (this is precisely the sort that Blake had most in mind) speaks with subdued but urgent voice of its desire to encompass a multitude: the belt of straw which Marlowe's shepherd promises to his love has not only the straw and "Ivie buds" to define its ties to nature but also "Corall clasps and Amber studs" to define its ties to artifice. The belt seeks totalization, a fullness of possibility, and so does the mode in which it takes so prominent a part.

In fact, what the belt quietly argues had been clear from the earliest pastorals as well as the forms of neo-pastoral with which Blake was thoroughly familiar. It was spoken with absolute clarity in Virgil's *First Eclogue* but was tuned down to the surreptitious in the pastorals closer to Blake's own time. Pastoral has always sought for a limited but entire world. It is a multi-levelled discourse, the point and purpose of which is to seek to bring together, within a single mode, not only straw and coral clasps but actors and an audience who come from different segments of society and different parts of the landscape—the citified/courtly group toward whom pastoral is directed, the shepherds and peasants who are the mode's principal agents. Whereas idylls of the sort described in, say, Rousseau's *Nouvelle Héloise*, may have as agents a set of figures who are much like its readers, the agents and audience of pastoral have to come from different sociological conditions (in rough terms city and country but more usefully seen in terms of degrees of awareness, a consciousness of levels of experience which takes in more than the sociological issues described by critics like Raymond Williams[1]). Agent and audience come together within the mode far more comfortably and coherently than they are ever likely to do within society itself. The concatenation which results from that meeting is the central, defining issued in William Empson's reading of pastoral, perhaps the most influential of our time.[2] "The essential trick of the old pastoral." Empson said,

> was to make simple people express strong feelings (felt as the most universal subject, something fundamentally true about everybody) in learned and fashionable language (so that you wrote about the best subject in the best way). From seeing the two sorts of people combined like this you thought better of both; the best parts of both were used.
>
> (11–12)

Put another way, the high and the low come together within the figure of the low, who stands as a synecdoche for society as a whole, that is, for an idealized vision of what we think it ought to be. Put still differently, Empson views the essence of pastoral as an act of coalescence in which the complex is put into the simple and the simple defines us all. Though Empson's concerns are finally social—he seeks to establish the mode's possibilities as a form of proletarian literature—what he does in his reading of pastoral turns it into a statement of universal import, its themes and its figures establishing truths for all of society, bringing all men together because they share in those truths. Though this is surely acceptable it cannot be the entire point, not all that pastoral looks for as it seeks to work out its world. It is not that pastoral seeks to undo *all* the distance between agent and audience; at one level it may pretend to do so, yet, as Blake's own pastorals show, that can never be more than an acknowledged fiction. Rather, pastoral seeks to create a full and coherent system in which agent and audience would each be essential aspects of an extraordinarily complex whole, a whole that wants to assert not only the presence of totalization but its productivity as well.

And yet there is more to this matter of multiple levels than the linking of social classes and the disguising of the high in the low.

For if there is a sense in which pastoral brings high and low together there is an equal and opposite sense in which it accents
the play of difference, the interplay of aspects which can never
be the same and which resist amalgamation however much we
may link them together. Frank Kermode's reading of pastoral
takes an opposite tack from Empson's and stands as a necessary
corrective to Empson's emphasis on the fusion of pastoral components. "The first condition of pastoral poetry," Kermode argues, "is that there should be a sharp difference between two
ways of life, the rustic and the urban."[3] That difference takes in
more than the location of pastoral agents: it goes on to take part
in one of the radical distinctions in experience, the "opposition
between the simple, or natural, and the cultivated" (an opposition which led Kermode, at another point, to treat *The Tempest* as
a version of pastoral[4]). Pastoral builds on that opposition, working from the imagery the simple offers to make all sorts of sophisticated statements that would be quite beyond the capacity of
its agents to understand. Still, if Kermode is a necessary corrective to Empson's universality we cannot take his reading alone
but have to bring it together with Empson's to get a fuller sense
of the mode, a sense which will include not only difference but
likeness, Kermode's argument for opposition and Empson's for
universality. Pastorals are fictions in which we envision ourselves
in an Other which is *both* other and ourselves. The mode takes
much of its effect from a system of surrogate selves, our stand-
ins in front of the flocks. But whatever their resemblance to us,
those surrogates inhabit a world that is radically different from
ours and must remain forever so. However much they stand in
for us our surrogates stand for modes of at-homeness in the
world, of the interplay of self and place, which can never be quite
like our own. The world from which we view our surrogates' at-
homeness—the Alexandria of Theocritus, the Versailles of Marie-
Antoinette, the London of Blake—requires a different sort of
arrangement in one's way of being-in-the-world than goatherds
or shepherds need, not to speak of Marie's milkmaids and Blake's
flying children. Even when the artist has a place within the pastoral world, as Wordsworth and Constable do, the difference between viewer and viewed is never less than emphatic. Pastoral
puts us through a peculiar sort of gymnastics in which we identify with our surrogates in an act of open desire, yet keep them
at a distance so that we can see, in a single glance, what and
where we are and what and where we are not. And indeed without those gymnastics pastoral would make no sense to its audience, have no viable meaning for them: for it is only in the play
of difference that pastoral's values emerge, only as the audience

sees in the Other the conditions it does *not* have that the function of pastoral comes clear. The difference in class between audience and agent which has been apparent since Theocritus means that pastoral is hierarchical: but since the Other we create is both other and ourselves pastoral is also oxymoronic, living with a play of difference which it needs in order to work but which, as long as it works, can never be reconciled.

It is part of Blake's achievement to take this elaborate play of likeness and difference and turn it back upon pastoral itself, undoing the pretensions of which the mode is capable, revealing what the mode had become in the hands of modern duplicity, showing the values of the city at work in these figments of rural order. It was inevitable not only that Blake would take such a tack but that he would take it in the way that he did. For one thing, he is the great urban poet of his time, perhaps the greatest in his country's literature. For another, he had begun his canon with some carefully canny pastorals, several in manuscript poems, others in *Poetical Sketches* and then as the basis of *The Book of Thel*, whose sardonic commentaries on pastoral possibilities had been engraved a few years before he completed the *Songs of Innocence*. *Thel* shows that Blake had brought to early mastery that combination of irony and the awareness of literary history which was to play throughout his work and determine a good deal of its tenor. In the case of the *Songs* that meant playing with the way in which the pastoral swain, the surrogate for whom we feel that oxymoronic tug of admiration and a sense of distance, can function within the conditions of contemporary urban order. Blake had to do as Gav and others did, collapse the distinction of locales, country and city, by placing the swain in an alien context: but he had also to keep attentive to the complexities of our stance toward the difficult demands of such figures, who asked more from their contexts, whatever their location, than most neo-pastoral realized. All of this comes to mean that there is far more of the pastoral in both sets of the *Songs* than just the introductory plates or even broadly pastoral poems like "The Shepherd" and "The Lamb." Blake's intention to both use and subvert pastoral by exposing its contemporary urban implications means that the fuller content of pastoral has to appear at all levels of the text and has to pick up with elaborate precision from the intensive instructions for reading with which the series began.

Take, for example, "The Chimney Sweeper" of *Innocence*. Striding within the swirling "C" of the title is the image of a sweep and his bag, while the "weep weep weep weep" of the third line is, as Geoffrey Keynes puts it, "both a Cockney version of the sweep's profession and a realization of his misery."[5] The color code that goes with these urban sounds and sights includes both black and white, the play of oppositions which begins with the shaving of Tom's white hair so that soot cannot spoil it. The same play appears later between the coffins of black and the bodies of the sweeps, which are made pure so that they can rise "naked and white, all their bags left behind." But there is another code at work in the total image, a code which brings along its own pattern of implications as well as its private set of colors. When that code works together with the one we have just seen, they fuse into a single complex the black of social oppression, the white of the order of transcendent purity and the colors which had helped to locate and define pastoral from the beginning of the series. Tom Dacre's white hair "that curl'd like a lamb's back" helps to link both of the codes. It takes in the play of black and white which is grounded in urban conditions, the soot which images the city's soul as well as the effect the city has; but it also takes in the figure of the lamb which had been part of the pastoral context in the first and third plates and turns up again in pastoral images like those in "The Shepherd" and "The Lamb." There is more to the code, however, than the figure of the lamb alone, because the colors which appeared in "The Shepherd" and "The Lamb" appear once again in "The Chimney Sweeper": while the plate plays black against white in the poem it plays against that code of colors not only the classic pastoral green but also the various shades of yellow that had appeared along with that green in each of the pastoral images up to this point in the series. The world beyond the coffins is, in the poem, a place with a green plain on which white bodies can sport; but in the illustration it brings in even more of the pastoral code, adding the various yellows of the sheep to the green and the transcendent white. Echoes and allusions both visual and verbal, both chromatic and active ("they rise upon clouds" just like the child in the frontispiece) not only link in a single complex the different worlds of each code but set up a situation in which the codes play at counterpoint, coming as each one does out of a different way of conceiving the self's at-homeness in the world.

What we have on this plate, then, is a play of chromatic difference; to put it in more detail, a play of the urban and achromatic (the black and white) against the pastoral and chromatic (the green and the various yellows). All of this material adds to the pastoral fullness of the image and to the range of its effect as it seeks after totalization. And yet as it acts out its pastoral heritage and moves toward a vision of wholeness the image undermines its own acts, its echoes of pastoral tradition, in a series of contrary gestures. The result of that contrariety is an undoing of pastoral assertions in the face of contemporary valorisation, the desires and commitments of the sociopolitical order for which such images are made. Take, for example, the linking of actor and audience in the Empsonian claim for universalism. What Blake's sweepers share with the audience, the group that buys books with pastoral images, is the sort of moral argument with which the poem ends, the sort that is supposed to turn the sweepers' sooted lives into a joyful purgatory: "So if all do their duty, they need not fear harm." Tom's dream of heaven and a heavenly father is a parody of consolatory ethics, the parody no less effective than the system it seeks to undo. The linking of actor and audience works with ironic efficiency and so do the sweepers, each sweeper doing his duty in the inspired knowledge that the soot cannot spoil his hair and that his duty will surely protect him. Of course the pastoral complex requires some sort of unlikeness to match the linking: pastoral cannot do without its Other. In this case that play of linking and difference which makes pastoral, at one level, an oxymoronic mode, works with full effect and leads the image ever deeper into the ironies that define it. The sweepers outside Tom's dream are precisely the same figures as the sweepers within it; but the sweepers within the dream live *out* the promise of consolatory ethics while those outside the dream can only live *for* it. And yet even with this drastic difference there is more substantial likeness in the play between the states of the sweepers than there is in the counterpart play between the boys and the audience which buys Blake's pastoral books, sends white haired boys down chimneys and promotes consolatory ethics. The only link between actor and audience is the promise of the bright river. All else is the stuff of difference, so much else in fact that the world laid out in this image is largely a land of unlikeness. What the sweepers have been taught by the pervading system of ethnics makes it possible for them to work out their own appropriate version of the self's at-homeness in the world; but the gap between actor and audience makes clear to all but the sweepers themselves that there are varying modes of at-homeness at work within this image, that in the radical acts performed by the selves which inhabit this world the play of likeness and difference is heavily weighted toward unlikeness. The result is a sardonic version of the pastoral oxymoron and another ironic reminder of that hierarchy of actor and audience on which all pastoral depends.

Still, there is more that is undone here than the claim for universalism. The instructions for reading with which the series of plates had begun stressed the plenitude of pastoral as well as its argument for its wholeness. (They did so with such intensity that we now can see, from this later point in the series, that we ought to have been more suspicious at the time, more open to the possibility of irony.) Parallel with those assertions was another that appears in many versions of neo-pastoral, its claims for the productivity of difference: urban and rural, high and low, as unlike as they are, together make a whole which works to the benefit of all, the happiness of the low, the consoled nostalgia of the high. That claim continues in the world of the sweepers, which produces a harvest proper to itself: the soot which the sweepers carry away is the precise and bitter equivalent of the produce that pastoral's richness should lead to, like the sheaves in Palmer's pastorals and the sheep of Marlowe's summertime scene as well as those in the frontispiece to these songs. But there is more to the parody of pastoral than even this ashy harvest, for in fact it is only in his sack of black soot and his dreams of a greener life that the sweeper can show any harvest at all, such fullness as there is in this urban pastoral. In place of the plenitude that defines the tradition there is plenty of the contrary, an abundance of emptiness. The sweepers are full of their dreams of green fields and clean bodies but of little else, while the plate as a whole is filled with little more than the results of the consolatory ethics which make their lives bearable. And how effective those ethics are: the tiny figure within the "C" who carries the sack of soot and the realities of their lives takes much less space on the plate than the green and yellow dream-shapes that inhabit the bottom of the plate. Other elements are not, however, so effective in their work. The claim of totalization through which pastoral argues that it is socially complete is supported by the poem but in a way that neatly undoes the intent of the claim: for if the instructions for reading had shown us a model that is whole and full of what it produces, "The Chimney Sweeper" shows another that is equally whole but stark with the emptiness that defines its moral space. What we see at work in this image is Blake's bitter, ironic awareness that the wholeness of a system need not imply a fullness for all of its inhabitants. Children can be exploited in a system whose contours leave them in a state of absolute lacuna, while those who use their services fill up their own conditions in a nastily inverse ratio (just that sort of working in ratio which Blake elsewhere sees as a property of corrosive Reason). The urban comes to stand for all that takes and takes away, while the discourse of neo-pastoral, with its built-in play with plenitude, is shown to be radically incapable of encompassing the conditions of contemporary social order; or, put another way, Blake shows that the discourse can work only when stood upon its head. Neo-pastoral's claim for a dense and coherent

condition cannot survive the urban pastoral of songs like "The
Chimney Sweeper." All of the fullness goes over to the side of
pastoral's implicit audience, the spectators who were always
there and who are now seen to be holding all of the better cards,
those which make it possible to find a desirable plenitude in the
conditions of urban order. Pastoral green and gold add up to an
empty chromatism that owns only its colors and the ironies that
shave the urban counterparts of lambs and send them down into
chimneys. In Blake's sardonic commentary on that fusion of low
and high to which Empson was to point, the pastoral and the
urban are shown to be able to fuse only at the cost of the former,
only with a radical taking-away. The world that emerges from
this plate is complete but so hollow that the sound of the sweeper's voice with which the poem begins echoes in every corner of
the city as it would in an empty house that has all of its exits
closed up. This is pastoral totalization but of quite another sort
than the elaborate straw and coral of Marlowe's shepherd's belt.

And yet it is not only the voices of the children that echo in the
corners of these texts but those of pastoral's audience as well.
Blake is fully aware that the landscapes of neo-pastoral from
which so many of his *Songs* derive are classic landscapes of desire, landscapes which embody what we do not have, toward
which our desires are therefore turned. The swains who stand in
for us in the pastoral landscape act out ways of being-
in-the-world which we cannot perform in our own. They are
there because we live a lack, because there are lacunae in our
lives that only figures like these can fill in. Whether we take pastoral with the playfulness of Marie-Antoinette or the more som-
ber pondering of dispossession in Virgil's *First Eclogue* the radical
theme of pastoral is always the same. The theme that propels the
mode is not the plenitude that Marlowe preaches and that Blake
shows in the *Songs*—the fullness of presence at the bright surface
of the text—but the absence, the deprivation, the sense of vacant
space which is the subtext of the mode and the substance of its
inner life. That radical sense of absence is what sets the desire
going that makes pastoral a permanent mode of the landscape of
desire. Blake plays upon that sense in a number of ways, all of
them sardonic, all designed to undo the pretensions of urban
pastoral while letting that pastoral speak. On the plate of "Holy
Thursday," one of the subtlest of Blake's parodies of the conditions of neo-pastoral, the regimented children from the charity
schools of London march in symmetrical order, boys and girls
apart, toward the cathedral where they are to sing and thank the
city for its support. But the fullness and wholeness imaged in the
marching groups are the same as those of the sweepers, an abundance of lack, a plethora of emptiness. In their particular case

there is an image of civic pride whose symmetry surrounds (and in that surrounding seeks to disguise) the vast void at its center. Thus, the echoes that Blake makes us hear in images like "The Chimney Sweeper" and "Holy Thursday" are the sounds of the urban audience as well as those of the children. The sounds that come out to us echo the audience's lacunae as well as those of the surrogate figures who work not only in the audience's chimneys and their charity houses but in their pastoral poems as well.

There is still more to the case of Blake's urban pastorals. His audience hears all those voices, its own and the juvenile swains, with a peculiar kind of resonance because of the size of the echo chamber created in the manifold hollowness of their world. The sense of elemental lack on which all pastoral is based is intensified and increased by the lack of essential substance in the lives of the sweepers and the charity children: and those absences work together to reveal that there are, in fact, several sorts of emptiness at play in the world of Blake's *Songs*. There is the existential lacuna in the lives of the audience, the sort that traditional pastoral was designed to fill in; but there is a moral one as well, a lack of social integrity (in all senses of the word) which the pastorals of consolatory ethics are designed to smooth over. Blake takes the subtext built into the pastoral tradition and adds to its radical theme a version that is proper to the modes of the London society in which his sweepers scrape and his charity children parade. Few of his predecessors had taken pastoral as seriously as he did, that is, taken it at its word—not just the words it speaks on the surface but those it represses in its effort to hide its origin, its commencement in absence. What Blake has managed to do not only reveals that origin but ties it to the facts of contemporary urban order. He wants us to see that though the absence which inspires pastoral may at one point have possessed a certain kind of innocence there is nothing at all innocent about the kinds of urban lack which continue the original absence but give it a new and mordant twist. It is not that Blake has written a different kind of pastoral but that he has taken that part of the text from which it derives its radical life and brought out what the subtext can show of a world of shaven swains who have little more to ponder than black soot and green consolation. He adds to the manifold levels of the mode a set of additional levels made for the London of his time.

NOTES

1. See Williams' seminal study, *The Country and the City*, New York: Oxford University Press, 1973.

2. *Some Versions of Pastoral*, New York: New Directions, 1974.
3. *English Pastoral Poetry from the Beginning to Marlowe* (New York: W. W. Norton, 1972). p. 14.
4. See his edition of the play, Cambridge, Mass.: Harvard University Press, 1958.
5. His comment on the poem in the edition of *Songs of Innocence and Experience* (London: Oxford University Press, 1967), unnumbered pages.

"THINGS CAN'T GO ON LIKE THIS":
A BEGGAR'S ITINERARY

Deborah Esch

> I wish to write of this . . . because it made so apparent what kind
> of power cities have over the imagination, and why the city, where
> people make the most thoughtless demands on one another . . .
> takes its revenge in memory, and why the veil it has covertly wo-
> ven out of our lives shows the images of people less than those of
> the sites of our encounters with others or ourselves.
>
> Walter Benjamin, *Berlin Chronicle*

I would like to indicate here what amount to the express stops on
an interpretive itinerary that departs from Walter Benjamin's
One-Way Street. Since his death in 1940, Benjamin has gradually
won recognition in Europe and America as an incisive analyst of
a range of philosophical and sociological texts; more specifically,
his essays on Marseille and Naples, the Moscow diaries, the autobiographical *Berlin Chronicle*, and the monumental *Paris, Capital
of the Nineteenth Century* establish him as one of the first to theo-
rize the function and consequences of urbanization for literature.
The opening sentences of *One-Way Street*, a work that he says
"found its form in Paris" and "owes much to the city,"[1] resituate
the locus of "true literary activity" in the face of the social dissolution of his time. What he calls the "brutal heteronomies
of economic chaos" are for Benjamin everywhere evident in the
cityscape against which he stages his theoretical reflection on
the possibility of writing, and reading, under the prevailing
conditions. Beneath the heading "Tankstelle" ("Filling Station"),
he writes:

> The construction of life lies at present in the power of facts far
> more than of convictions, and of such facts as have scarcely ever
> become the basis of convictions. Under these circumstances, true
> literary activity cannot aspire to take place within a literary frame-
> work—which is, rather, the habitual expression of its sterility. Sig-
> nificant literary effectivity can only come into being in a strict
> alternation between action and writing: it must nurture the incon-
> spicuous forms that better fit its influence in active communities
> than does the pretentious, universal gesture of the book—in leaf-
> lets, brochures, newspaper articles and placards. Only this prompt
> language shows itself actively equal to the moment.[2]

One-Way Street, entitled in an early draft "Plaquette für Freunde" ("Little Placards for Friends"), sought to put directly into practice the theory of literary activity articulated in its opening passage: it was first published in Berlin in 1928 in pamphlet form, with a typographical design that evoked the shock-effects of advertising; the cover was a photo-montage of urban images stamped with phrases culled from newspaper ads, posters and circulars. The work takes the form of what Benjamin calls an "Aphorismen-büthlein," a constellation of fragments captioned with placards in an imperative mode: Post No Bills; Germans, Drink German Beer; Caution: Steps; Detour.

It is noteworthy that Benjamin's terms for the material crisis that precipitated the new conditions of possibility for literary activity—in an historical moment when the force of facts has supplanted the power of persuasion—are remarkably close to Rousseau's in the *Essai sur l'origine des langues*, a text that claims to trace the natural development of languages out of human need. In it final chapter, on "The Relationship of Languages to Government," Rousseau asks: What is the use of eloquence, or of popular speech, in a time, like his own, when public force [*la force publique*] has supplanted [*suppléé*] persuasion? "Societies," he writes "have assumed their final form: no longer is anything changed except with arms and money [*avec du canon et des écus*]; and since there is nothing to say to the people except give money [*donnez de l'argent*], it is said with placards on the street corners or with soldiers in the houses. It is not necessary to assemble anyone for that. On the contrary, the subjects must be kept apart. That is the first maxim of modern politics."[3]

Benjamin's recognition in *One-Way Street* of the waning power of persuasion in the face of inflationary pressures—under the caption "For Men," he writes that "Überzeugung ist unfruchtbar" (87), persuasion is fruitless—recalls Rousseau's account in the *Essai* of the dispersion of subjects and the disruption of communal interaction with the institution of social distance under oppressive government.[4] For purposes of the present reading, Rousseau's text is notable for its specification of what is inscribed on the mute and impersonal placards that paper the city street corners, supplanting the proximity of face to face encounter—"Give money"—for it anticipates a pivotal figure in Benjamin's text. Under yet another emphatic caption that reads "Begging and Peddling Forbidden," Benjamin elaborates:

> All religions have honored the beggar. For he proves that in a matter at the same time as prosaic and holy, banal and regenerative as almsgiving, intellect and axiom [*Geist und Grundsatz*], consequences and principle [*Konsequenzen und Prinzip*] are miserably inadequate.

We deplore the beggars in the south, forgetting that their persistence in front of our noses is as justified [*gerechtfertig*] as a scholar's before a difficult text. No shadow of hesitation, no slightest wish or deliberation in our faces escapes their notice. The telepathy of the coachman who, by accosting us, makes known to us our previously unsuspected inclination to board his vehicle . . . is of the same order.

(German 146, English 102–103)

Benjamin, who claims (in a letter to the editor of the *Neue Schweizer Rundschau* in 1931—*Briefe* II, 523) that there exists "a mediation, however tense and problematic" between his "very special point of view as a philosopher of language and the outlook of dialectical materialism," constructs an analogy in which his readers—scholarly city-dwellers that they are—find themselves doubly implicated. The persistence of beggars (in saying "give money") is as justified, as rightful, as our persistence in the face of a difficult text (like Benjamin's). What is more, the beggar is able to read our faces, telepathically, as Benjamin asserts—that is, without mediation, without the difficulty we ourselves undergo in the face of the opacity of the text. As Terry Eagleton has noted in another context, "Oppressed people are natural hermeneuticists, skilled by hard schooling in the necessity of interpreting their oppressors' language. They are spontaneous semioticians, forced for sheer survival to decipher the sign systems of the enemy, and adept at employing their own opaque idioms against them."[5] Benjamin's analogy suggests that it is this that we deplore in the beggar—our vulnerability as a text to his or her hard-won skill as a reader.

On this one-way street, then, the scene of beggary is staged as a scene of reading, in which the onlooker is in turn looked upon as a text, and in which our axioms and principles (of charity, as of reading) prove miserably inadequate. And it is not only a scene of reading, in Benjamin's terms. For the theorist attempting to mediate, however problematically, between his philosophy of language and dialectical materialism, it is also an attempt to establish an image of history, as he writes in a letter to Scholem, out of "its most inconspicuous fixtures [*unscheinbarsten Fixierungen*] of existence, its rejects" (*Briefe* II, 684–85). In the philosophy of history posited in Benjamin's *Theses*, the past gathers itself into a moment—in a "dialectical image," like Klee's "Angelus Novus"—and as such enters the collective *mémoire involontaire* of mankind, where it is readable (though with difficulty) by the philologist, Benjamin's "true historian." Despite our own willed forgetting of his right to do so, the beggar, that inconspicuous fixture of contemporary urban existence, makes his persistent demand—"give money"—at the intersection of reading and history.

His activity, as Benjamin frames it in the opening passage of *One-Way Street*, seeks out the prompt language of the street corner, the alternation between action and writing that is possible only in the "inconspicuous forms" (the pamphlet, the placard) which alone are equal to the historical moment.

I propose now to follow Benjamin's avenue of interpretation back to another literary-historical juncture, another scene of beggary—this one inscribed in the "pretentious, universal" narrative form that is neither epistemologically nor politically true to Benjaminian history. It is perhaps doubly scandalous when read in this context, for it is a story of what happens when the beggar and his placard become conspicuous. The city is London, and the onlooker, the Wordsworth of *The Prelude*.

Book VII, entitled "Residence in London", begins with the poet's retrospective account, narrated from his present position "fixed amid that concourse of mankind" (69),[6] of his naive preconceptions of the great city: "what my fond simplicity believed / And thought of London" (85–86). He recounts one of "those ingenuous moments of our youth / Ere we have learnt by use to slight the crimes / And sorrows of the world" (331–33)—in this case, an early hermeneutic effort to read the significance of London in the face of a boyhood companion.

> . . . One, a cripple from his birth, whom chance
> Summoned from school to London; fortunate
> And envied traveller! When the Boy returned,
> After short absence, curiously I scanned
> His mien and person, nor was free, in sooth,
> From disappointment, not to find some change
> In look and air, from that new region brought,
> As if from Fairy-land. Much I questioned him;
> And every word he uttered, on my ears
> Fell flatter than a cagèd parrot's note,
> That answers unexpectedly awry,
> And mocks the prompter's listening.
>
> (91–102)

The poet recovers from the disenchantment attendant on this failed reading attempt, and on his subsequent arrival in the city

> looked upon the living scene;
> Familiarly perused it; oftentimes,
> In spite of strongest disappointment, pleased
> Through courteous self-submission, as a tax
> Paid to the object by prescriptive right. (144–48)

The "endless stream of men and moving things", composed of "the comers and the goers face to face, face after face," exerts its own force on the onlooker, "[s]olicit[s] [his] regard" (467)—in the poem's terms, "taxing him by prescriptive right." The brutal impositions of life in Wordsworth's London dictate an ethical imperative, "a thing that ought to be", in the line of the 1805 version omitted in the 1850 text—in this case, a figurative version of Rousseau's "give money." It is readable everywhere, in the "Advertisements, of giant size" that "from high / Press forward, in all colours, on the sight" (194–95), "fronted with a most imposing word" (197), with "symbols, blazoned names . . . like a title—page" (158–160); or again in the "staring pictures and huge scrolls,/Dumb proclamations of the prodigies"—the placards that line the Bartholomew Fair midway—and indeed in "every character of form and face", including a figure visible "among less distinguishable shapes, / The begging scavenger, with hat in hand" (212–13), an anticipation, added in the text of 1850, of the more conspicuous beggar soon to follow.

Book VII proceeds to recount the poet's experience of the London theatre, whose "prompt forms", to recall Benjamin's terms, evoke in Wordsworth a prompt, but limited, response.

> For though I was most passionately moved
> And yielded to all changes of the scene
> With an obsequious promptness, yet the storm
> Passed not beyond the suburbs of the mind;
> Save when the realities of act and mien
> . . . called forth
> By power of contrast, made me recognise,
> As at a glance, the things which I had shaped,
> And yet not shaped, had seen and scarcely seen,
> When, having closed the mighty Shakspear's page,
> I mused, and thought, and felt, in solitude.
>   (473–85)

"Wrought upon by tragic sufferings", the mind itself, in this passage, is urbanized, in the phrase "suburbs of the mind".[7] The city becomes a figure for the mind—as it does, to bring this gesture closer to home, in the less conspicuous literary form of a remarkable article by Samuel Freedman that appeared in the *New York Times Magazine*, under the title "Metropolis of the Mind". That text begins:

A beggar staggers up the aisle of a Broadway local subway and into the next car. In his wake sits a woman reading *One Hundred Years of Solitude* by Gabriel García Márquez. On a sidewalk off Times Square, near a souvlaki stand and a pornographic bookstore, 10 men bend over 5 chessboards. These are scenes of the

intellectual life of a city, New York City. This life of the mind is not
a graft on the metropolitan body; it is something organically, naturally, often anonymously part of the constitution of New York.
It is the contrast, or perhaps the coexistence, between life ascen-
dant and life descendant: chess next to pornography, a book and a
beggar.[8]

Both Freedman's "Metropolis of the Mind" and Wordsworth's
"Suburbs of the mind" are *Denkfiguren,* rhetorical structures like
those that *The Prelude* claims "the mind / Builds for itself" (625–
26, 1805) (or has built for it, in the terms of Benjamin's *One-Way
Street,* which is dedicated to the woman who, "as engineer, cut it
through the author"). But if the force of the city is here enacted
rhetorically—if the city becomes a figure for the mind as the locus of thought, thus allowing for the appropriation by interiorization of the city's "power of contrast"—the pivotal genitive in a
phrase like "suburbs of the mind" allows as well for reading the
mind, in turn, (indeed, turned inside out) as a figure for the radical externality of the city. In all three texts, from newspaper article to pamphlet to poem, it is in the context of an analogy with
reading and the solitary reflection it prompts that the figure—
however it is to be read—confronts the reader.

   To return to the canonical example: in the subsequent passage
in *The Prelude,* the "realities of act and mien" supplant in succes-
sion theatrical entertainment as well as the eloquence of Burke
and the London rhetoricians, which had earlier made itself felt:
"Not unfelt / Were its admonishments, nor lightly heard / The
awful truths delivered thence by tongues / Endowed with various
power to search the soul" (545–48). The eloquence of the
"tongue-favored men" is displaced by the living scene, the over-
flowing streets of the city itself. The account of what the poet
calls "a few conspicuous marks" sets the stage for the blind beggar, a "candidate for regard" of another order—an order in which
the mute force of fact produces its own eloquence:

>   . . . one feeling was there which belonged
> To this great city by exclusive right:
> How often in the overflowing streets
> Have I gone forwards with the crowd, and said
> Unto myself, "The face of everyone
> That passes by me is a mystery."
> Thus have I looked, nor ceased to look, oppressed
> By thoughts of what, and whither, when and how,
> Until the shapes before my eyes became
> A second-sight procession, such as glides
> Over still mountains, or appears in dreams,

And all the ballast of familiar life—
The present, and the past, hope, fear, all stays
All laws of acting, thinking, speaking man—
Went from me, neither knowing me, nor known.
And once, far travelled in such mood, beyond
The reach of common indications, lost
Amid the moving pageant, 'twas my chance
Abruptly to be smitten with the view
Of a blind beggar, who, with upright face,
Stood propped against a wall, upon his chest
Wearing a written paper, to explain
The story of the man, and who he was.
My mind did at the spectacle turn round
As with the might of waters, and it seemed
To me that in this label was a type
Or emblem of the utmost that we know
Both of ourselves and of the universe,
And, on the shape of the unmoving man,
His fixèd face and sightless eyes, I looked,
As if admonished from another world.

                                        (593–623. 1805)

The figure of the beggar is here conspicuous, by "power of contrast" with the teeming background, the mass of faces that are insignificant for the onlooker who is, as he confesses, unable to read them. This failed hermeneutic effort to interpret the faces of the passers-by (anticipated in Book IV, 58–9, where the poet writes that "The face of every neighbor whom I met / Was as a volume to me") has consequences more drastic than the childhood episode narrated earlier in the book: it entails, in fact, the collapse of "all the ballast of familiar life—The present, and the past"—that is, history, and with it, "All laws of acting, thinking, speaking man." It is at this moment of failure of moral, intellectual and linguistic imperatives that the onlooker is forcibly struck, amid the moving pageant of the street, by the fixed face and affixed label of the beggar.[9]

The beggar's force of fact, like the power of Burkean eloquence and pulpit oratory, is registered with the word "admonished"— the specific effect of this figure, in other words, is to put the onlooker in mind of his duties, with a tacit reference to the penalty of failing to fulfill them. In this he functions like Wordsworth's earlier, suburban fixture, the old Cumberland beggar, in whom the villagers

Behold a record which together binds
Past deeds and offices of charity,
Else unremembered, and so keeps alive
The kindly mood in hearts which lapse of years,

> And that half-wisdom half-experience gives,
> Makes slow to feel, and by sure steps resign
> To selfish and cold oblivious cares.

The old Cumberland beggar, a "silent monitor" of the villagers' moral life, is also a Benjaminian image of history, a record binding together past acts of charity which without him would be consigned to oblivion. As such he insures present and future compliance with the imperative "Give money." What distinguishes the onlooker's reaction to the London beggar is the attribution of his feeling "to this great city, by exclusive right"—by the prescriptive right that taxes the onlooker, demands that he give, submit, fulfill his duty.

Wordsworth's response to the demand is again a hermeneutic one; he understands the beggar's written paper to "explain the story of the man, whence he came and who he was"—interprets it, that is, as an allegorical sign pointing to his own autobiographical project in *The Prelude*. In all rigour, however, this interpretation would entail his confronting in the beggar a figure for the poet who is quite literally unable to read his own text.[10] That the poet is unwilling to face such a consequence is borne out in the next lines, which turn the inscription on the beggar's chest into a "spectacle," one that marks the onlooker's failure to read. No mention is made of what the beggar's placard obviously says, must say, to the extent that the beggar is defined as one who lives by asking alms—who is, in effect, a personification of the demand "give money." For the paper to say "who he was," it must say "give money." In the face of this intractable demand, the smitten poet is himself beggared, becomes one who begs the question, begs off the imperative that confronts him in the person of the blind beggar.

This elementary reading error, moreover, is not restricted to the specific encounter, but is universalized, as the poet casts the beggar's label, understood as his life-story, as a "type or emblem of the utmost we can know, both of ourselves and of the universe." With this arch-ideological gesture that turns a specific historical configuration into a universal type, obliterating its fundamental antagonism, the onlooker misreads "the power behind the beggar's fixity of stance," in a misreading that takes the form of an appropriation of the beggar's power as knowledge and self-knowledge.[11] In fact—by force of fact—the beggar, in his radical externality, is arguably to be read as a figure of resistance to this interiorization, this appropriation as knowledge. If the beggar's text is an emblem, a type, it is not of the utmost we can know, but rather, as Rousseau's text makes apparent, of the least we can do—give money. In Benjamin's terms, the poet and his particular literary form are unequal to the demand of the moment—in this case, the demand of reading the beggar as an image of history "in its most inconspicuous fixtures of existence, its rejects." The subsequent passage in Wordsworth's text speaks obliquely about this failed reader response, this begging of the question:

> But these, I fear,
> Are falsely catalogued; things that are, are not,
> As the mind answers to them, or the heart
> Is prompt, or slow, to feel. What say you, then,
> To times, when half the city shall break out
> Full of one passion, vengeance, rage or fear?
>
> (668–673)

Wordsworth's text and Benjamin's intersect at such a time, in a moment when the beggar, subjected to the brutal heteronomies of economic chaos, threatens to break out of this type-casting, gives notice, in Benjamin's ironic usage in *One-Way Street*, that "things can't go on like this." Truly catalogued, the beggar and his placard are readable—and unreadable—as a figure for what *The Prelude* calls "blank confusion, and a type not false / Of what the mighty city is itself"—what we might otherwise label the urban sublime, the city's own resistance to interiorization and appropriation by the mind as a figure for the mind. What such an interiorization willfully forgets is, in Wordsworth's terms, the things that are, but are not as the mind answers to them; in Benjamin's terms, the force of fact, of a history whose claim, like the beggar's, cannot be settled cheaply.[12]

NOTES

1. Benjamin, *Briefe* I, ed. Gershom Scholem and Theodor W. Adorno. Frankfurt am Main: Suhrkamp, 1966, 446 and 459. Cited hereafter in the text as *Briefe*.
2. Benjamin, *Gesammelte Schriften* IV, 1 (Werkausgabe Bd. 10), ed. Rolf Tiedemann and Hermann Schweppenhauser. Frankfurt am Main: Suhrkamp, 1980, 85. I have quoted (and where necessary modified) the English translation from *One-Way Street and Other Writings*, trans. Edmund Jephcott and Kingsley Shorter. London: NLB, 45. Page references to both the German and the English editions will be cited hereafter in the text.
3. Rousseau, *Essai sur l'origine des langues*. Paris: Bibliothèque de Graphe, 1970, 542. An English translation is provided in *On the Origin of Language: Two Essays by Jean-Jacques Rousseau and Johann Gottfried Herder*, trans. John H. Moran and Alexander Gode. New York: Frederick Ungar, 1966, 72.
4. Jacques Derrida analyzes Rousseau's account in *De la grammatologie*. Paris: Editions de Minuit, 1967, 235–378.

5. Terry Eagleton, "The Uses of Criticism," *The New York Times Book Review,* December 9, 1984, Sec.7, 45.
6. Unless otherwise indicated, all line numbers refer to the 1850 text.
7. Cf. the "straggling breezes of suburban air" (192) that, earlier in Book VII, fail to refresh the claustrophobic midway.
8. *The New York Times Magazine,* Part 2, November 4, 1984, 32.
9. Cf. Geoffrey Hartman, *Wordsworth's Poetry 1787–1814.* New Haven: Yale University Press, 1964, 241–42.
10. In "The Ring of Gyges and the Coat of Darkness: Reading Rousseau with Wordsworth," Cynthia Chase argues that "In the blind beggar Wordsworth confronts an image of the autobiographical poet unable to read his own text" (in *Romanticism and Language,* ed. Arden Reed. Ithaca: Cornell University Press, 1984, 72).
11. Hartman's claim (242) is that Wordsworth here "divines," rather than appropriates, this power. For another suggestive reading that tries to take account of the beggar's radical externality, see Frances Ferguson, *Wordsworth: Language as Counter-Spirit.* New Haven: Yale University Press, 1977, 141 ff.
12. See the second of the theses "Über den Begriff der Geschichte", *Über Gesammelte Schriften,* I, 2, 694. Translated by Harry Zohn as the "Theses on the Philosophy of History" in *Illuminations,* ed. Hannah Arendt. New York: Schocken, 1969, 254.

Rakoczy/Art Resource. Empire State Building, New York.

7

CONTEMPORARY CITIES: TRAFFICKING AND FILMING

LAS VEGAS DALLAS LOS ANGELES MIAMI All nowhere cities, all so well rehearsed in their outrageousness. Is there something in us that demands the oversize place for the undersize underhero we want to have become? Futurism and all its bigness have led us to a series of parking lots, for long term non-dwelling in some machine; in the short term, all those films speed by in their Flippy-Floppiness, too fast except for serialized space and being. Here is—even if it is a sort of nowhere—where we are.

TRAFFICKING IN PHILOSOPHY: LINES OF FORCE IN THE CITY-TEXT

Laura Rice

From 1975 to 1982 the French artist Arman occupied himself with the creation of the sculpture *Long-term Parking*. The piece, sixty-five feet high by twenty feet square, is a stack of sixty automobiles embedded in concrete. A monolithic reification of the social relations at work in Late Capitalism, it makes us think about what it means to live in a society in which machines, especially inoperative ones, become the gigantic and expensive totem of the culture. Arman himself calls *Long-term Parking* "a visual accumulation [of] the most typical object of the twentieth century, an invasion of cars, to which we are all witness."[1] Before this totem we feel first, perhaps, horror, and then fascination with the way in which the use-value of the automobile has been immobilized. And in fact, the exchange value too has been jammed by this multi-storied grid-lock sculpture. What we are left with is a spectacle of accumulation. *Long-term Parking* embodies, then, the three moments of capital which America has undergone. In terms of the history of cities, David Gordon speaks of these three moments as the Commercial City—a port that siphons off the wealth to the metropolis abroad; the Industrial City—the site of heavy production; and the Corporate City—a high tech environment where information is hoarded or exchanged.[2] This shift has also been characterized as one from marketplace to factory town to "no town."[3] In literature, Fredric Jameson has seen these stages as concomitant with realism, modernism and postmodernism, and noted that in technology there is a similar movement from the steam-driven motors of 1848 to the electric and combustion motors of the 1890s to electronic and nuclear-powered apparatuses after the 1940s.[4] And in terms of the social relations we practice, we might see these stages as shifts from products, to money to credit, or, as Guy Debord does in *Society of the Spectacle*, from being to having and from having to appearing.[5] What becomes clear when we superimpose these various layers of historical change is that somehow, something has become nothing, as embodied in the spectacle, and nothing has become something, as imaged in the idea of credit. A tremendous amount of trafficking goes on in the "no towns" of the sunbelt and the old towns of the East, but it often amounts to circulation devoid of substance. In *Long-term Parking*, for all its seeming solidity, what we see is an image of absence, for what kind of society needs long term parking, if not a society which is no longer at home with itself?

As these shifts have taken place, the car, which once was the symbol of urban dynamism and technological meliorism, has come to stand for alienated and atomized living. In his 1909 "Furturist Manifesto," the Italian poet F. T. Marinetti saw in the automobile the emblem of the energy that was to generate an explosive future: "We affirm that the world's splendour has been enriched by a new beauty: the beauty of speed. A racing car whose hood is adorned with great pipes, like serpents of explosive breath—a roaring car that seems to ride on grapeshot—is more beautiful than the *Victory of Samothrace*."[6] Classical sculpture, like the classical architecture of Italy's great cities, symbolized a stasis and an order that were antithetical to Futurism's vision of an avant-garde world—a world of flux, speed and motion, always forward motion moving toward an ameliorated, liberated future. The over 100 art works futurist painter Giacomo

Balla did of speeding automobiles evidenced the importance of the car as a tool of personal power which allowed the driver to transform stasis into speed. Paintings of cars, poems about cars, even concerts like Luigi Russolo's *Meeting of Airplanes and Automobile* which included the sounds of motors backfiring and engines droning, led English writer and artist Wyndham Lewis to label Futurism mere "Automobilism."[7] The Futurists voiced, in extreme form, what was a far more general faith in technology at the turn of the century.

The International Expositions of 1889 and 1900 in Paris marked a change in direction, away from the Banquet Years and the Ancien Regime and toward Americanization, eventually called Fordism and Taylorism. The 1889 Exposition, visited by Thomas Edison, featured a pavillion dedicated to the incandescent light bulb. Here Edison bought an allegorical statue called "The Fairy of Electricity" which was "a winged woman crouching on a dilapidated gas jet, surrounded by a Volta battery, telegraph key, and telephone, and brandishing an incandescent bulb," all done in Carrara marble.[8] Edison bought it for his lab in West Orange. But the center of the fair was, of course, the Eiffel Tower, the very image of technical prowess. The scientific innovations exhibited at these two fairs reflected the face of the coming century. They included the internal combustion engine, the diesel engine, the steam turbine; electricity, oil and petroleum as sources of power; the automobile, the motor bus, the tractor, and the airplane; the telephone, the typewriter, the tape machine, in short, the modern bureaucratic office; and the new productions of the chemical industry—dyes, synthetics and plastics. In 1900 there were in France a total of 3,000 automobiles. By 1907, that number had jumped to 30,000 and by 1913, France itself was producing 45,000 automobiles a year. Given the rapidity of the rate of change, it is little wonder that the Futurists were so enamoured of speed and science. The futurist city—based on the American skyscraper city—would be a centrifugal dynamo rather than a centripetal, centered city that brought people together for the purpose of either government or exchange. As the painter Umberto Boccioni wrote in his 1914 futurist "Manifesto of Architecture":

> We have said that in painting we shall put the viewer in the center of the picture making him the center of emotion rather than a mere spectator. The architectural environment of the city is also being transformed to include people. We live in a spiral of architectural forces. In the past, construction unwound in a successive panorama: one house followed another, one street followed another. Now around us we see the beginnings of an architectural environment that develops in every direction: from the luminous basements of large department stores, from the several levels of the

tunnels of the underground railways to the gigantic upward thrust
of American skyscrapers.[9]

This image of the American city as the ameliorative environment
of the future was widely shared in Europe. In 1906 H. G. Wells
saw New York in terms of "limitless bigness"; "One has a vision," he wrote, "of bright, electrical subways . . . of clean, clear
pavements . . . spotless surfaces, and a shining order of everything wider, taller, cleaner, better."[10] And later in 1913, *The New
York Tribune* published an interview with newly-arrived, indepen-
dently wealthy Dada artist Francis Picabia, who said: "I see
much, much more, perhaps, than you who are used to it see. I
see your stupendous skyscrapers, your mammoth buildings and
marvellous subways, a thousand evidences of your great wealth
on all sides. . . . Your New York is the cubist, the futurist city. It
expresses in its architecture, its life, its spirit the modern
thought."[11] The modern cityscape, for Picabia, was one in which
the line and the vector had replaced the city center, the cube had
replaced the matrix. Like Wells, Picabia and Boccioni, the futurist
architect Sant Elia saw in America the hope of a social order
based on purity of line and rationality of organization. Architecture was the art of the future—a merging of art, science and
technology to create a total artistic environment: the city. Following the same line of thought as Sant Elia, Ozenfant, Le Corbusier
and Neutra saw the American city as the emblem of the future.

Other Europeans like Kafka, Céline, Sartre and Lévi-Strauss
would find the American city, as it moved from the industrial
stage to the corporate stage, a more ambiguous and less than rational environment that would end by isolating and atomizing its
inhabitants. Far from being the center of the city—as Boccioni
had envisioned them—the urban dwellers of the metropolis
risked being transformed into serialized automatons pushed
across the spaces of the city by forces beyond their control and
beyond their comprehension. This more negative side of modernity was also embodied in some of the manifestos of the Futurists
as they voiced the "need to Americanize ourselves by entering
the all-consuming vortex of modernity through its crowds, its
automobiles, its telegraphs, its noises, its screeching, its violence,
cruelty, cynicism and unrelenting competition; in short, the exaltation of all the savage and anti-artistic aspects of our age."[12] The
Futurists deplored the historic city with its cathedrals, palaces
and podiums—elaborated architectures that expressed royal authority and ecclesiastical power: "We are the men of the great
hotels, the railway stations, the wide streets, colossal ports, covered markets, luminous arcades, straight roads and beneficial

demolitions."[13] The new authorities are those who command
these forces and environments of change and exchange: bankers,
businessmen, and leaders of fashion. In his excoriation of the Ve-
netians in his 1910 speech, Marinetti shouted that the putrid, ancient city would be paved over by the men of modernity: "Trains
and tramways racing along the great thoroughfares built over
your canals, filled in at long last, will bring you mountains of
merchandise, amidst a crowd of shrewd, wealthy, bustling manufacturers and tradesmen.[14]

What the inevitable shift from the European historic city to the
new world commercial nexus to the contemporary corporate city
has meant for social relations is both disturbing and ambiguous.
If, as French sociologist Henri Lefèbre has argued in his book *La
Production de l'espace*, every mode of production involves the production of built space that corresponds to that mode in a coherent way,[15] then the shift from guild city to grid city to "no
town" suggests a movement from a system where power and
control were visible and identifiable although not accessible to
all, through an arrangement of competing sites of exchange and
production to a system where power seems disembodied, decen-
tralized and continually displaced through computerized information networks—corporate headquarters are nowhere and everywhere at the same time. The grid city was generated, as Louis
Mumford has noted, by the actions of land speculators who
"treated the individual lot and the block, the street and the avenue, as abstract units for buying and selling, without respect for
historic uses, for topographic conditions, or for social needs."[16]
The grid city, then, generated by the forces of investment was a
planned city, albeit the planning was far from democratic. Its topography was born from the overlapping and contradictory development of many private, competitive enterprises. The mode of
generation of the high tech city is more difficult to grasp because
it develops less out of the forces of investment and reinvestment
than out of the act of diversifying investment and speculating
about investment returns.

It makes sense, then, that Europeans might be especially sensitive to the ways in which American cities move us, given that
they have experienced the space of two very different modes of
production—the historic city and the commercial city. As Alan
Trachtenberg points out in *The Incorporation of America*, despite
the major upheaval caused by the Industrial Revolution, "European cities have, on the whole retained a residue of earlier
stages; medieval structures survived as 'old towns,' marking a
center as a visible memory of an older, more coherent and uni-
fied social order."[17]

It is perhaps this visible memory which leads French anthro-
pologist Levi-Strauss to find the difference between European cities and American cities to be based on a contrast "not between
new towns and old towns, but between towns with a very short
evolutionary cycle and towns with a slow evolutionary cycle.
Certain European cities sink gently into a moribund torpor; those
of the New World live feverishly in the grip of a chronic disease;
they are perpetually young, yet never healthy."[18] And just as
Levi-Strauss experiences American cities as sites "which pass
from freshness to decay without ever being simply old," Jean-
Paul Sartre finds, in his phenomenological encounters with
American cities, an extreme fluctuation in their topology, but his
understanding is tied much more closely to the mode of production which created the city space. He writes:

> Removals [from one place to another] indicate fluctuations in
> American fortunes. It is customary, in the United States, for the
> fashionable neighborhoods to slide from the center to the outskirts
> of the city; after five years the center of the town is "polluted." If
> you walk about there, you come upon tumble-down houses that
> retain a pretentious look beneath their filth; you find a complicated
> kind of architecture, one-storey frame houses with entrances
> formed by peristyles supported by columns, gothic chalets, "colo-
> nial houses," etc. These were formerly aristocratic homes, now in-
> habited by the poor.[19]

Sartre points to two separate issues here, the hodgepodge of historical styles and the shifting configurations of the cityscape.

In the centers of many historic cities, the monumental buildings display varied facades that echo earlier styles. Yet, however
disparate the styles of these monumental copies, they do demonstrate at least some unity between the historical facade and the
interior function. Carl E. Schorske in his study *Fin-de-siècle Vienna*, for example, explores the way that the buildings were created and disposed on the Ringstrasse. The Ringstrasse, a wide
boulevard encircling the inner imperial city of Vienna, cut the
inner city off from the surrounding suburbs. The plan adopted in
1859 for the grand boulevard did not seek to tie the two parts of
the city together by organizing "vast vistas oriented toward the
central, monumental features" of the old city; rather it "suppressed the vistas in favor of stress on the circular flow."[20]
Schorske goes on to demonstrate that the great representational
buildings of the bourgeois architects of the Ringstrasse become
equivalent moments in undifferentiated space: "Alternate centers
of visual interest, they are related to each other not in any direct
way but only in their lonely confrontation of the great circular

artery, which carries the citizen from one building to another, as from one aspect of life to another. The public buildings float unorganized in a spatial medium whose only stabilizing element is an artery of men in motion."[21] Perhaps we have here in old-world fashion, the beginning of the serialized experience which is so typical of American cities.

The buildings of the Ringstrasse, however, share with each other their sameness as monuments to bourgeois culture—the Parliament, the Townhall, the University, the theater—and the unity of their historicized facades with their interior functions. However different they are from one another in style, their style does bear some relation to their use. The gothic townhall is liberal Vienna's attempt "to evoke its origins as a free medieval commune, now reborn after a long night of absolutist rule"; the theater, in Baroque style, commemorates "the era in which theater first joined together cleric, courtier, and commoner in a shared aesthetic enthusiasm"; the Renaissance-style University celebrates liberal dedication to knowledge; and the Greek style of the Parliament, with its statue of Athena in front, symbolizes justice.[22] It is this unity of form and function that seem to get lost in the new world.

In *The Incorporation of America*, Trachtenberg notes that in cities like Chicago,

> the sight of upheaval was commonplace: old landmarks destroyed, new structures of a different kind hoisted in their place, a new scale of tall building obliterating older buildings; neighborhoods changing their face as well as their ethnic and social character, as homes of the formerly rich became sites of multiple flats and crowded rooms. Surely the many faces of the city belonged to a single body. But unity seemed dispersed in a multiplicity of appearances, and especially appearances which disguised—department stores dressed in a garment more appropriate to Italian Renaissance palaces, or railroad stations represented as cathedrals. Height and size as gratuitous statements of power appeared in their most pure form in the relatively useless towers of railroad stations, in the elegantly picturesque designs of New York's Grand Central, Boston's Park Square Station, and Chicago's Illinois Central. These massive downtown structures, usually identified with the center of the city, served multiple functions . . . functions [which] represented travel, interconnection, coordination, the spatial form of placelessness, of being neither here nor there, but on the way.[23]

The cities of the new world, then, have gone Vienna's Ringstrasse one better, we might say, by combining buildings with circulation while at the same time devoiding style of its historical content—both time and space are emptied.

Sartre is especially struck by the furious cycles of construction-destruction-reconstruction: "Changes are continually made within the same place. An apartment house is bought to be demolished, a larger apartment house is built on the same plot. After five years, the new house is sold to a contractor who tears it down to build a third one. The result is that in the States a city is a moving landscape for its inhabitants, whereas our cities are our shells."[24] These shifts in configuration are tied specifically to the mode of production by historian David Gordon, who notes that as early as the commercial city we begin to see the emergence of a grid pattern. As the industrial city emerged, the huge factories were concentrated downtown near rail and water outlets, the workers were segregated into housing districts, that is tenements, near work and the middle and upper classes, who could afford to travel, gradually moved into rings beyond the city limits. At the turn of the century, the great shift reversal of factory location began as capital moved its product operations to the outskirts, separated its workers from each other because they were prone to striking and even striking in sympathy, and located its corporate headquarters downtown.[25]

This shift from industrial capital to monopoly capital, as it is played out on the grid of New York, is imaged by Franz Kafka in his novel *America* and by Céline in his *Journey to the end of Night*. Kafka's main character, newly emigrated Karl Rossmann, looks over New York from the balcony of his rented room: "What would have been at home the highest vantage point in the town allowed him here little more than a view of one street, which ran perfectly straight between two rows of squarely chopped buildings and therefore seemed to be fleeing into the distance."[26] New York is for him a chaotic welter of sight and sound, reminiscent of Russolo's mechanical concert:

> That street was the channel for a constant stream of traffic which, seen from above, looked like an inextricable confusion, forever newly improvised, or foreshortened human figures and the roofs of all kinds of vehicles, sending into the upper air another confusion, more riotous and complicated, of noises, dust and smells, all of it enveloped and penetrated by a flood of light which the multitudinous objects in the street scattered, carried off and again busily brought back, with an effect as palpable to the dazzled eye as if a glass roof stretched over the street were being violently smashed into fragments at every moment.[27]

Despite the mental confusion Karl feels when confronted by his small section of Manhattan, he is also dimly aware that there is some mysterious force holding it all together and orchestrating the serialized existences of the city-dwellers. He senses that his street is "only one small section of a great wheel which afforded no hand-hold unless one knew all the forces controlling its full orbit."[28]

Karl does get some vague idea of how corporate New York controls the everyday lives of the citizens when he visits his Uncle Jacob's firm. The firm sells no product, rather it is a sort of information and man-power intermediary and a trafficker in moveable goods. "It was a sort of commission and despatch agency such as, to the best of Karl's knowledge, was probably not to be found in Europe. For the business did not consist in the transference of wares from the producer to the consumer or to the dealer, but in the handling of all the necessary goods and raw materials going to and between the great manufacturing trusts. It was consequently a business which embraced simultaneously the purchasing, storing, transport and sale of immense quantities of goods and hand to maintain the most unintermittent telephonic and telegraphic communication with its various clients. . . . In the telephone hall, wherever one looked, the doors of telephone boxes could be seen opening and shutting, and the noise was maddening."[29] To Karl the business is only so much circulation and circuitry without real substance. He is more than happy to escape this frightening world of commerce when he is invited to be the guest at the suburban house of one of his uncle's colleagues. As Karl and this Mr. Pollunder drive out of the city at night, they have to take side roads rather than the main thoroughfare because the main streets are all tied up with strikers demonstrating and marching. At this point, we are told that "Karl merely leaned back happily on the arm which Mr. Pollunder had put round him; the knowledge that he would soon be a welcome guest in a well-lighted country house surrounded by high walls and guarded by watch-dogs filled him with extravagant well being."[30] It is only after Karl gets kicked out of Mr. Pollunder's house and hits the road that he notices the tenements where the workers live on the outskirts of the city near the factories: "By the side of the road were badly tilled fields clustered round big factories which rose up blackened with smoke in the open country. Isolated blocks of tenements were set down at random, and their countless windows quivered with manifold movement and light, while on all the flimsy little balconies women and children were busy in numberless ways, half concealed and half revealed by washing of all kinds, hung up or spread out to dry, which fluttered around them in the morning wind and billowed mightily."[31] Along the highway which skirts these tene-

ments, streams of cars five abreast move humans to market as
consumers or commodities in terms of labor power: "there were
no pedestrians, no market women straggling singly along the
road towards the town, as in Karl's country, but every now and
then appeared great, flat motor-trucks, on which stood market
women after all, craning their necks to oversee the traffic in their
impatience for a quicker journey."[32] There were similar trucks
taking cattle to market and taking day wage-laborers to the city,
human cargo transported by the Jacob Despatch Agency. Karl's
travelling companions tell him that this trafficking in humans is a
"scandalous fraud" and that Uncle Jacob's firm is "notorious."[33]

As Karl looks back at the city from the ridge of a suburban hill,
he sees "the panorama of New York and its harbour extending
more and more spaciously below [him.] The bridge connecting
New York with Brooklyn hung delicately over the East River, and
if one half-shut one's eyes it seemed to tremble. It appeared quite
bare of traffic, and beneath it stretched a smooth empty tongue of
water. Both the huge cities seemed to stand there empty and pur-
poseless. As for the houses, it was scarcely possible to distin-
guish the large ones from the small. In the invisible depths of the
streets life probably went on after its own fashion, but above
them nothing was discernible save a light fume, which though it
never moved seemed the easiest thing in the world to dispel."[34]
The beauty of New York's lines, vectors and cubes, of its technology, emerges most clearly when the city is seen from an inhuman distance, far from the alienated and atomized lives being
lived on a pitifully human scale, in the midst of all that traffic,
those buildings, that noise.

Celine's Bardamu in *Journey to the End of Night* doesn't need
any panoramic distances to recognize the sterility and inhumanity of life lived in the city, perhaps because he arrives in the city
a down-and-out immigrant without the influential relatives Karl
used to buffer him from the cityscape. As Bardamu escapes his
quarantine on Ellis Island and heads for the big city, he knows
that Americans think that people without money are "all anar-
chists," so he stuffs his pocket with a wad of paper so he would
"look more or less like a businessman when (he) hit town." He is
terrified by the enormous scale of the city and immediately gets
carried off in its current, a small particle of humanity.

Raising my eyes to the ramparts, I felt a kind of reverse vertigo,
because there were really so many windows and so much alike that
whichever way you looked that it turned my stomach. Flimsily
clad, chilled to the bone, I made for the darkest crevice I could
find in that giant facade, hoping the people would hardly notice

me in their midst. My embarrassment was quite superfluous. I had nothing to fear. In the street I had chosen, really the narrowest of all, no wide than a good-sized brook in our part of the world and extraordinarily dirty, damp and dark at the bottom, there were so many other people, big and little, fat and thin, that they carried me along with them like a shadow. They were going to town like me, on their way to work no doubt. Poor people like everywhere else.[35]

Dark shadows, high winds and domination are what Bardamu feels in the skyscraper city: "Those people were pushing life and night and day in front of them. Life hides everything from people. Their own noise prevents them from hearing anything else. They couldn't care less. The bigger and taller the city, the less they care. Take it from me. I've tried. It's a waste of time."[36] Disgusted by New York, Bardamu does something which seems almost inexplicable to readers now, he moves to Detroit.

Why Detroit? He's heard that jobs there are easy to get, are well-paid uncomplicated and undemanding. So much may well have been true. At the River Rouge Ford plant, however, Bardamu discoveres the inhumanity of Taylorism and Scientific Management. The exterior of the plant—which contained forty-four buildings, had 110 miles of railroad tracks, 81 miles of conveyer belts and 4 bus lines and covered an area more than a mile and a half long and three quarters of a mile broad—was vast, quiet and inhuman. This is the aspect of the plant we see captured in the many photographs and paintings the artist Charles Sheeler did of it: for example *River Rouge Plant—Power House* (1927); *Tunnel* (1927); *River Rouge Plant* (1932); and *Classic Landscape* (1931). By 1927 the Rouge had fulfilled Henry Ford's dream of being able to build a car from beginning to end, from the making of steel to finishing touches, in one plant. Perhaps it is the self-sufficiency of the Rouge which caused Sheeler to entitle this painting of it *City Interior* (1936). The interior of this plant was vast, noisy and inhuman. As Bardamu says, "Actually it was worse than everywhere else."[37] Sheeler did take a few interior photos, *River Rouge Plant-Stamping Press* (1927) and *River Rouge Slag Buggy* (1927), which begin to suggest what Bardamu says of the environment inside:

Everything trembled in the enormous building, and we ourselves, from our ears to the soles of our feet, were gathered into this trembling, which came from the windows, the floor, and all the clanking metal, tremors that shook the whole building from top to bottom. We ourselves became machines, our flesh trembled in the furious din, it gripped us around our heads and in our bowels and

rose up to the eyes in quick continuous jolts. . . . Still, you resist;
it's hard to despise your own substance, you'd like to stop all this,
give yourself time to think about it and listen without difficulty to
your heartbeat, but it's too late for that. This thing can never stop.
This enormous steel box is on a collision course; we, inside it, are
whirling madly with the machines and the earth. All together.
Along with the thousands of little wheels and the hammers that
never strike at the same time, that make noises which shatter one
another, some so violent that they release a kind of silence around
them, which makes you feel a little better.[38]

The silent tumult that is Ford is what the Mexican socialist
painter Diego Rivera captured in his murals *Detroit Industry*
(1931–33). It is probably the Rivera murals that Charlie Chaplin
modeled his mass production sequences after in *Modern Times.*
Rivera's murals begin to reflect the real working conditions at
Ford which were the cause of strikes and clashes with local police
in the thirties. Meanwhile, consuming America was urged to see
the automobile as the transport to a dream while poverty-stricken
America tried to survive the depression. This is reflected in photographer Margaret Bourke-White's 1937 *At the Time of the Louis-
ville Flood*, a photograph of a gigantic billboard picturing a
middle-class white family packed in the car to go to the beach;
below the billboard, in real life, a long line of poor Blacks wait in
a soup kitchen line. The American precisionist Sheeler remains
calm and keeps his faith in technology through all this. His industrial paintings are devoid of humanity, not because the industry is unhuman but because humanity gets in the way. Sheeler. is
rumored to have once remarked that he was interested in a manmade world, depopulated landscapes. It is his illustration of
what a beautiful world it would be if there were no people in it.
His 1940 *Conversation—Sky and Earth*, which images telephone
transformers against a blue sky, sums up the shift toward a world
in which the apparatuses of communication are more important
than either human agents or any particular content.

Before the war when industrialists tried to institute American
methods in French plants, the workers suspected that there was
indeed an inhuman side to scientific management and dubbed
Taylor's time-motion efficiency scheme "systematized sweating"
and the effort to use it "generated a spate of unfavorable publicity
and ended abruptly in a series of violent strikes throughout the
region of Paris in 1913." In the article " 'Architecture or Revolution': Taylorism, Technocracy, and Social Change," Mary McLeod
traces the fascination of Le Corbusier with scientific management. However set against this dehumanization of work people
were before the war, the devastation of the war—"6,147 public

buildings . . . were razed; 293,039 dwellings were completely de-stroyed; another 435,961 homes severely damaged; and 52,734 ki-lometers of highways needed to be rebuilt. Much of northeast France was reduced to rubble"[39]—caused a reversal and gave Taylorism a new lease on life in Europe. "Fordism joined Tay-lorism as a model of rationalization; the assembly line, standard-ization, and the expansion of a mass market through higher wages and lower prices gave impetus to the belief that social problems could be alleviated within the boundaries of capi-talism."[40] In short, greater efficiency meant greater profits, and greater profits—of course—meant more for everyone. Technical Nirvana. But what looks, on the one hand, like socialism, looks on the other more like authoritarianism, because somebody has to run the show. Le Corbusier wanted to extend this system-atized efficiency to prefabricated housing, and eventually to cit-ies, as did so many other utopian architects. Traffic and people, public space and private life all needed to be smoothly inte-grated. In 1910, Edgar Chambless proposed *Roadtown*—a con-tinuous house with a promenade on the roof and high velocity trains in the basement. This was one way to avoid urban sprawl.[41] Le Corbusier's 1921-22 Contemporary City revealed the more conservative assumptions of the industrial utopians. Ac-cording to McLeod,

> the most apparent of these was the proposed hierarchy of power. Taylorism, which purported to transcend political divisions in its guise of neutrality, was by no means egalitarian. Casting aside tra-ditional determinants of power—wealth, family, and class—the system . . . predicated rank on capacity and expertise. As Le Cor-busier himself explained: 'the right man for the right job is coldly selected; laborers, workmen, foremen, engineers, managers, ad-ministrators—each in his proper place; and the man who is made of the right stuff to be a manager will not long remain a workman; the higher places will be open to all.' This vision of a hierarchy of talent takes material form [in Contemporary City.][42]

The professional managerial class—engineers, industrialists, fin-anciers and artists—work in the skyscrapers at the center of the city. They live nearby. The workers and the other subordinates live around the periphery in Garden Cities, and are brought into work by the two major highways which bisect the city in the form of a cross.

Frank Lloyd Wright's 1925 project for a "City of the Future" would have us all live in a single unit of reinforced concrete, a forty-acre building erected on a floating foundation. It too was never built because capital while it accumulated in fewer and fewer corporate hands did not concentrate in these cities—it dispersed multinationally, it diversified instead of reinvesting, and this shift can be read on the landscape of the South and West where the "no where" cities were built, as the sunrise inequality of Silicon Valley replaced the sunset inequality of Detroit and New York. In the Bronx now we see a purposeful attempt to divorce facade and content in the name of pure spectacle: in 1983 the Reagan administration gave New York City $300,000 to improve the image of its neighborhoods, including the Bronx by pasting cheerful vinyl decals—flower pots, venetian blinds, sunning cats—over the smashed, gaping windows of abandoned buildings. This *tableau mourant* was to be pasted up so that potential developers zooming by on the Cross Bronx Expressway would not move their investment to, say, Houston. Decaling the Bronx is a tour de force when it comes to making something (poverty, misery and desperation) into nothing. According to *The Nation*, the commissioner of New York's Department of Housing Preservation and Development explained it this way: "Perception is reality."[43]

As we move to looking at the cities of the sunbelt, we realize that we no longer need the distance of the European gaze to feel the phenomenological weight of these cities. Not even Americans are very much at home in these "no where" cities. One of the first reasons this is so is that we don't walk in the cities, we drive. Getting grid-locked is not a danger in Los Angeles like it is in Manhattan. And even in Manhattan we need to get into the city somehow. We do so by vast freeway arteries. As early as 1957 Lewis Mumford warned America that it was going to be sorry if it did not begin to think about the implications of the enormous freeway system it was building:

> The major highway systems are conceived in the interest of speed, as linear organizations, that is to say as arteries. That conception would be a sound one, provided the major arteries were not overdeveloped to the exclusion of all the minor elements of transportation. Highway planners have yet to realize that these arteries must not be thrust into the delicate tissues of our cities; the blood they circulate must rather enter through an elaborate network of minor blood vessels and capillaries.[44]

Nobody listened, of course. The result, for me at least, is that entering most American cities on the freeway system is like being in the movie *Fantastic Voyage*—that was the movie where a medical team and a submarine are miniaturized to microbe size so that they can enter the circulatory system of an important scientist and remove a blood clot from his brain by laser surgery. The

hemonauts, who have been injected into the carotid artery, get
caught in a whirlpool which throws them into the jugular vein
unexpectedly. There they are zooming down the stream away
from the brain and toward the gnashing, throbbing heart. I know
how they feel.

Still in most of the "no where" cities we don't have to navigate
the heart because there is no center. As Gertrude Stein put it:
"There is no there, there." But we still have to worry about de-
bouching at some horribly inappropriate or dangerous place. The
car gives us some power of domination over this freeway landscape, but anyone who's ever run out of gas on the freeway
knows how fragile this power is. That may be one reason we
have so much suppressed car hatred in contemporary art. Consider Andy Warhol's *Five Deaths Twice* (1963); Tom Wesselmann's
Landscape #5; John Chamberlain's *Ravyredd* (1962); Cesar's *Com-
pression* (1980); Robert Longo's *Love Police: Engines in Us (The
Doors)* (1982–83); Claes Oldenburg's *Soft Airflow—Scale 2* (1966);
Francesco Torres' *Snap and/or in the Spirit of the French Commune*
(1982); Arman's *White Orchid* (1963)—an exploded MG sportscar;
Ant Farm's *Cadillac Ranch* (1974); or Jim Wines' *Ghost Parking Lot*
(1978), twenty automobiles sunk to different levels in a suburban
shopping mall parking lot, each covered with gray asphalt.
Wines captures the gray, static yet disembodied experience of
suburban life.

This last installation points to how "nowhere" cities move us. I
think they work something like the shopping center, as a geography. Shopping Centers, as Fred Pfeil demonstrates in a piece
called "Center of the Dream: Mass Culture in the Shopping
Mall"[45] are most successful when they cover about a 600,000 sq.
ft. area and contain three anchor stores. We enter the shopping
malls like small ionized particles and are drawn from one to another of these anchor or magnet stores. On the way we pass and
are sometimes drawn into "secondary traffic attractors"—stores
like Baskin-Robbins, or Brentano's—to drop a few bucks. Shopping center manuals (aimed at the builders of malls) suggest that
benches in malls should look nice but should not be too comfort-
able; "They can be constructed with slat seats, which become tir-
ing after a while; they can be built without backrests and spaced
away from walls."[46] These benches are also usually built right
into the flow of traffic so that rather than enjoying a vista, the
bench sitters feel like they've just stopped in the middle of the
Ringstrasse.

William H. Whyte in his book *The Social Life of Small Urban
Spaces* discusses some of the ways cities have to keep us on the
move. In a March 1985 lecture given at the Dallas Public Library,

Whyte told his audience what he'd discovered about Dallas after seven years of research. "Asked to identify the 'center' of Dallas, fewer than one-third of the 560 respondents named any downtown location. One-tenth said the city's center was on one freeway or another."[47] Whyte also found there were few places to sit in Dallas, even when one could find the center, and there were no newspaper kiosks or food vendors to clutter up the city, so why sit down anyway. Typical of the new architecture of "nowhere" city is the mirror-walled building. Fredric Jameson best describes the emptiness and disorientation these buildings create in his description of Los Angeles' Bonaventura Hotel:

> Now one would want to stress the way in which the glass skin repels the city outside; a repulsion for which we have analogues in those reflector sunglasses which make it impossible for your interlocutor to see your own eyes and thereby achieve a certain aggressivity towards and power over the Other. In a similar way, the glass skin achieves a peculiar and placeless dissociation of the Bonaventura from its neighborhood: it is not even an exterior, inasmuch as when you seek to look at the hotel's outer walls you cannot see the hotel itself, but only the distorted images of everything that surrounds it.[48]

Like the older cities of the East, the "nowhere" city enjoys an eclectic architecture. Rather than engaging in historicism, some cities are now having ruins built to house their goods: for example, at the Best Products Co. showroom, built by James Wines, just outside Houston, the walls are built already in the process of tumbling down, and at his Drive Through Showroom at Cutler Ridge near Miami, the main wall is ripped asunder making the building merely a gutted shell. Wines also has an answer to the American desire to participate in city life, but still retain the benefits of the suburbs like private property and single family houses. His *High-Rise of Homes*, which he maintains is feasible both commercially and structurally, would be eight to ten stories high and would contain diverse single family houses in "picturesque eclectic" American style, five or so to each skyscraper level. But, Dolores Hayden's description of the "nowhere" city captures the reality we already have:

> A few tall buildings downtown tower over parking lots and garages. Perhaps there will be a park and some apartment houses. Then a tangle of porno shops, discount stores, fast food places and gas stations will lead to freeway ramps, and the freeway will connect miles and miles of similar, large single family houses on landscaped lots with shopping malls, industrial parks and the

occasional school or church. In the American city, all the themes, styles, and features of the speculative builder's prevalent jargon preclude architectural style in the same way that a string of expletives precludes coherent argument.[49]

What gives this landscape physical continuity, according to Hayden, are precisely the apparatuses of circulation—the infrastructure of roads, sewers, utility poles and wires. And following Lefèbvre's concept of built space reflecting the mode of production, Hayden sees a cityscape whose development has been based on land speculation, cheap, non-renewable energy and private transportation.[50] Symbolic continuity, she sees in the endless sales pitch for mass consumption.

Contemporary society—whether we call it 'high tech,' the media generation, or the information society—seems to have moved beyond buying products to selling itself. Networking is an integral part of working. One reason this shift may have taken place is suggested by Fred Pfeil in his essay, "Makin' Flippy-Floppy: Postmodernism and the Baby-boom PMC": The PMC, or technical intelligensia, is mainly made up of baby-boomers; the overwhelming majority of people who were between 25 and 35 in 1980 are members of the PMC. "Of the 37.4 million citizens between those ages, 22.2 million were employed in managerial and professional specialty occupations. . . . that's 59% of all 25–35 year olds, and 82% of all those employed."[51] The information monger and the image maker can live in cities which are dispersed through space, even in an energy-scarce age; it has become so possible to move information so that we don't have to bother with moving people.

The city envisioned by the futurist architect Fortunato Despero in his 1916 Aerial City was to be an "aerial and mobile city of leisure,"[52] a thing of beauty. What America created instead was Las Vegas, the ultimate landscape of spectacle—the capital of entertainment; the city of lights. Here's a "nowhere" city that is really nowhere. The t.v. private eye, Dan Tanna who worked the strip in Las Vegas and parked his car in his living room is a media version of *Long-term Parking*, one in which home and absence have become synonymous. Architect Robert Venturi in *Learning from Las Vegas* sees the signs of Las Vegas, those architectures in the night, as creating a rich semiological field. Tomas Maldonado in "Las Vegas and the Semiological Abuse" points out that the signs of Las Vegas are hardly polyvalent symbols rife with ambiguous meanings.[53] Rather, they are the flip side of the repetitive facades of the architects of the international style in that the tumult of sensory input they trigger can lead to sensory satiation as deadly as the sensory deprivation of a monotonous cityscape. The visual barrage echoes the auditory barrage Bardamu found at the River Rouge plant. The signs in Las Vegas are simply that—neon signs. Inside the buildings they tower over, according to Joan Didion, "the level of frustration and nervous boredom is so pronounced that a crowd will form around the search for a dropped dime."[54] Boredom, as Marx defined it, is "the nostalgia for content."[55] Outside, the spectacular skyline is merely specular; when the lights go out, in the light of the day, as Stein has put it, "There's no there, there."

NOTES

1. Gerald Silk, *Automobile and Culture* (New York: Abrams, 1984), 160.
2. David M. Gordon, "Capitalist Development and the History of American Cities," in *Marxism and the Metropolis: New Perspectives in Urban Political Economy,* William K. Tabb and Larry Sawers, eds. (New York: Oxford, 1978), 25–63.
3. Dolores Hayden, "Capitalism, Socialism and the Built Environment" in *Socialist Visions,* Stephen Rosskamm Shalom, ed. (Boston: South End Press, 1983), 59–81; David R. Goldfield and Blaine A. Brownell, *Urban America: From Downtown to No Town* (Boston: Houghton Mifflin, 1979).
4. Fredric Jameson, "Postmodernism, or The Cultural Logic of Late Capitalism," *New Left Review,* 146 (Summer 1984), 53–92.
5. Guy Debord, *Society of the Spectacle* (Detroit: Black and Red, 1977), section 17.
6. F. T. Marinetti, "The Futurist Manifesto" in *Futurismo & Futurismi,* catalogue to an exhibition organized by Pontus Hulten, Palasso Grassi, Venice (Milan: Bompiani, 1986), 452.
7. Silk, 58.
8. Roger Shattuck, *The Banquet Years: The Origins of the Avant-Garde in France, 1885 to World War I* (New York: Random, 1955), 17.
9. *Futurismo & Futurismi,* 452.
10. H. G. Wells, *The Future of America* (New York: Harper and Brothers, 1906), 40.
11. Francis Picabia, "A Post-Cubist's Impressions of New York," *The New York Tribune,* 9 March 1913.
12. *Futurismo & Futurismi,* 452.
13. *Futurismo & Futurismi,* 459.
14. *Futurismo & Futurismi,* 452.
15. Cited and translated in Dolores Hayden, "Capitalism, Socialism and the Built Environment," 63.
16. Louis Mumford, *The City in History,* 421.
17. Alan Trachtenberg, *The Incorporation of America: Culture & Society in the Gilded Age* (New York: Hill and Wang, 1982), 115.
18. Claude Lévi-Strauss, *Tristes tropiques,* trans. John and Doreen Weightman (New York: Atheneum, 1974), 96–97.
19. Jean-Paul Sartre, "American Cities" in *The City: American Experience,* Alan Trachtenberg, ed. (New York: Hill and Wang, 1982), 199.
20. Carl E. Schorske, *Fin-de-siecle Vienna: Politics and Culture* (New York: Random, 1961), 32.
21. Schorske, 36.
22. Ibid., 36–44.

23. Trachtenberg, *Incorporation*, 118, 120.
24. Jean-Paul Sartre, "American Cities" in *The City: American Experience*, Alan Trachtenburg, Peter Neil and Peter C. Bunnell, eds. (New York: Oxford, 1971), 199–200.
25. See Gordon, 35, 43, 47.
26. Franz Kafka, *America* (London: Penguin, 1967), p. 44–45.
27. Ibid., 44–45.
28. Ibid., 48.
29. Ibid., 51–52.
30. Ibid., 57–58.
31. Ibid., 104–05.
32. Ibid., 103.
33. Ibid., 104.
34. Ibid., 105–06.
35. Céline, *Journey to the End of Night*, 165.
36. Ibid., 180.
37. Ibid., 192.
38. Ibid., 193–94.
39. Mary MacLeod, " 'Architecture or Revolution': Taylorism, Technocracy, and Social Change," *Art Journal* 43,2 (Summer 1983), 134.
40. MacLeod, 135.
41. Lawrence Halprin, *Freeways* (New York: Reinhold Publishing Corporation, 1966), 215.
42. MacLeod, 138–39.
43. *The Nation*, 237 (1983), 524.
44. Lewis Mumford, *The Highway and the City* (New York: Harcourt, Brace and World, 1963), 236.
45. Fred Pfeil, "Center of the Dream: Mass Culture in the Shopping Mall," *Moving On* (December/January 1980), 11–15, 20.
46. Pfeil, 15.
47. *Corvallis Gazette Times* (Sunday, March 24, 1985), A8.
48. Jameson, 81.
49. Hayden, "Capitalism," 59.
50. Ibid., 63.
51. Fred Pfeil, "Makin' Flippy-Floppy: Postmodernism and the Baby-Boom PMC.
52. *Futurismo & Futurismi*, 418.
53. Tomas Maldonado, *Design, Nature and Revolution: Toward a Critical Ecology* (New York: Harper & Row, 1972), 62–63.
54. Joan Didion, "Getting the Vegas Willies," *Esquire* 87, 44.
55. *Zur Kritik der Nationalokonomie—Okonomisch-philosophische Manuskripte*, 66, quoted and translated in Maldonado, 64.

CITY/CINEMA/DREAM

Jon Lewis

Summoned to lay down the rules for the foundation of Perinthia, the astronomers established the place and the day according to the position of the stars . . . Perinthia—they guaranteed—would reflect the harmony of the firmament; nature's reason and the gods' benevolence would shape the inhabitants' destinies.

Following the astronomers' calculations precisely, Perinthia was constructed; various peoples came to populate it; the first generation born in Perinthia began to grow within its walls; and these citizens reached the age to marry and have children.

In Perinthia's streets and square today you encounter cripples, dwarfs, hunchbacks, obese women, bearded women. But the worst cannot be seen; guttural howls are heard from cellars and lofts, where families hide children with three heads or with six legs.

Perinthia's astronomers are faced with a difficult choice. Either they must admit that all their calculations were wrong and their figures unable to describe the heavens, or else they must reveal that the order of the gods is reflected in the city of monsters.[1]

"New York, New York / Sweet city of dreams;" or so the rap song goes. LA: for some dreamers of the golden dream—milk and honey, Chicanos, Watts and Charles Manson. The city as dream . . . in recent years such a romantic notion seems hardly useful. It has become a qualified dream, a reconciled dream, a dream colored by the mass media (and do any of us dream without their help these days?).

"When Hemingway called Paris 'a movable feast' he was not talking about its gastronomy," Charles Michener muses, "Paris has long been a dream about a dream—in this case about the City of Light; a place where buildings glimmer, clothes shimmer . . . and sex flickers."[2]

But when Jean-Luc Godard, tongue firmly in cheek, projected the Paris of the near future as ALPHAVILLE, with its swimming pool executions (of people who have shown emotion, of people who read poetry) and its cinemas furnished with electric chairs, he made no attempt to change the landscape. Instead he shot the entire film in familiar Parisian locales. For Godard, Paris was the city of dreams all right—but the dream was not of light, but of a constant physical and moral darkness; a darkness one can not hope to change, one can only hope to escape. For Godard, Paris, the city of dreams, had lost its fundamental humor, its intrinsic poetry. Salvation (and this is why he remains so perplexing to the lettered French) lay in American popular culture; ironically, in the literature of Raymond Chandler and Dashiell Hammett and the B-cinema of the thirties and forties that so captured the post-industrial American city milieu.

In John Carpenter's ESCAPE FROM NEW YORK, the rampant crime that now characterizes America's cities results in the conversion of Manhattan into a maximum security prison island. Carpenter's city/film-set, like Godard's, involves no "industrial light and magic." Rather, the film was shot on location in contemporary New York City, Gary, Indiana and Minneapolis, Minnesota. His projection of garbage-laden streets and a city society based on the racially drawn prison hierarchy is both an inside joke and a chilling social comment. Vincent Canby remarked that ESCAPE FROM NEW YORK was like "the hallucination of someone riding the subway at 3 AM . . . Manhattan becomes a sort of Roach Motel: the inmates check in, but they don't check out."[3]

Urban historian Lewis Mumford refers to the city as "a stage upon which the drama of social life may be enacted . . . with the actors taking their turns as spectators and the spectators as actors."[4] Such a point of view is suggestive on several levels: (1) it affirms the relationship between the aesthetic and the social, the functional and the cultural; (2) it refers to the "double game" of acting and spectating—the drama of participation and alienation; (3) it alludes to the dreamwork: does one appear as an actor in one's dreams? or is one simply a captive spectator? or both? and (4) it offers a metaphor to the subjective dialectic posed by the cinema, here a troubling reference given one's powerlessness in the throes of the film spectacle. For Mumford, the individual's relationship to the city is to a great extent a speculary phenomenon. One stands before the built environment that is the city like a spectator in a dream; like the viewer of a film.

The social dimensions of such a theory of subjectivity or spectatorship is noted by Christian Metz in the following:

> (The spectator) lives in a sort of acquarium which differs from real acquaria only that it is a bit more sparing with its windows (keeping something back is part of the scopic game). Besides, the fish are on the other side, eyes glued to the glass, like the poor of Proust's Balbec who watched the guests at the grand hotel eating.[5]

Metz then discusses the ideological underpinnings of cinematic spectatorship, but one can hardly miss his theory's usefulness with regard to urban subjectivity:

The cinematic institution demands a viewer who is immobile and silent, a secret viewer, constantly in a state of sub-mobility and hyper-perception, alienated and happy, acrobatically attached to himself by the invisible wire of sight, a viewer who only retrieves himself as a subject at the last moment, by a paradoxical identification with his own self, stretched to the limit in the pure act of watching.[6]

The situationists, a post-critical group of radical ideologues, focussed much of their pre-Paris 1968 attention to the structure, function and ideological significance of the urban environment. Echoing the city/cinema/dream metaphor set up by Mumford, situationist theorist Ivan Chtcheglov (in an essay titled: "Formulary For a New Urbanism") argues that: "Architecture is the simplest means for articulating time and space, of engendering dreams."[7]

In THE SOCIETY OF THE SPECTACLE, Guy Debord describes "urbanism" as "capitalism's seizure of the natural and human environment." Debord argues that space in and of itself is ideological, and that the agenda of all ideologies serves the logic of absolute domination. In the city, as Debord sees things, such an ideological agenda is served as the "totality of space" evolves into a (film-like) setting; a well planned space conducive to the operations of late market capitalism.[8]

The following characterizes Debord's sense of the speculary with regard to the cinematic spectacle:

The spectator's consciousness, imprisoned in a flattened universe, bound by the screen of the spectacle behind which his life has been deported, knows only the fictional speakers who unilaterally surround him with their commodities and the politics of their commodities. The spectacle, in its entirety, is his mirror image. Here the stage is set with the false exit of generalized autism.[9]

According to Debord, the city systematically packages the dominant culture's political and social and moral imperative—a process completely in line with the function and ideological effect of mass media in contemporary society. The individual's role, position and range of activity vis a vis the dream or the cinema, Debord argues, coordinates a profound and chilling metaphor regarding anomie in the contemporary urban environment.

Debord argues that the organization of city space, which could encourage frequent and fruitful interactions between different social classes and ethnic groups, has instead developed into a built, ideological space that "safeguards class power." The post-industrial city scheme has, according to Debord, effected "the atomization of workers who had been dangerously brought together by the urban conditions of production;"[10] a situation that clearly serves the agenda of the dominant culture.

As Mumford, Chtcheglov and Debord describe things, the city can be viewed as a ritual version of one's own heavily mediated imaginative state, subtly and completely formulated in advance of our humble arrival. In such terms, the built environment is, as Metz describes the filmwork, "always already there."[11]

LA: "Reality is that which, when you stop believing in it, doesn't go away."[12]

The single most perpetrated city myth is LA. Via daily television and Hollywood cinema, the world (as urban, suburban and rural) has been reproduced not only in and by LA, but reproduced (commercially, morally and politically) as LA. If there was ever any doubt that capitalism manifests systems in which commodity production involves the reproduction of the means (and in this case the locale) of production, LA does well to dispel such foolish notions once and for all.

Within its expansive borders, LA provides a multitude of city and country film sets: sea and sand, mountains, plains, desert, skyscrapers, crowded urban streets, slums, ghettos, development house and lawn suburbs and ridiculous and sublime mansions. From this selection, LA renders the film-set city as LA_1or LA_2— stipulating a kind of generic nature to the American urban film environment. (That LA has accomplished this feat suggests the frightening conclusion that future cities have learned, not from Las Vegas, but from TV and film replicas of cities gestated in and as LA.)

The concept of the generic is taken to extremes in REPO MAN, Alex Cox's near-future vision of LA. In REPO MAN, food in the icebox is just labeled food. Drinks are just drinks; beer, beer. REPO MAN's focus on the unglamorous, East-LA city-scape depicts the city as just one very large bad neighborhood—a neighborhood contained and produced within the confines of LA. As opposed to Italo Calvino's romantic notion that one city can be all cities if one just has the imagination to see it, REPO MAN posits the less lofty view that one city is the same as another, is the same as another . . .

"People get so hung up on specifics, they miss the whole thing," Miller (REPO MAN's oddball truth-teller) muses while burning garbage under the polluted but beautiful LA sunset. "I do my best thinking on the bus," he continues, "the more you drive, the less intelligent you are." His remarks offer a critique of the new American city, "a nowhere city," described by Dolores

Hayden as follows: "a private city dependent on automobiles . . .
commercial strips and dispersed production sites."[13]

Miller, whose bizarre philosophisizing is validated just as the
Hispanic, black and youth-punk "work ethics" are not, exits the
film aboard a flying, radioactive automobile which soars above
the night-lit city. And even in this panorama, or perhaps especially in this parody of clichéd helicopter sequences from other
city movies, LA is aestheticized just as it is rendered indistin-
guishable from the other cities it comes to represent in other
films.

The restrictive, stupefying city milieu in REPO MAN offers explanation for why urban teenagers are so screwed up. Otto, the
film's crew-cut punk hero, and his straight friend Kevin, are, in
the beginning of the movie, employed in a local quick-stop market. Labelling cans, a symbolic process indeed, Kevin sings:
"Feelin' 7-up, I'm Feelin' 7-Up . . . " In a later scene, Otto exits a
party alone, after his girlfriend dumps him for his best friend.
Stopping at the railroad tracks (on the wrong side of Our Town),
Otto testifies to his loneliness and despair, singing: "Don't want
to talk about anything else / We don't want to know / We're just
dedicated / To our favorite show / 'Saturday Night Live' / 'Monday Night Football' / 'Dallas' / 'The Jeffersons' / 'Gilligan's Island' / 'The Flintstones . . . ' "

Later, we find both Otto and Kevin unemployed, and Kevin
faces the want ads head on. "There's room to move as a fry
cook," he argues, "in two years I'll be assistant manager . . . It's
key!" Such is the state of things in the Pepsi generation.

REPO MAN romanticizes the city because it is filthy and corrupt, because social mobility there is such a joke. For the punks,
the city is an underground in itself. The film's frenetic, loud
punk music score, the characters' fascist posturings and rehearsed outrageousness, identify the repo men as heroes in an
urban battleground. Certainly REPO MAN is to a great extent
parody, and at times pretends to the postmodern; but the city, as
the film sets it, is a very real wasteland, an unconquerable wilderness in which only a particular and peculiar style of heroism
can endure.

There is a progressive argument to be made about REPO
MAN—a critical position seldom stated with regard to punk art
and lifestyle. Fred Pfeil argues that REPO MAN "reproduces the
relation between the bone-numbing vacuity and circularity of
daily life . . . " noting that the film's "sudden jolts of idiotic violence" offer a profound, if parodic (and Pfeil would argue post-
modern) critique of "the nowhere city." Pfeil then comments on
"the simultaneous desire and dread of some ultimate, externally

imposed moment of truth" in REPO MAN, a moment that "once and for all (would) put an end to the endless, senseless repetitions of which our lives seem to be made."[15]

REPO MAN accurately reveals the punk critique of the city as the locale for "the decline of western civilization" (the title of Penelope Spheeris' dazzling inside-punk documentary set and shot in LA in the late seventies). Since such an eventuality is apparently upon us, or so the punks argue, the city becomes both home and toilet—home and cause célèbre. The punks, whose vision dominates REPO MAN just as it pervaded youth culture in LA in the late seventies, completely acquiesced to the aesthetics of ugliness that characterize downtown LA. For them, the city is a graffiti-decorated, obscenity-filled sewer—a metaphor regarding the state of things in American culture in general. This particular vision is exemplified in the lyrics of the punk anthem "I Love Livin' in the City" by the LA based punk band Fear:

> My house smells just like a zoo
> It's chock full of shit and puke
> Cockroaches on the walls
> Crabs are crawlin' on my balls
> Oh, I'm so clean cut
> I just want to fuck some slut
>   chorus: I love livin' in the city
>   I love livin' in the city
>   (lyrics by Lee Ving
>   copyright: Toxic Tunes)

Making his home in nearby Anaheim, home of Disneyland, Knotts Berry Farm and the California Angels, science-fiction novelist Philip K. Dick has become something of a visionary on the subject of LA. His novel, DO ANDROIDS DREAM OF ELECTRIC SHEEP (re-titled BLADE RUNNER on its seventh printing following the success of Ridley Scott's film adaptation of the novel) projects the future city as a last refuge for assorted misfits and "chickenheads" (mutant-humans too damaged to be allowed to genetically poison the "suburban" off-world colonies).

The novel and film focus on the issue of empathy as a signifier of humanity. The film posits the ironic conclusion that near human may be close enough, but this very much runs against the grain of Dick's novel. In "How to Build a Universe That Doesn't Fall Apart Two Days Later," Dick argues that all his fiction attends to a single issue: the fake versus the real. And there is no ambiguity at all in Dick's rather spiritual sense of things.

In DO ANDROIDS DREAM OF ELECTRIC SHEEP, J. P. Isidore's victimization at the hands of the super-androids and later

Deckard's fall from grace following an intimate evening with a radically new simulated human are presented as the stupid and unpleasant results of a city-world subsumed in the ideology of capital and the accompanying poverty of the spiritual. In fact, there are no chickenheads at all in the film. Isidore is renamed Sebastian and he is a "genetic engineer", a mastermind for the renamed Terrel Corporation.[16]

Dick cleverly connects this malady with the capital-in-reproduction city of Disneyland, a metaphor Dick lays out as follows:

> Fake realities will create fake humans. Or, fake humans will generate fake realities and then sell them to other humans, turning them, eventually, into forgeries of themselves. So we wind up with fake humans creating fake realities and then peddling them to fake humans. It is just a very large version of Disneyland.[17]

In the film, BLADE RUNNER, the staggering, spectacular visuals of the opening sequence immediately set up the social conditions of LA in the not so distant future. The sky is black and filled with rain. The camera hovers along with the futurist hover crafts high above the ground. City space is separated as the masses are. The higher above ground you are, the better off. Those on the ground engage in a kind of sub-culture, street-wise, cottage industry. Street stands with fast food compete for the patronage of the throngs crowded into the devastated habitat; everyone speaking in short-hand, gutter-speech.

Those inhabiting the overcrowded streets are strange ethnic variations: Mexican-Chinese, Vietnamese-Black, Irish-Spanish-Japanese. The cross-bred culture, completely confused ethnically and thus assimilated into the trap of petty bourgeois capitalism, occupy the now defiled turf of their dreams.

And above their heads they are policed from the sky. Giant neon billboards form the skyline, advertising social mobility (via immigration to the off-world colonies) and mass market commodities (like Coca-Cola). These messages occupy the same sign structure, linked together by a neon dissolve.

The terrain is organized as an aesthetic-corporate scheme, in which architecture is both art and advertising; in which the lived environment is both served by and servant to the commodity. In the film, even the acid rain black sky and overcrowding on the street are aestheticized. Via camera movement and the ongoing Vangelis electronic music score, the film superimposes its ironic detective story over Dick's spiritual, anti-capitalist fable of the evil of the simulacrum, epitomized for Dick by the Abraham Lincoln exhibit at Disneyland and horrifyingly dramatized in the novel by the Rosen Corporation's unapologetic mass production of simulated humans.

The city in the novel has lost its essential humanity. It is an atomized society in which the people blindly worship a TV clown and receive simulated sexual and emotional gratification in the safety (or is it prison?) of their own apartments. In both the film and the novel, the city effectively organizes a powerless spectator culture; one which is alienated from the promise of the off-world as well as the legendary cities of the past. In the film, the city invokes a living space for those not ethnically pure enough to escape, but at the same time romanticizes city-life through its evocation of the American film noir detective myth.

Providing the final word on LA, Dick poses the following ironic conversation in FLOW MY TEARS THE POLICEMAN SAID:

"I don't like LA," Ruth Rae whimpered. "I haven't been there in years. I hate LA." She peered wildly around.
"So do I," the (policeman) said . . . "But we must learn to live with it: it's there."[18]

Miami: "All space is occupied by the enemy."[19]

Perhaps more than any other "new" city, Miami has come to epitomize the changing face of urban America. The allure of fun and sun has been amended to "fun, sun and guns": in Miami, as elsewhere, racially motivated violence has all but negated whatever claims to integration and assimilation city-planners and politicians have ever held.

Miami may well be America's second city spectacle (behind LA)—a spectacle of the decline of urban America and the idiocy of American imperial foreign policy. In the new, uncontrollable, violent, Hispanicized city environment of Miami, America is paying for its sins abroad.

Comparisons between the 1950 and 1960 census reports were among the first official signals of the changing face of the American city. In Washington, DC, for example, the non-white population rose from 35% to 55%. Statistics revealed that blacks living in Chicago paid one third more for comparable housing; and there seems to be ample proof that the white-male controlled banks conspired to deny blacks mortgage insurance and thus blocked their exit to the promised land of the suburbs.[20]

Banks and urban planners systematically supported highway construction over decent inner-city public housing. The highway became the city's focus and the city became the focus of the highway. The accompanying glamorization of the automobile further isolated the "new" city from its moneyed economic base and further isolated its citizens from any real control over its development.

In "Situationist Theses on Traffic," Debord argues that efforts to re-design urban architecture to serve the "parasitical existence of the private automobile" elaborate a connection between contemporary city planning and mass market monopoly capitalism.[21] Warning against a "progressive urbanism" that accepts the automobile as its central theme, Debord resists the "new," postmodern architecture; a style wholeheartedly embraced by the Atlantis Condominium Project and Paradise Business Complex in downtown Miami.

Both the Atlantis and Paradise were designed by the controversial Miami architecture group, Architectonica. Laurinda Spear, a 3-D designer for the group, noted the following in a recent interview: "We want our designs to stand out at 55 miles per hour."[22] Such a remark offers no less than the degree zero for viewing postmodern architecture—perhaps for viewing in general—in the American eighties.

This 55 mile per hour spectacle offers an introduction to the visual formula embraced by the still popular NBC-TV show, MIAMI VICE. Indeed, the show successfully speeds up the TV cop show formula, updating the genre with trendy clothing, a splashy blue and white (and more recently muted blue and grey) color scheme, an emphasis on camera movement (as opposed to the static shot/reverse shot "conventional" TV editing formula) and the now familiar Ferrari open road montages set to upbeat pop songs (alluding to music video as well as affirming the show's awareness of its audience).

MIAMI VICE is an unabashed expolitation, and veritable catalogue of fashionable, "youth" and yuppie culture. References abound: to MTV, to a new vogue in fashion, to the glitzy, hyperconsumptive lifestyle of the unembarrassed, upwardly mobile white city dweller; to postmodern architecture; to a society on the move, on the road, too impatient and too busy and too information-obsessive to deal with the old slow-moving cop show formula.

The show features two handsome male stars, both of whom have benefitted from the layered nature of television promotion. They have parlayed their visibility on MIAMI VICE into guest spots on MTV, Friday Night Videos, Live Aid, Monday Night Football and a television miniseries. In addition, there have been fashion layouts in GQ, JET, ESQUIRE and COSMOPOLITAN. Philip Michael Thomas (Tubbs) has recently secured a recording contract and Don (Sonny) Johnson's HEARTBEAT topped the charts a few years back. Clothing manufacturers are mass-producing baggy belt-less pants, loose fitting jackets and pastel colored tee-shirts after Don Johnson's ultimate Miami wardrobe. Such apparel, along with a line of tuxedos and sunglasses already bear the Miami Vice logo.

Via the pages of America's popular news, fashion, features, television and entertainment magazines—along with high-profile "free" advertisements on MTV and radio—MIAMI VICE has co-ordinated a monopoly style of production unparalleled in the history of American television. With MIAMI VICE, it's not so much a media blitz as a vertically integrated corporate blitz. And for a show so in tune with up-scale life in one of America's most wealthy and controversial cities, its packaging is hardly inappropriate.

Demographers project that by 1990 more than half of the population living within the city limits of Miami will be Hispanic. As of 1986, whites accounted for less than 30% of the population. Blacks, who also accounted for just under 30%, have not been able (for a variety of reasons) to re-locate;[23] a situation similar to what was going on in the New York area some twenty-five years ago.

But despite the fact that MIAMI VICE attests to the racial instability in Miami these days, the show's local support is considerable. A recent AP story quotes a Miami official remarking that the show gave the city "an image of adventure and glamour." Syndicated columnist Bob Greene recently mused over what he observed as a "MIAMI VICE swagger" in the gait of residents and tourists alike. Due in large part to the image purveyed by the show, Greene argues that now "Miami seems more vibrant . . . the stereotype in the 1970's was of a dying city, old and sort of fading . . . Now it's more international."[24]

The opening credit sequence on MIAMI VICE is a veritable tourist bureau's dream ad—in form and content a spectacle of the commodity Miami and not the real Miami. In THE SOCIETY OF THE SPECTACLE, Debord argues that all spectacles, despite content, are positive; supporting the old ad agency adage that all publicity is good publicity (especially if it's for free). As Debord puts it:

> The spectacle presents itself as something enormously positive, indisputable and inaccessible. It says no more than "that which appears is good, that which is good appears." The attitude which it demands is passive acceptance which in fact it already obtained by its manner of appearing without reply, by its monopoly of appearance.[25]

The opening credit sequence on MIAMI VICE begins with the now familiar theme music—a catchy pop instrumental by Jan Hamer (which received its share of AM and FM and even MTV airplay in the first few years of the show). The opening visuals include a low-angle shot of blue sky through palm trees, pink flamingoes and an overhead (helicopter) tracking shot over blue water. These visuals set up both the dominant cinematographic formula and the show's color scheme. As the camera tracks, the MIAMI VICE logo (a reference to the rising significance of commercial art) and "Stereo" are supered over the image. Indeed, from its opening three shots, MIAMI VICE affirms its sense of itself on the cutting edge.

Because the opening credit sequence is the show's thirty second advertising signature, information is jammed together via jump cuts, a technique characteristic of television commercials. The next cut moves from the sea to a tan woman's breasts barely held in her bikini top, decorated by a gold chain. Then we cut to jai-alai (offering further reference to tourism and gambling). The subsequent cut leads back to the water as the opening tracking shot continues over the vast city docks, showcasing Miami's ultra-chic leisure boating community (where Sonny lives on the show). The next cut is unusual; it's a cut on reverse movement presenting yet another gambling and tourist attraction: horse racing. The aesthetics of wealth and the high life are emphasized throughout, with subsequent cuts to a Rolls Royce showroom and a tracking shot of the famous Miami Beach hotels.

The subsequent ten shots reinforce the visual scheme, the pace and the thematics of tourism, gambling and the high life: (1) more water, (2) birds (the tropics, paradise), (3) more water, (4) the dog track, (5) a low angle shot of the new Miami skyline, (6) a tracking shot of construction in progress (aestheticized so that even construction is seen as art), (7) more women in bikinis (this time shot from behind in a high angle shot), (8) more boats, panning up to the next shot (9) the city at night (as the song hits its last ominous chord), and (10) a fade to black (followed by the first sequence of television ads).

Despite its conspicuous absence in the opening credit sequence, the crime problem in Miami is attended to (perhaps even sensationalized) on the show. The heroes on MIAMI VICE (one white, one black, one Hispanic) are working class cops (with great clothes) in a city clearly out of control; a city in which criminals are well armed, where violence on the streets is relatively commonplace (see here also Brian DePalma's remake of SCARFACE) and where the Dodge City lawlessness is underwritten by a network of white, white collar organized crime.

True to its updated visuals and corporate-production scheme, MIAMI VICE is "hip" to the financial underpinnings of big money industry (including crime) in America. In the two hour season premiere episode of MIAMI VICE in 1985, the criminal seat of power was revealed outside the city limits—in fact the heroes track their case to a pristine office in a New York high-rise on Wall Street. When they enter, they are greeted by a gaunt WASP named Johnson (played by controversial Living Theater avatar Julian Beck), who gives them a lesson in the nature of organized crime in America in the 1980's:

> Money is a commodity . . . like oil or water. And that American dollar is the best brand in the world. And those of us who have it, can make more of it by lending it to those who don't . . . Not so long ago, our bank loaned a lot of money to our friends in Latin America . . . We are talking about hundreds of millions of dollars . . . Now they aren't going to repay that by selling straw bands and clay pots . . . If these Latin borrowers default, we would be decimated . . . and we are America . . . We are the entire free world . . . When we sneeze, (he snaps his fingers), everybody catches cold. That's why it's very important that we nurture our Latin brothers' major cash crops.

But despite such lessons, which are weekly fare on the show, the fact remains: Miami looks good. The Hispanic criminal element, the shoot 'em up streets and the unapologetic profiteering by white collar criminals simply reinforce Miami's newest attraction: its mean streets. MIAMI VICE presents the new city as the final frontier of adventure—a simply amazing bit of hucksterism the best public relations firm could never have accomplished on purpose.

Las Vegas: "The Circus Circus is what the whole hep world would be doing on Saturday night if the Nazis had won the war."[26]

In ONE FROM THE HEART, Francis Coppola's much underrated Zoetrope Studio debut, set-designer Dean Tavoularis replicated the famous Las Vegas strip on the old Hollywood General Studio lot. The art as artiface / artiface as art aesthetic, the hallmark of Coppola's Zoetrope Studio efforts (THE OUTSIDERS, RUMBLE FISH, THE COTTON CLUB, HAMMETT, MISHIMA and THE ESCAPE ARTIST), well suited its subject; as Las Vegas is the one American city most clearly tied up in its own fabrication(s).

Like Las Vegas, ONE FROM THE HEART revolves around a single aesthetic and political issue: scale. The film is primarily about its own production, as is Las Vegas, a reading keyed by the curtain opening and closing at the start and end of the film, the obtrusive camera movement, the neon-dominated oversized sets matched to the little boring characters, the secondarization of the narrative dialog track to the more evocative but less realistic romantic music track (featuring Tom Waits and Crystal Gayle) and the repeated references to the magic of the image and the insubstantial nature of everyday life. In ONE FROM THE HEART, Las Vegas is a city of dreams; but the characters soon learn that even the most simple dreams of escape simply don't include them. That such a moral may well be the point of Las Vegas, a city that wears its dreams on its sleeve, seems hardly worth arguing.

The individual's relationship to the system at work in Las Vegas is clearly marked by the architecture: big sign, little building, tiny human. That such a drama is played out on a couple of streets in the middle of the desert that people pay to go to clearly marks the tiny human's willingness to play the subject in a completely unrepressed discourse of American mass society.

Las Vegas is a city without embarrassment. In the production of a milieu, a system of signs and then an elaborate, manipulated system of signification—after all, the Las Vegas production understands and anticipates its audience—there is no effort to obfuscate the post-industrial, late capitalist intrusions into artistic design. Rather, such intrusions are part of the form and part of the politics involved as well. The big signs in the city—the most lucrative design firm in Las Vegas is not surprisingly YESCO, the Young Electric Sign Company—correspond to and coordinate an unabashed, spectacular celebration of the very system that produced them, that supports them; and in the final analysis, it is the system itself that these signs refer to.

And yet Las Vegas maintains an image of egalitarianism—despite, or because of its superficial celebration of money and the various "dreams" (leisure-oriented things) money can buy. Certainly racial tensions do not readily surface in Las Vegas, because the only color of significance is green. And since the city's motto is "easy come, easy go," as long as you can play the part, nobody cares what neighborhood you're from.

This superficial egalitarianism is the essence of Las Vegas, positing the spurious capitalist myth that everything money can buy is available (and money can buy anything) so long as you've got money to spend. That Las Vegas gambling and entertainment, like the Miami drug trade, is underwritten by white-collar, organized crime simply underscores the model society Las Vegas spectacularizes.

One lesson Las Vegas teaches is that in America even egalitarian models are based on the unequal distribution of wealth. That

Las Vegas thrives—that it is seen as romantic—stipulates the mystifying power of capitalist mythologies. One can hardly fear the odds; that they are long is precisely why they cry out to be played.

Thomas Disch, whose postmodern novel THE BUSINESSMAN provides a tour de force on the subject of the idiocy of capitalist mythologies, lampoons Las Vegas' superficial egalitarianism as follows:

> I think Las Vegas is the secret capitol of the country. The one place where democracy really works . . . Stand by any crap table or roulette wheel and look at the mix of people around you. Where else in the world would you find millionaires on speaking terms with ordinary riff-raff like me? Not in many churches for all their talk of brotherhood. No, the real melting pots these days are the casinos, and I think it's because people can express their deepest feelings there.[27]

What enables Las Vegas to maintain its image (its dream) of pure capitalist divertissement and its ability to mask its nastier underpinnings is its unapologetic sense of humor about itself. When Tom Wolfe muses that the signs that comprise the night time Las Vegas skyline (and the opening sequence of Coppola's ONE FROM THE HEART): "soar in shapes before which the existing vocabulary of art history is helpless . . . Boomerang Modern, Palette Curvilinear, Flash Gordon Ming Alert Elliptical, Miami Beach Kidney . . . ",[28] he echoes Calvino's point that one city (in this case Las Vegas) can be any city, if that's the way you want it (and if you can pay your own way). Looking at Las Vegas from this point of view, it is truly America's repository, if not its provider, of dreams.

Finally, we are a culture in love with such dreams; such cities of dreams. As Morris Lapidus puts it:

> People are looking for illusions. They don't want the world's realities. And I asked, where do I find this world of illusion? Where are their tastes formulated? Do they study it in school? Do they go to museums? Do they travel in Europe? Only one place—the movies. They go to the movies. To hell with everything else.[29]

NOTES

1. Italo Calvino, INVISIBLE CITIES, trans. by William Weaver (NY: Harcourt, Brace and Javanovich, 1972), pp. 144–145.

2. Charles Michener, "Paris," ESQUIRE, October, 1986, pp. 76–77.
3. Vincent Canby, "ESCAPE FROM NEW YORK," New York Times, August 2, 1981, p. 15. ESCAPE FROM NEW YORK reminds Canby of ALPHAVILLE as well, but for him, it's as if ALPHAVILLE "had not been directed by Jean-Luc Godard but by Federico Fellini."
4. Lewis Mumford as cited by Marty Jezer in THE DARK AGES: LIFE IN THE U.S. 1945–1960 (Boston: South End Press, 1982), p. 182.
5. Christian Metz, "History/Discourse: Note on Two Voyeurisms," trans. by Susan Bennett, EDINBURGH MAGAZINE, no. 1, 1976, p. 24.
6. Ibid., p. 24.
7. Ivan Chtcheglov, "Formulary For a New Urbanism," in THE SITUATIONIST INTERNATIONAL ANTHOLOGY, ed. and trans. by Ken Knabb (Berkeley, CA: Bureau of Public Secrets, 1982), p. 2.
8. Guy Debord, SOCIETY OF THE SPECTACLE (Detroit: Black and Red, 1977), section 169.
9. Ibid., section 218.
10. Ibid., section 172.
11. A major critical point in film theory generally credited to Metz. See: "History/ Discourse: Note on Two Voyeurisms" and "The Imaginary Signifier," in THE IMAGINARY SIGNIFIER, trans. by Ben Brewster (Bloomington, IN: Indiana University Press, 1975) pp. 1–98.
12. Philip K. Dick, "How to Build a Universe That Doesn't Fall Apart Two Days Later," in I HOPE I SHALL ARRIVE SOON, ed. by Mark Hurst and Paul Williams (Garden City, NY: Doubleday, 1985), p. 4.
13. Dolores Hayden, "Capitalism, Socialism and the Built Environment," in SOCIALIST VISIONS, ed. by Steve Rosskam Shalom (Boston: South End Press, 1983), p. 60.
14. Fred Pfeil, "Makin' Flippy Floppy: Postmodernism and the Baby Boom PMC," in THE YEAR LEFT (London: Verso Press, 1985), p. 285.
15. Ibid., p. 286.
16. The films changes the name of the company that produces the simulacra from Rosen (clearly a Jewish name) to Terrel (a familiar, but not so ethnic company name of a contemporary race car manufacturer)—an effort, no doubt to tread lightly on such sensitive turf.
17. Philip K. Dick, "How To Build a Universe That Doesn't Fall Apart Two Days Later," p. 6.
18. Philip K. Dick, FLOW MY TEARS THE POLICEMAN SAID, (NY: Daw, 1974), p. 112.
19. Guy Debord, "Theses on a Paris Commune," in THE SITUATIONIST INTERNATIONAL ANTHOLOGY, p. 315.
20. Jezer, pp. 176–181.
21. Guy Debord, "Situationist Theses on Traffic," in THE SITUATIONIST INTERNATIONAL ANTHOLOGY, p. 57.
22. John Dorschner, "Miami's Brave New Look," MACLEANS, February 27, 1984.
23. "Ethnic Strife, Crime Lurk Behind Miami Skyline," (AP), Corvallis GAZETTE TIMES, November 18, 1985, p. A6.
24. Ibid., p. A6.
25. Debord, SOCIETY OF THE SPECTACLE, section 12.
26. Hunter Thompson, FEAR AND LOATHING IN LAS VEGAS (New York: Warner Books, 1971), p. 46.
27. Thomas Disch, THE BUSINESSMAN (New York: Harper and Row, 1984), p. 77–78.
28. Tom Wolfe cited by Robert Venturi, Denise Scott Brown and Steve Izenour in LEARNING FROM LAS VEGAS (Cambridge, MA: MIT Press, 1972), p. 53.
29. Venturi, Brown and Izenour citing Lapidus, p. 51.

Jan Lukas/Art Resource. View of Brooklyn Bridge, New York.

8

ENACTMENT AND LASTNESS

*What sort of finality might a reader of the city expect to be
summoned to? A walk into the picture replaces the stroll along
the streets of the picturesque. Too much has crowded in, and the
dog baying at the lostness of it all, just the dog alone and the
horizon remains. Where we are.*

THE LAST MANIFESTO

Richard Kuhns

Nur zu Zeiten erträgt göttliche Fülle der Mensch. Traum von ihnen
ist drauf das Leben.

Only at times can our kind bear the full impact of gods. Ever after
our life is a dream about them.

Hölderlin, *Bread and Wine*

Coming into possession of a cultural tradition, and in turn being
seized by that tradition, evolves slowly over a life lived in self-
conscious community. And no community lacks self-consciousness; that is the mark of social life lived and passed on through
generations. We, from our late twentieth century vantage point
have mapped the past, interpreting primitive myth and urban
design as stages preliminary to our own. We are now becoming
more and more aware of the degree of continuity—perhaps even
sameness of basic outlook—that occurs repeatedly in human history. Yet each age and each city retells the story of growing up in

culture in its own way. Our cultural products tell the story we tell ourselves, and present to others the world outlook of our own time. So we have established *our* sense of being in a cultural tradition. Our own artifacts can be used to discover myths of origin and destiny we express as our own, and appropriate from others. Our tradition is unique in its incorporation of other traditions as partial realization of itself. Yet in our total comprehensiveness we are as culturally parochial as the peoples we would see beyond.

In 1866 Walt Whitman gazed out over New York harbor as he crossed from Brooklyn to Manhattan; his poetic vision both created and recorded the buildings ringing the waters:

CROSSING BROOKLYN FERRY

Lines: 123–132

Thrive, cities—bring your freight, bring your shows, ample and
sufficient rivers,
Expand, being than which none else is perhaps more spiritual,
Keep your places, objects than which none else is more lasting,
You have waited, you always wait, you dumb, beautiful ministers,
We receive you with fresh sense at last, and are insatiate hence-
forward,
Not you any more shall be able to foil us, or withhold yourselves
from us,
We use you, and do not cast you aside—we plant you perma-
nently within us,
We fathom you not—we love you—there is perfection in you also,
You furnish your parts toward eternity,
Great or small, you furnish your parts toward the soul.

Walt Whitman both creates and passively receives the city whose existence relies upon the poet as the poet is created by the objects he responds to. Mutual interdependence of objects and creators, of coming into the city which delivers a tradition, and making the tradition a part of oneself as one lives a life—that is the condition we call "culture." Whitman's vision sees the mythic possibilities for America and creates an American Manifesto, a manifesto of the New World, measuring itself against, as it uses elements of, the European inheritance. Truly, the American Manifesto declares the beginning of our modern era, of "modernity" in the sense exploited by the art of our time.

The wedge that forced open the space we now look back to as "modernity" was given its first thrust by Immanuel Kant's strange, difficult rumination, "The Critique of Aesthetic Judgment." And the filling of that space with objects was overseen and justified by a cultural object in its own right, the 19th and early 20th century manifesto. The more radical declarations of cultural renovation (for example, Corbusier's *Vers une architecture*) turned the 19th into the 20th century, artistically speaking, as Kant's Third Critique turned the 18th into the 19th century. The one hundred years between Kant's enlightenment hallowing of art, and the radical exploitation of art's political potential, is the most revolutionary in the history of Western cultural objects.

The objects I shall discuss in the following essay are all implicated in the revolution we call "modernity, although their production was, of course, oblivious to the weight of future interpretations. We tell the story of "modernity" in part as a joke played on our unsuspecting forbears; and as I say this, I wonder what ends will be assigned to our far less ingenious products.

Among the objects whose "aim" was to bring modernity to birth, the manifesto as a strict document, and the manifesto as a covert theme in the cultural products of the past, counts itself as an object, and in its claims can be rightfully set alongside the cultural products we refer to as "philosophies of art." Manifestoes, however, are documents whose difference from philosophies of art produced by those calling themselves "philosophers" should be carefully noted.

A philosophy of art explores epistemological, metaphysical, logical, and often ethical issues in its pursuit of the nature of art, and the terms it articulates are of a sort that would hardly—or rarely, except in the most devious ways—interest artists themselves. And yet those terms may, often in unconscious ways, profoundly influence the way an art, school, congregation of artists, produce, interpret, and develop an ideology of art.

Manifestoes, for their part, are the products of artists themselves who freely pillage the thought of philosophers, kooks, journalists, critics, and workers in a variety of domains. Manifestoes may rise to poetic heights, sink to flapdoodle depths; they are often obscure, silly, eloquent, visionary, acute, dull by turns. Yet they too have an influence far beyond their manifest audience, since they are read by philosophers, novelists, popular journalists, and end their days as documents full of "meaning" in the archives of art historians.

Any effect upon art production that manifestoes may have follows from their genesis in dissatisfaction and self-conscious reflection, for manifestoes are symptoms of an attitude and a practice within the arts which J. C. F. Schiller termed "sentimental." The term "sentimental" Schiller contrasted with the term "naive," in that famous essay now little read, though known today through the reference to it by Nietzsche in the *Birth of Tragedy*, "On Naive and Sentimental Poetry." Schiller's distinction cuts to the center of artistic visions, separating out the artist who creates unselfconsciously and without artifice—for example, Homer, Shakespeare, and, Schiller believed, the great Goethe— from the artist who is all self-consciousness, often a revolution- ary who requires a screen of artifice and of theory to interpose itself between himself and his art, for example, Wagner, certainly Nietzsche himself, though he aimed at the naive (it's a contradic- tion just to say that); and then, of course, Walt Whitman, who tried desperately to overcome the sentimental and reassert the naive, but once again, just to think that thought condemns one to sentimentality in Schiller's sense. The sentimental artist, Isa- iah Berlin observed, is identified as one who pronounces mani- festoes "as a symptom of revolt, reaction, personal or collective, that is to say, manifestoes are an acute phase of sentimentality." (I. Berlin, "The Naiveté of Verdi," *Against The Current*, New York Penguin Books, 1982, pp. 257–295). And, indeed, this very con- versation I carry on with you is an expression of our natural, per- haps inescapable, proclivity for the sentimental. Let us then exploit our sentimentality by setting out to write The Last Mani- festo. I must warn you that I cannot be held responsible for the document we shall begin to sketch out here; the product, the ob- ject I begin to delineate, takes its shape from the city itself, from the city we today celebrate.

America has been writing "The Last Manifesto" ever since the North American continent was settled; it was envisioned to be the fulfillment of ultimate destiny, and the apotheosis of Euro- pean tradition. Not only the religious sects who settled the new land, but the intellectuals revivifying Western European thought believed that there could be, at last, an end to the restless change and conflict that characterized the 5½ millennia since creation. And in the last one hundred years, with the establishment of "the modern," "last manifestoes" are issued regularly! And now I offer my ultimate manifesto, the *very* last, for I shall not declare the end of time, nor the end of cultural diversity, but simply an inclusive and exhaustive classification of all the objects we can ever make, the inventory of cultural products. Whatever the fu- ture reveals, the made things will find a place in my matrix. And they will be so accommodated because it is a matrix generated by myth.

Our mythic vision requires that we talk about *everything*, since the last manifesto, the Noah's Ark of finality, cannot omit any beast that clamors to be aboard; all beasts regard themselves as worthy of being saved from the deluge of post-modern destruction. For that is the cultural obliteration we have devised for our-selves, and is part of our mythic telling of our story, where we are and where we are going. Modernity is at an end; the era of the post-Modern is upon us, an era which is doomed to be a re-prise of the tradition as it now finally exists. Our inheritance is put to a use: it reflects, represents, regards itself.

That is the fate of the post-Modern, to tell the story of cultural objects over and over again. And therefore to create in its own makings repetitions of the makings of the past. And the grand container of our time in which and through which the represen-tations take place is the city. All cultural objects from the past shall find their place in it; it itself is part of the display, and it expresses the commentary upon both itself and the objects it con-tains. Our cultural situation today is thus a museum as habita-tion, for the city is a museum, though it contains within it collections that are referred to as "museums." And the Last Man-ifesto is the document that describes this grand container and contained, as if the city could reflect upon itself: the Last Mani-festo is the consciousness of the post-Modern city.

So let us imagine the city now—join with me as we create our semblance—a huge box, chock-a-block full of the objects we post-modernists preserve, restore, protect, squabble over, and even adore; objects we pray to, venerate, honor, find inspiration in, and teach our children to respect. We have in our excessive fondness allowed culture to swallow up nature.

My manifesto, now that it is in search of completeness, seeks a visual image that can serve as a *metaphor* of its dedications. We might reproduce Corbusier's *Vers une architecture* to serve, for it itself is a miniature, pocket-sized museum and might function as the metaphor, but it shows the scruffiness of modernity and poor plates. No, I need something beautiful in itself to set us off on our search for objects to occupy the cubby holes of my final clas-sification. Perhaps an object fitted with an internal organization where, as in the city, objects are already neatly boxed.

The painting *Gersaint's Shopsign* tells us a great deal about our-selves and the contents of the Last Manifesto, for the painting is a box, and we shall, in our Final Document, put a lid on the box. *Gersaint's Shopsign* is a metaphor for the city and for the ac-cumulation of cultural objects the city perpetuates and sustains. In the presence of Watteau's great representation we see the opening wedge of modernity as I want us to consider modernity in this post-modern accounting. Produced when modernity as we live that phase of history was just coming into consciousness, the *Shopsign* betokens the new presence, the merchant of art, and the clientèle for objects that are cultural objects, the rich bourgeoisie who, then as now, buy from a shop. No longer is art directly and simply commissioned by monarchs; now they too must frequent the shop if they want possession of objects; or their agents must search the shops, where art is bought and sold, as did in fact the agent for Frederick the Great, the agent who bought the Watteau painting and sent it to the Charlottenberg Palace. There it was divided into two, hung in—some say the music room, some say the dining hall—and thus began the passion of the simple shop-sign raised by our taste into greatness.

Several sufferings were imposed upon the object we are regarding. Originally, the top of the painting was slightly rounded, and when you see the original you see that the space of the painting needs the roundness; and the painting was trimmed on the right, probably so the right half could be fitted into a panel in the palace wall. And the painting which had been on two pieces of canvas was divided so each side of the room had a piece of it. And then in 1760 a marauding Russian soldier put a sword through it; and it finally found relief from its divided and slashed state, joined again into one, and framed (inappropriately) only in 1930. Despite all its wounds, we see it as both a shop-sign (painted in 1720 for the art dealer Gersaint, No. 35 Pont Notre-Dame) and as a monument that moves from the streets of the city to the final resting place of cultural objects spawned by the city, the museum. And it possesses the immediacy of city life, as it enshrines painting itself.

We may be gazing at Gersaint's family who pose in the shop; and therefore since the painting was originally hung at the entrance of the shop it established a set of internal and external references that we today, we post-modern semioticians, love. It is a painting whose semantical intricacies have generated semiotic gabble; I shall try to avoid that, but the Last Manifesto, whose opening page is the Watteau painting, cannot avoid altogether reflecting some of the preoccupations of our time—a silliness that must creep into every manifesto. For what is the seriousness of purpose of one age to the interpretations of another?

We are looking into a shop interior seen from the street, the middle of the street, for the first frame we move through after the gilt restorer's frame of 1930 is that of the street and the curb, the cobblestones, and the narrow passageway afforded pedestrians. Upon the outer footing stands a man lost in thought, sightlessly turning to the packing box, drawing our sighted attention to the box into which a painting (it happens to be of Louis Quatorze) is being put; and also on the outer footing is a dog going after a flea, or—since interpreting dog-intentions is difficult—relieving an itch. Of all the figures painted, only the dog looks out at us, we the viewers who are unseeingly seen by the dog, as we adjust ourselves to seeing into the shop. We viewers seek admittance; the dog has no need to see since all his perception is directed to the itch; and the peasant or city dweller looks inwardly, lost in fantasy. Then only we and the attentive painting-mongers in the painting are exercising the voraciousness of sight, although, as is clearly represented, the modes and manners of seeing within the painting are of several sorts.

Still staying outside the shop, we might reflect that we are not of the class with the peasant-city dweller lost in thought; and to be sure today there are no longer inward-looking dispossessed hanging around the curb of the Metropolitan Museum of Art— our equivalent to the shop. Rather, they are *in* the Met, rubbing elbows with the art history students and the hungry professors who are always starved for objects. In our world the contemplative peasant is replaced by jugglers and mimes who self-consciously entertain as we descend the long steps towards the well-designed all-beef frankfurters and their vendors.

Watteau's fantasier is outside the box of the painting, but in the box of the painting that contains all the paintings, and we, viewers in the Met, confront a nest of boxes. The biggest box is the city; inside it is the Met; inside it the room, the frame of the painting; and inside the painting the frame of the curb and sidewalk, the sides of the shop and the box in the shop and the painting sliding into the box, as we slide into the box of the city and the box of the Met and the room and the frame and the curb and the mysterious window we see through but cannot penetrate.

But we can see into and move through the box of the painting where a luscious luminescence pervades the perfumed atmosphere; within, all the clients are looking at the accumulated treasures of art, just as we in moving through the rooms of the Met incorporate the trove of past objects whose representations of the gods are all we possess of powers that once determined our lives, as in like abjection to representations, the people in the painting attend to the goddess, her thighs spread apart to be gazed at by the overdressed aristocrats who bend over displaying their huge besilked and belaced behinds as they regard the nude presence of painted godesses in the little shop where the gods have their final dwelling.

As we move through the interior of the shop, looking at the past and present representations, we suddenly see ourselves seeing, for the shop is not only a mirror of art but fitted out with mirrors and time pieces. Reflections and the fleeting are everywhere in the painting: On the right at the counter a beautiful woman entertains the expression of one looked at; a glorious silk dress slides over her knees in a cascade of texture that can only be looked at for it defies description; and the woman looks askance, not looking into the mirror before her because she knows she is being looked at, and the look she possesses is the look of self-conscious awareness, of being admired and deliciously basking in the look of our looks as we look. And behind her are two fops who are looking—or one of them is—into the mirror in sheer self-adulation, needing nothing but himself to be himself and to glorify himself as he basks in his own reflection. And behind him we see the fop whose reflection is behind him, in the mirror where we see his head in its unappearing-to-him back that he shall never see, but we shall see through the representation of a representation in the mirror. And there behind the shop is a mysterious blue space, access to which is gained by going through the half-opened French doors with slightly undulating gauze-like white curtains: shall we pass through it?? If we do we shall come out into the emptiness of the post-modern in which art is dead, gone, done with, overcome its service as the narcissistic presence for the rich. And we shall leave the dreaming peasant outside the narcissistic realm of representation, and the dog who truly looks at us—the only one who looks out of the box right into our eyes, but unseeing, unreflecting, unselfconscious doggy look as he nibbles on a flea, intent on scratching the itch, *that* is doggy reality, and perhaps as substantial as the reality of the ladies and gentlemen with their lorgnettes casting piercing gazes at the great thighs of the goddess who responds to the lusts of the gods about her, as the ringed mortals are right then and there responding to their lusts, their itches, their gormandizing on the cultural edibles of their tradition to which they sit as at a feast.

Manifestoes, sentimental documents of persons and ages that feel themselves alienated from a true cultural reality, express an ambivalent attitude towards the vast accumulation of cultural objects. Indeed, it is just the warehousing of the past that contributes to sentimentality, forces the opening between daily life and the past. And hence new myths need to be forged in the pressures of sentimentality: we here, in America, have told ourselves the story of culture with a plot and characters never before realized in our tradition, yet the plot and characters are all derived from the tradition.

One obsessional concern of modernity (now under reconsideration) was to separate out the preservable bit from the monstrous

de trop. To decry the detritus of the past became part of the win-
nowing process, for revolutionary art might draw strength and
derive authority from a vision of the death of past art. The fantasy of killing off the past has been confirmed in a realistic de-
structiveness punctuating the modern period. In *The Place
Vendome in Ruins*, painted by Pils in 1871, we see greatness leveled, the column, an imitation of Roman triumph, and the statue,
the fallen emperor. There is a thrill at seeing our own force and
power to destroy. In *The Tuilleries in Ruins*, painted by Meissonier
in 1871, an even more directly metaphoric representation here
gathers together all the elements of art and power in one great
wreckage. Metaphoric extensions move not only to the museum,
but to the contents, allowing us to entertain the possibility of
starting afresh.

Response to these two paintings is complex: a mixture of sad-
ness, even shock, and then for some, relief at having at last a
clear view of the destruction; and the metaphor of rebirth is right
there in the Triumph of Peace on top of the arch of triumph,
erected by Napoleon the First. Each viewer will have a slightly
different feeling about the sharply etched Triumphal Monument
as it appears in the distance. Faced with the paintings by Pils and
Meissonier, we join in the construction of metaphors to carry us
through the destruction to the effort at reconstitution. But there
is another and companion response, that of the historian in all of
us who wants above all to preserve the past.

I suspect *that* is the response of most of us: to the historian, the
collector, the cultural attaché, accumulation is greatness. And
thus the famous cry of the manifesto, "Less is More," is returned
by the insistent echo of the curator: "More is Renown." We today
no longer join in the rejection of the museum that the modernist
manifesto proclaimed. Marinetti's angry threat, his tenth thesis,
hardly stirs a vibration: "We will destroy all museums and libraries and academies . . . " And *we* cannot regard anything as passé:
"When then will you disencumber yourselves of the lymphatic
ideology of your deplorable Ruskin, whom I intend to make utterly ridiculous in your eyes . . . " Marinetti's spleen cannot taint
us for we are at home in all ages, styles, periods, schools.

To be at home in all ages, periods, schools would seem to confer upon us, once again, the naive as Schiller defined it, for are
we not as Homer and Shakespeare, now completely settled in
our world, protected against alienating chasms? Perhaps we post-
moderns fall outside both the naive and the sentimental, and are
now arrived at the cultural anesthetic in which no feeling pre-
dominates; we are world-weary, without exclusionary values,

open to everything. Then we are neither naive nor sentimental; and our mythic visions entertain possibilities of wholesale destruction as much as of total preservation. We have come to the point where anything can be accepted into the museum, and once an object has been "exhibitionized" it is thereafter companionable, our cultural friend. That degree of openness and liberality contains its negation within it, the exhibitionizing of total annihilation, visions that were given substance with the atomic bomb. But we have even repressed the anxieties we once felt, in the near past—the 1950's—about atomic holocaust. We no longer actually picture the end of the city, though we recently did just that. New York was considered a prime target for nuclear destruction, and we even drew pictures of its "look". Our mythic entertainments have gone beyond the simple image of burning docks; we now speak of "nuclear winter" and obliteration of all forms of life.

Both forces, those of Futurist renovation and of fantasies of destruction on the one hand, and the greediness to amass on the other—miss the complex urban reality for a simplifying ideological expression. The domain of objects is more complex and worth closer scrutiny than either the avant-garde manifesto or the museum curator can recognize. Responding to their simplifications, my purpose here in writing the Last Manifesto is to lay out a matrix to house an imaginary modern heap, to sort out the different kinds into the wings of a vast philosophical museum that would classify without hard boundaries all that we object-mongers clutch, preserve, label. And thus I shall sketch an album of our cultural passions and actions, a map of our deep feelings.

Our deepest feelings in the realm of cultural objects have been, as is always the case, ambivalent and complex, for it is readily evident that the modern manifesto gathered its force to attack a formidable greed, a lust to conserve absolutely everything, even in the age of artistic revolt. How formidable the need is well illustrated by the heap of canoes, shelters, implements taken in the south Seas by Captain James Cook (1728–1779) who might be blamed, if we want to find an initiator, for the modern collection since that 18th century hoard can be seen today in the Dahlem Museum, West Berlin. We are at home today with such objects because the ethnographic display has become common. But one of the obsessions of the modern manifesto was to make the recognition of such odd juxtapositions possible, and then to reject the traditional past for a new vision. When, therefore we return to Corbusier's *Vers une architecture*, we are bombarded with objects of all sorts, jumbled together in what then was an odd combination, but seems to us quite reasonable. In one sense the manifesto won out, in just the sense it wanted to suppress. All of these photographs appear in Corbusier's book: temples, grain elevators, automobiles, aeroplanes, turbines, classical ruins, Renaissance plans, and the architect's own sketches—all set the stage for the manifesto's proposal.

Manifestoes are the right spokesmen for the modern museum; and the museum has become for us in our day the keeper of the myth through which we read our past, take to ourselves the heroic achievements of our cultural journey. Having given up, or lost, the scop, gleeman, bard, keeper of story who keeps our past alive, we substitute, by easy stages of development, the collection. Its objects not only gratify for their intrinsic qualities and heralded *provenances;* the objects themselves function symbolically, metaphorically beyond their immediate presence to project a grander reality. And part of that reality is dependent upon myths of peoples now gone, for we have been as assiduous in collecting and preserving "the myths of all peoples" as we have to enshrining the fine art of our own making. And again, for the same function, for myths of all peoples, however remote, function symbolically for us, shaping a reality that in its meta-cultural inclusiveness establishes *our myth.* We are the people of inheritance, who have appropriated *all* traditions to make *our* tradition.

To be able to think the Last Manifesto at all, and to think it as a compendium of cultural diversity and plenitude, follows from a utopian ideal of community that we project for the postmodern city. For however much we consciously reject the manifestoes of the tradition, to which I shall return in a moment, we ourselves have never given up an inherited progressivism about ourselves and our powers to be fruitful and multiply. We perpetuate Enlightenment optimism, and attitude in *Kant,* in *Whitman,* and in *Corbusier,* cultural models already mentioned. We are still seeking the liberation of a new vision with a frenzy of cultural production that threatens to overwhelm us as we enlarge the capacities of our museums, now becoming coincident with the city itself.

Corbusier expresses that optimism when he established the buildings, such as the Marseille apartment house.

But something went wrong; not only have we failed to realize the values of democratic liberalism, the very buildings themselves suffered a sickening decline. Failure and Wanhope peeped out from the barracades of poured concrete. It is true that somehow the originality of design no longer satisfies our spiritual wants, and it may be the case for us that Hegel's anticipations of the death of art were prophetic, though we deny it with increased energy and cultural experimentations. Indeed, the great plentitude of cultural objects that I have investigated suggests that the Lyre of Hermes still sounds its twanging tones at the falling of dusk.

Our post-modern vision of the city should be drawn in shades of grey, rather than the garish colors preferred by the post-modern designers. But may it not be a mode of construction to hide the emptiness of our cultural world, so rich in its diversity that now everything, but *everything*, counts as a cultural object? To make everything into culture obliterates the distinction of nature and culture that has been so important to us in coming to understand the appropriate human ways of dwelling. And one reason why we should think through the Last Manifesto is that the modernist manifestoes were deeply flawed.

When we regard artists' statements about the nature of art and the future shape that art should possess, we find a driving need to dominate the future in its form as the city. *Corbusier*, my model manifesto writer, sought not only the approval of architects, but more importantly to him, the recognition from the deep thinkers of his time. He sought approval from the learned establishment and drew courage from every indication that his thought might be taken seriously by non-architects. He reports his meeting with Albert Einstein as follows:

> I had the pleasure of discussing the 'Modulor' at some length with Professor Albert Einstein at Princeton. I was then passing through a period of great uncertainty and stress: I expressed myself badly. I explained the 'Modulor' badly. I got bogged down in the morass of 'cause and effect" . . . At one point, Einstein took a pencil and began to calculate. Stupidly, I interrupted him, the conversation turned to other things, the calculation remained unfinished. . . . In a letter written to me the same evening, Einstein had the kindness to say this of the 'Modulor': "It is a scale of proportions which makes the bad difficult and the good easy." There are some who think this judgment is unscientific. For my part, I think it is extraordinarily clear-sighted.
>
> It is a gesture of friendship made by a great scientist towards us who are not scientific but soldiers on the field of battle. The scientist tells us: 'This weapon shoots straight: in the matter of dimensioning, i.e. of proportions, it makes your task more certain.' (*Le Modulor*, p. 58)

In seeking domination and recognition from the strict-thinking physicists, Corbusier reveals the contradiction in his imperialism.

Once the revolution is installed in the academy, and once the professional school training future architects accepts the manifesto, the transvaluation of values for which the manifesto stands becomes unthinkable. For the manifesto is the expression of artistic individuality, of the artist's own rules, so far as there can be rules, for his own design. Corbusier made the mistake of thinking that the *Modulor*, as he called it, could be a template for all building in the future; based upon the golden section, derived from the standing human figure, it was to be the standard against which all proportions in building were to be measured, from which derived. But the genius of the artist does not allow formulable rules—as Kant readily saw—and thus when Corbu seeks rules for others he but seals his own fate. No set of rules for art can be taught or transmitted, and the very writing of a manifesto is a self-contradiction if it seeks to lay down rules for all future art.

Here indeed is the paradox of the modern manifesto, and the internal contradiction that allows my design of "The Last Manifesto" to gain a momentary life since it points to the contradiction in the object itself. As soon as modernity proclaims that its rules could be the rules for all the making of the future, freedom is denied. And that denial expresses the inner contradiction which dooms *Vers une architecture*, for if the manifesto of modernism were to achieve its aim, it would fail as a creative vision; and if it fails, on the other side, to impose itself upon the future as it hopes to do, then it is saved to be what it truly aims to be as *itself an artistic expression:* an enactment whose meaning can be grasped as an enactment, and responded to as an enactment by making an other object according to an other—perhaps even radically distinct—vision. And we have just made such an object, THE LAST MANIFESTO. Like all the others it is doomed.

And what we are left with is THE DANCE BEFORE THE BRONTOSAURUS (Gene Kelly: "On The Town.") And the final panel in Goya's house, *La Quinta del Sordo,* the dog with whom we began, contemplating the emptiness of the universe. From the House of the Deaf.

CONTRIBUTORS*

Jane Augustine teaches in the English Department of the Pratt Institute. She is the author of essays in *Sagetrieb* and *Paideima* and poems in numerous literary magazines.

Mary Ann Caws teaches in the English, French, and Comparative Literature Ph.D. Programs at the Graduate School of the City University of New York. She is the author of *The Eye in the Text: Essays in Perception, Mannerist to Modern, Reading Frames in Modern Fiction,* and *The Art of Interference: Stressed Readings in Visual and Verbal Texts.*

M. J. Diamond teaches French at Rutgers University. She is the author of *Flaubert: The Problem of Aesthetic Discontinuity* and *Crossings: A Novel.*

Deborah Esch teaches Comparative Literature at the University of Toronto. She is the author of *The Senses of the Past* and the editor of *New Essays on the House of Mirth.*

Wendy Faris teaches in the English Department of the University of Texas, Arlington. She is the author of *Carlos Fuentes* and *Labyrinths of Language: Symbolic Landscape and Narrative Design in Modern Fiction.*

Fred Garber teaches in the Comparative Literature Department of the State University of New York in Binghamton. He is the author of *Self, Text, and Romantic Irony, Thoreau's Fable of Inscribing,* and *The Poetry of Encounter.*

Sima Godfrey teaches in the French Department of the University of British Columbia. She is the author of *Baudelaire and the Poetics of Nostalgia* and numerous articles on Baudelaire and other 19th century French authors.

---

* The titles of publications have been limited to three—in many cases it serves only as a sampling.

Michael Heller teaches in the ESL Program at New York University. He is the author of *Conviction's Net of Branches*, on the objectivist poets; his most recent volume of poetry is entitled *In the Builded Place*.

Gerhard Joseph teaches in the English Department of Lehman College and the Graduate School of the City University of New York. He is the author of *John Barth*, *Tennysonian Love: A Strange Diagonal*, and *The Texture of Tennyson*.

Alfred Kazin teaches in the English Ph.D. Program at the Graduate School of the City University of New York. He is the author of *A Walker in the City*, *New York Jew*, and *An American Procession*.

Richard Kuhns teaches in the Philosophy Department at Columbia University. He is the author of *Structures of Experience: Essays on the Affinity Between Philosophy and Literature*, *A Psychoanalytic Theory of Art: A Philosophy of Art on Developmental Principles*, and *Tragedy: Contradiction and Repression*.

Jon Lewis teaches Film and Literature in the English Department of Oregon State University. He is the author of *From Romance to Ruin*, a book on youth culture and teen movies.

Charles Molesworth teaches in the English Program at Queens College and at the Graduate School of the City University of New York. He is the author of *Gary Snyder's Vision*, *The Ironist Saved from Drowning: The Fiction of David Barthelme*, and *Marianne Moore: A Literary Life*.

Eugène Nicole teaches in the French Department of New York University. He is a novelist (*L'oeuvre des mers*), one of the editors of the new Proust edition, the co-editor, with Mary Ann Caws, of *Reading Proust Now*, and a frequent contributor to *Etudes proustiennes*.

Christopher Prendergast teaches in the Comparative Literature and French Ph.D. Programs of the Graduate School of the City University of New York. He is the author of *Balzac: Fiction and Melodrama*, *The Order of Mimesis*, and the forthcoming *City of Dreams: Paris in 19th Century Literature and Painting*, of which the essay in this volume forms a chapter.

Laura Rice teaches in the English Department of Oregon State University, Corvallis, Oregon. She is the author of "Nomad Thought: Isabelle Eberhardt and the Colonia Project," and, with

A. Karim Hamdy, of a translation and commentary on the work of Eberhardt.

Steven David Ross teaches in the Philosophy and Comparative Literature Departments of the State University of New York at Binghamton. He is the author of *A Theory of Art: Inexhaustibility by Contrast, Inexhaustibility and Human Being* and *Metaphysical Aporia and Philosophical Heresy*.

Susan Merrill Squier teaches in the English Department at the State University of New York at Stony Brook. She is the author of *Virginia Woolf and London: The Sexual Politics of the City*, the editor of *Women Writers and the City: Essays in Feminism*, and the co-editor of *Arms and the Woman: Gender and Literary Representation*.

Arnold Weinstein teaches in the Comparative Literature Department of Brown University. He is the author of *Fictions of the Self: 1550–1800* and *The Fiction of Relationship*.

Steven Winspur teaches in the French Department at the University of Wisconsin. He is the author of *Saint-John Perse and the Imaginary Reader*, of many articles on French poetry and poetics, and the guest editor of *Sub-Stance* for the issue *Writing the Real*.

INDEX